TEACHERS AND ACADEMIC PARTNERS IN URBAN SCHOOLS

'Showing how critical thinking and local democracy can be a spur to very real educational development within schools that are facing severe challenges, this book provides us with one very valuable contemporary resource of hope.'
Ian Menter, *Professor of Teacher Education, University of Oxford, UK*

Teachers and Academic Partners in Urban Schools identifies and addresses a major problem for practitioners – teachers, student teachers and teacher educators – working in urban schools burdened by highly restrictive teaching methods and pressures to meet unrealistic benchmarks set by government. In this book, Lori Beckett investigates how to negotiate these tensions and challenges and offers an account of how to elevate practitioners' professional voice on quality teaching along more democratic lines.

The book addresses key issues for teachers in urban schools, such as:

- fractures in teachers' professional communities;
- impacts of imposed marketizing policies and forced performative practices on schools;
- the complexities of teaching and teachers' concerns about practice, as well as teaching practitioners' perception of educational/schools policy.

Both academic and teacher partners contribute to the work, showcasing the ways they have engaged with each other in joint work and with local government. Through this, the book supports a professional and politicized dialogue about teaching and teacher education, offering a meaningful account of how to fashion a form of educative schooling for students and families with complex needs.

Written by a dynamic and experienced author, this book brings Beckett's experience to bear on a controversial and complex area – addressing the general trend towards increased regulatory policy in education. It is an essential read for anyone interested in a rich analysis of how practitioners can work to reassert their professional voice and regain control of schools and teacher education, and will also appeal to those interested in the larger project of restoring school democracy.

Lori Beckett is the Winifred Mercier Professor of Teacher Education at Leeds Beckett University, UK.

Teacher Quality and School Development Series
Series Editors: Christopher Day and Ann Lieberman

The Teacher and the World: A study of cosmopolitanism and education
David T. Hansen

Raising Achievement in Schools: Learning to succeed
Alma Harris, David Crossley, Graham Corbyn and Tracey Allen

Self-Study and Inquiry into Practice: Learning to teach for equity and social justice
Linda Kroll

The New Lives of Teachers
Christopher Day and Qing Gu

Teacher Education Around the World: Changing policies and practices
Linda Darling-Hammond and Ann Lieberman

The Professional Identity of Teacher Educators: Career on the cusp?
Ronnie Davey

Resilient Teachers, Resilient Schools: Building and sustaining quality in testing times
Christopher Day and Qing Gu

Promoting Early Career Teacher Resilience: A socio-cultural and critical guide to action
Bruce Johnson, Barry Down, Rosie LeCornu, Judy Peters, Anna Sullivan, Jane Pearce and Janet Hunter

Teachers and Academic Partners in Urban Schools: Threats to professional practice
Lori Beckett

TEACHERS AND ACADEMIC PARTNERS IN URBAN SCHOOLS

Threats to professional practice

Lori Beckett

LONDON AND NEW YORK

First published 2016
by Routledge
2 Park Square, Milton Park, Abingdon, Oxon OX14 4RN

and by Routledge
711 Third Avenue, New York, NY 10017

Routledge is an imprint of the Taylor & Francis Group, an informa business

© 2016 Lori Beckett

The right of Lori Beckett to be identified as author of this work has been asserted by her in accordance with sections 77 and 78 of the Copyright, Designs and Patents Act 1988.

All rights reserved. No part of this book may be reprinted or reproduced or utilised in any form or by any electronic, mechanical, or other means, now known or hereafter invented, including photocopying and recording, or in any information storage or retrieval system, without permission in writing from the publishers.

Trademark notice: Product or corporate names may be trademarks or registered trademarks, and are used only for identification and explanation without intent to infringe.

British Library Cataloguing in Publication Data
A catalogue record for this book is available from the British Library

Library of Congress Cataloging in Publication Data
Names: Beckett, Lori, author.
 Title: Teachers and academic partners in urban schools : threats to professional practice / Lori Beckett.
 Description: New York, NY : Routledge, 2016. | Series: Teacher quality and school development | Includes bibliographical references and index.
 Identifiers: LCCN 2015031283| ISBN 9781138826250 (hardback) | ISBN 9781138826267 (pbk.) | ISBN 9781315739441 (ebook)
 Subjects: LCSH: Professional learning communities--Great Britain. | Teachers--Professional relationships--Great Britain. | Teachers--Training of--Great Britain. | School autonomy--Great Britain. | Urban schools--Great Britain. | Education and state--Great Britain.
 Classification: LCC LB1775.4.G7 B44 2016 | DDC 371.1/06--dc23
 LC record available at http://lccn.loc.gov/2015031283

ISBN: 978-1-138-82625-0 (hbk)
ISBN: 978-1-138-82626-7 (pbk)
ISBN: 978-1-315-73944-1 (ebk)

Typeset in Bembo and Stone Sans
by Florence Production Ltd, Stoodleigh, Devon, UK
Printed in Great Britain by Ashford Colour Press Ltd

We should see the English situation as a warning, not as a system from which to learn.

Lingard, 2009

*For my mother,
Margery Berenice Phillips
(1923–2005)*

CONTENTS

Series editors' introduction ix
CHRISTOPHER DAY AND ANN LIEBERMAN
Foreword xi
IAN MENTER
Acknowledgements xiv

1 A 'choreography of policy conflict' in urban schools   1

2 'Local' solutions to 'failing' schools   21

3 Critical democratic work   41

4 Academic partners and the 'university project'   61

5 Making common cause   85

6 Teachers' voices   112

7 Professional control over schooling   134

Bibliography   155
Index   169

SERIES EDITORS' INTRODUCTION

Christopher Day
University of Nottingham, UK

Ann Lieberman
Stanford University, USA

This series is intended as a showcase for the most recent scholarship on teacher and school development internationally and this book provides a significant addition. Its author focuses on the work of teachers and their academic partners in schools in the northeast of England that serve socially and economically disadvantaged urban communities. However, the stories which the author tells about disjunctures between policies and practices will be recognisable in many other jurisdictions. The author presents partnership work with schools in urban settings which takes place within the broader and now well-established policy context of performativity and high stakes accountability which pervades the school system in England, to the extent that many in schools no longer question its undue emphasis upon the metrics of student performance against which the 'effectiveness' of schools is largely judged. Lori Beckett writes passionately, persuasively and sometimes angrily about her opposition to this, and in particular the added disadvantage it brings to those who already suffer multiple deprivation through the circumstances of birth and environment. Her stories of localised struggle within the persistence of external national, undifferentiated external assessment frameworks provide a reality check against the rhetoric of standards-raising agendas and 'No Child Left Behind'. Yet the underlying story which she presents is one of hope. The chapters provide powerful examples of practitioner–partnership research between schools in urban settings and university academics which refuse to cast teachers as passive victims of the policy system. Rather, she claims that their contextually driven inquiry work enables them to better speak truth to power through the development of local solutions to local issues. In doing so, they act in the 'real' interests of students in disadvantaged settings as they attempt to 'wrestle back' professional control from what she describes as 'authoritarian education politicians' through their collective actions.

The book is overtly political in its intent, challenging current dominant neoliberal policy orthodoxies in the English education system. It is likely to cause disquiet amongst those outside schools who continue to set the agenda through monitoring and inspection regimes in what the author calls 'Austerity Britain'. It is not, therefore, easy reading, for it is unashamedly assertive in tone and direct in its critique of the short-term chasing of improved, narrowly defined test and examination results where this further disadvantages those who are already disadvantaged. Yet it is also a testament to the possibilities for schools and universities to work together in changing policy contexts. For some, then, the book may be regarded as just another 'rant' by a privileged academic against a system that cannot be changed, such is its force. For others, it may, however, be read as an attempt to provide a different voice in the ongoing debate about what 'standards' really mean when judged against equity and inclusion.

FOREWORD

Ian Menter
Professor of Teacher Education, University of Oxford, UK
President, British Educational Research Association, 2013–2015

Writing this Foreword in the aftermath of the 2015 UK General Election means that it is impossible not to have very mixed feelings about the contents of this important book. Professor Lori Beckett has been working in the north of England for more than 10 years and has been collaborating with teachers in schools where the impacts of 'austerity' have been most severe. This book is not only a powerful testament to her own work but also to the work of the teachers, head teachers and others in those schools.

There is a strong personal narrative which runs through the book that reminds us not only that things may be different in other parts of the world but also that things have been changing dramatically within English schools as well over recent years. Beckett describes the culture shock she experienced arriving in England and finding how teachers were being widely disparaged by politicians, inspectors, the media and some policymakers, something that she had not experienced in Australia, at least not to anything like the same extent. But also, in coming from Australia, she already had significant experience in working in close partnership with teachers and drawing on some of her compatriots in developing critical transformative approaches to teacher inquiry. I am thinking of scholars such as Stephen Kemmis, Marie Brennan and Susan Groundwater-Smith, all of whose work has clearly been an important influence on Beckett's approach throughout her career. But also, we see the influence of Bob Lingard, R.W. Connell and John Smyth, other Australians whose work on teachers and 'close to practice' research has been so significant.

Certainly, schools in England have experienced one of their most volatile periods ever over the last 10 years, with curricular and assessment reforms tumbling one after the other, but also with new schooling structures being introduced by each government in turn. First we saw the academy programme of New Labour which was then picked up and accelerated by the Coalition Government from 2010, but that government also introduced the curiously named 'free schools'. When I was a student teacher in the 1970s, free schools were institutions that were based primarily on strong links with their local community and developed their curriculum democratically in association with parents and students. Now in the twenty-first century it seems that a free school is a school that is directly managed by central government without a locally elected intermediary, such as a local education authority, and has an independent governing board which can determine its own admissions policy and can decide whether or not the teachers employed need a teaching qualification.

The Conservative Government elected in 2015 has made a commitment to maintain current levels of 'per pupil' spending in education. This means that there will in effect be further cuts, as each pound in a school's budget gradually lessens in value over the next 5 years. The Conservatives did pledge to maintain what was perhaps their most progressive policy – albeit a policy pushed into place by their Liberal Democrat coalition partners, that of Pupil Premium. The targeted approach to provide extra funds for each pupil from a low income household has been used effectively in many schools around the country, and it is certainly to be hoped that this will continue. In many ways this has been a more effective policy than some of those earlier policies that sought to achieve similar effects, such as Educational Priority Areas or Educational Action Zones.

It is the urban context that fascinates Beckett and which her teacher partners are working in. She draws on the work of English scholars, such as Gerald Grace and Geoff Whitty, who, with others, did so much to develop our understanding of 'urban education' during the 1970s, 80s and thereafter. In particular she draws on Grace's concept of 'complex hope', a concept that draws our attention to the multiple facets of urban challenge. This phrase captures the strong potential for community action and for social solidarity that exists in working class communities which nevertheless is constantly being undermined by punitive and divisive welfare policies (such as the notorious 'bedroom tax') and by continuing disruption in local economies. In English education these complex processes are being analysed by a new wave of scholars on whom Beckett also draws, such as Ruth Lupton and Diane Reay.

The book gives teachers a voice. We see how the pressures on them in these settings can provoke outrage and anger. We see how managerialist governance can seek to exclude the voices of hardworking and committed professionals. We see how governing bodies can be badgered if not bullied into changes that are strongly counter-intuitive and undemocratic. All of these are revealed in Beckett's powerful volume. But we also see how teachers can respond in ways that enhance criticality and democracy at least at a local level. We see the complex hope being translated into progressive and positive action on the ground, through critical systematic inquiry (see BERA-RSA, 2014), leading to the provision of a much more meaningful education for young people in these communities. This is an education that can inspire and liberate learners in a not dissimilar fashion to the pioneering work of Paulo Freire in the 1970s (Freire, 1972).

But this is not a call for a return to the progressivism of the 1960s and 70s, even if some of the inspiration may lie there. It is a realistic and profound critical response to the contradictions of the public education in urban settings in twenty-first century England. Throughout the book Beckett draws on the work of Edward Thompson, the social historian who wrote about the development of the English working class (Thompson, 1963/68). One of Thompson's fellow travellers was the cultural theorist Raymond Williams. A collection of his papers that was published not long after his death in 1988 was entitled *Resources of Hope* (Williams, 1989). In developing the idea of complex hope and showing how critical thinking and local democracy can be a spur to very real educational development within schools that are facing severe challenges, this book provides us with one very valuable contemporary 'resource of hope'.

References

BERA-RSA. (2014). *Research and the Teaching Profession: Building the capacity for a self-improving education system*. London: British Educational Research Association.

Freire, P. (1972). *Pedagogy of the Oppressed*. Harmondsworth, England: Penguin.

Thompson, E. P. (1963/68). *The Making of the English Working Class*. Harmondsworth, England: Penguin.

Williams, R. (1989). *Resources of Hope*. London: Verso.

ACKNOWLEDGEMENTS

This book could be considered a companion volume to my edited collection, also published by Routledge, when I first called on academic and teacher partners to help demonstrate the intellectual activity needed to regain professional control in teaching and teacher education given corporate takeovers in the global neoliberal policy context. I am appreciative for this second opportunity to share the details of one local struggle to bring such work into being, so my sincere thanks go to Anna Clarkson and Chris Byrne at Routledge for their encouragement along with sympathetic and expert editorial advice. I am lucky to have received one-off benefits from anonymous reviewers of the book proposal, plus Ann Lieberman who discussed the ideas from the outset and who delivered the Series Editors' Introduction co-authored with Christopher Day. The ideas about the school–university partnership project have been enriched by ongoing conversations with Ian Menter who kindly authored the Foreword.

The research and teaching that informed the material for this book was supported by Carnegie faculty, Leeds Beckett University. I am grateful to the entire staff but particularly to Carlton Cooke, Marie-Odile Leconte, Jon Tan and Linda Hepworth, who, in their own ways, provided vital backing and assistance. I am also grateful to colleagues who came to be called consultant academic partners and who provided instrumental advice: Bob Lingard, Susan Groundwater-Smith, Ruth Lupton and Geoff Whitty. I owe much to retired academic colleague Iain Poole who consistently worked as Research Assistant to lend inordinate help in response to questions and queries. Two academic colleagues read most of the draft book manuscript and provided critical constructive feedback so I would here like to acknowledge Doug Martin and Terry Wrigley. Three teacher partners read the whole draft manuscript and provided invaluable annotated comments throughout so I owe more than overarching acknowledgement to Nikie Arthurs, Kathleen Gallagher and Amanda Nuttall. The remaining cohort of teacher partners, called

Trailblazers and RaTs (research-active teachers), along with academic partners Jon Tan, Chris Ford and Terry Wrigley, provided support and encouragement more than they know.

I would also like to thank the school Heads for their interviews; Linda Hepworth for all the transcriptions; local NUT officers Christine Raftery, Richard Raftery and Patrick Murphy for important teacher union advice; and Rachel Thornton for securing all the copyright permission. Two doctoral students, Ian Kaplan and Aneela Ali, consistently challenged me to critically understand teacher education and clarify my arguments. On a more personal note, I would like to acknowledge and give heartfelt thanks to family and friends who unswervingly provide love and support, but especially Lin Williams, Sibyl Fisher, Mary Roddick, Chris Evans, Betty Barnes, Jan Lonie and Carol Henderson who also offer intellectual companionship. Mention must be made of their empathetic patience because not once did they complain about holiday time being taken up by my work in England! On a more serious note, this book is dedicated to my mother long gone but who set me on this path to take urban schooling seriously as a means to work our way out of poverty. She had great faith in the worth of education and the collectivity of trade unions. I trust her example has a far reach and others will benefit from her wisdom.

1
A 'CHOREOGRAPHY OF POLICY CONFLICT' IN URBAN SCHOOLS

Introduction

This book describes the specific details of one local struggle to establish professional learning communities of teachers and academic partners to focus on poverty and cumulative multiple deprivation in a network of urban schools in a former industrial northern city of England. This city of nearly a million people claims 22.5 per cent of children aged 0–15 live in low income families often registered among the top 10 per cent most deprived neighborhoods in England, according to the latest census figures and the Index of Multiple Deprivation (IMD)[1]. Not surprisingly social and economic disadvantage is writ large in these urban schools, variously called 'challenging schools', 'underperforming schools', and 'socioeconomically challenged' schools but mostly 'failing schools' if not 'disadvantaged schools'.

Whatever they are called, these urban schools invariably have the distinction of being the focus of political attention, especially given concerns about students' performance and achievement. This is welcome when it is positive discrimination, for example through additional funding, which inevitably supports compensatory measures such as facilitating access to schooling and the curriculum through learning support[2]. This is at least some recognition of student disadvantage flagged up by designated labels, such as free school meals (FSM), which is an official categorization in student census data indicative of low socioeconomic status family background given parents'/caregivers' receipt of welfare benefits. Curiously there is rare acknowledgement of how/why this might be a social determinant of students' learning much less the social and educational inequalities that are reflected by it[3]. The history is seemingly lost. In a discussion of working people's fightback attempts over time, the historian E.P. Thompson (in Winslow, 2014) noted Bradford Independent Labour Party[4] fought *against* infant mortality, and *for* nursery schools, council houses and free school meals. This was a long-fought campaign, a stand against hardship, and should give pause to consider the attention on students in poverty by former Conservative Secretary of State for Education Michael Gove[5]:

> My priority this year has to be to invest any savings . . . in measures that most directly affect attainment for the poorest pupils.

While the rhetoric might sound convincing, this is political opportunism at its most brazen. It smacks of false sentiments about urban schools living on a precarious edge between success and failure (MacBeath et al., 2007) and negative stereotypes that drive policy making (Maguire et al., 2006). It glosses over the impact of unequal access and provision of education as well as current debates of choice, self-management, accountability, standards and the role of the state in education (Thrupp, 1999). Worse, Gove's pronouncement heralds scorn and blame, which connects with the politics of so-called 'failing' schools, a term I reject particularly when it is bandied around by politicians, policymakers and powerbrokers to signify some dubious claims about urban schools' inadequacies[6]. These are invariably followed by high-pressure policy and time demands from the imposition of national standardized performance indicators twinned with a 'one size fits all' approach to teaching and learning (Lingard, 2009; Mahony and Hextall, 2000). This includes dictates to 'raise achievement', 'close the gap', increase students' levels of progress, meet floor targets and national benchmarks, harnessed to what has come to be called toxic forms of accountability (see Park, 2013) and threats of sanctions.

This is all part of the vernacular of neoliberal globalization in England's system of schooling (Ball, 2012; Lingard and Rizvi, 2009), a peculiar form of the global educational reform agenda, or GERM (Sahlberg, 2011), rolled out by neoliberal governments, whether Conservative or Tory, New Labour or Liberal Democrat. The government's constant demands for testing and results are compounded by directions from the Office for Standards in Education, Children's Services and Skills (Ofsted), a semi-privatized and supposedly independent arm of government (Gorton et al., 2014)[7], in school inspection judgements. These very often portray criticisms of urban schools' work as 'inadequate or 'requires improvement', and likewise in regional reports. For example, the Ofsted (2014) *North East, Yorkshire and Humber Regional Report* opening sentence declares that:

> much remains to be done to tackle variations in school performance and pupils' achievement. . . . The biggest challenge facing the region is the poor performance of secondary schools. . . . The stark reality for too many 16–19-year-olds continues to be life without a job, training or further education.

This is captivating language but it too is not quite convincing because it ignores everyday life in urban schools in socially disadvantaged areas and the extent of challenges facing school Heads and teachers. These practitioners struggle on a day-to-day basis to provide worthwhile and meaningful schooling experiences for students marked by poverty and cumulative multiple deprivation. Witness teachers' concerns about disadvantaged students' health and welfare, lack of sleep, tiredness, hunger, bringing personal/family problems into school, which can result in lateness, emotional tensions and being ill-prepared for the day's school work; then there is lack of interest, disaffection, disengagement, alienation, absenteeism, the list goes on[8]. Such concerns provide some professional insight into the social realities for teachers in urban schools and more seriously the social and economic fallout of Conservative Government policies in Austerity Britain.

This should begin with key social and economic patterns in the region, which align with the politics of place, social geography and neighborhood studies (see Lupton, 2003; Thomson, 2007). These reflect the deep structures of capital and inequalities (see Piketty, 2014a, 2014b; Ball, 2006), which point to stark social and economic disadvantage in urban school communities (Angus, 1993) that gives rise to differential patterns of learning and achievement (see Hayes *et al.*, 2006). Rather than acknowledge poverty and deprivation as 'mitigating circumstances', a phrase coined by one of my teacher partners (Arthurs, 2012, 2013), instead the regional report proffers a set of myths that teachers need to be told again they have it wrong. This seemingly sits with a history of the New Right marked by what Ball (1990/2012) called 'discourses of derision' from the 1970s and 1980s throughout Thatcher's era. It is a classic demonstration of 'blame the victim' (Ryan, 1971) where urban schools are stigmatized (see Pink and Noblit, 2007), which takes shape through the willful insistence of politicians, policymakers and powerbrokers to take so-called 'failing' schools in the state system to affect quasi-marketization and semi-privatization.

This links to Jones' (2011) analysis of the demonization of the working classes, which has given way to the term 'feral underclass', or CHAVS, in a deeply unequal society, a myth at the heart of British politics, so as to entrench the idea that there are entire communities crawling with feckless, delinquent, violent and sexually debauched no-hopers[9]. I suggest the charge of 'failing' school is an expression of the demonization of urban schools, as 'no-hopers' at least, which requires drastic action. This is a sad reflection on the teachers and students whose experience of social and educational disadvantage finds expression in the urban school classroom. Such demonization sits well with Jones' (2014) argument about establishment mentalities that those at the top deserve to be there; those with talent, skill and determination will climb the social ladder; and those who fail to improve their circumstances have only themselves to blame. This echoes Piketty's (2014a) assertion that 'losers' are often made responsible for their situation – because their productivity is too low for example.

A prime case is forced school closure, a drastic 'structural' solution to so-called underperformance by successive neoliberal governments to facilitate privatization via corporate sponsors' takeover and relinquishment of Local Authority ties. This fate is captured by Harvey's (2005) concern that the processes of neoliberalization

4 A 'choreography of policy conflict'

entail the 'creative destruction' of institutional frameworks and powers, which happens in urban schools supposedly 'failing', very often contrary to local school-community interests (see Beckett, 2012a). This calls into question the so-called democratic mandate that elected governments have to reform and reorganize the state system of schooling.

A confusing and difficult problem is the ways authoritarian politicians and civil servants or officials at the local and national levels line up with business leaders and entrepreneurs intent on profit making from schooling and education including teacher education. Previously I reported on Gove, formerly a journalist for *The Times*, which is owned by the Murdoch Press in the UK[10] (see Beckett, 2013a). Again this links to Jones' (2014) analysis in *The Establishment* of powerful groups who protect their position in a democracy. He includes mention of Gove, named as part of the political elite with close ties to big business in the Policy Exchange think tank, which calls for the wholesale privatization of public services, and Gove's appointment of a businessman as non-executive member of the Department for Education Board. These non-educationalists then come to dictate the terms of teaching and teacher education, which results in the loss of democratic professional control (see Beckett, 2013a).

Another difficult conundrum is to ascertain *what sort of professional response is appropriate*, because in this time and in this place, the odds are stacked against a locally determined professional response: not only is there the central regulation of teachers' work and the increased role for quasi-markets, which has diminished the professional influence on policy and practice (Apple, 2009; Gewirtz *et al.*, 2009). There is an erosion of both the teacher and academic voice, marked by a deliberate and ongoing sidelining of research insights and what is called 'the university project' (see Furlong, 2013; Menter, 2013; Whitty, 2014). This includes recognition of the relationship between students' achievement, family and social backgrounds (Mortimore and Whitty, 1997/2000), or as I prefer to put it, a critical understanding of the interconnections between disadvantaged students' lives, learning and urban schooling experiences.

In this book I want to give voice to some of the inherent difficulties for a professionally determined 'local' solution facilitated by teachers coming together, working collaboratively and building theoretically informed practical knowledge about poverty and cumulative multiple deprivation given support from academic partners. This is not to dwell on the negative experiences, mindful England has the dubious distinction of being 'a warning' to other systems globally (Lingard, 2009), but to look for the positives and to the future. Hence it is important to look closely at the distinction between the two solutions, one 'structural' and the other 'local', not just because of cogent arguments that teaching is a research-informed profession (Lingard and Renshaw, 2010; Menter and Murray, 2011; BERA-RSA, 2014a, 2014b) or school–university partnership ways of working protect and advance staff professionalism (Hargreaves, 2006). Political wit to the fore because Gove argued on the strength of teachers' professionalism in a letter to the National Association of Head Teachers:

I would like to see if we can reform our system of assessment and accountability to take into account of those concerns that have been raised by committed professionals.

This appeal could rely on any number of forms of professionalism (Furlong et al., 2011) though my concern is with 'democratic professionalism' (Whitty, 2008) to realize the transformative potential of school–university partnership work in urban schools to help identify the most suitable interventions. This draws on my records of teaching and research in this local network of urban schools, which derives from my work as academic partner in Australia before recruitment to England in 2005 as Professor of Teacher Education, invited governor on local urban schools' Boards of Governors, and elected regional representative on the now defunct citywide Governors' Forum. Of necessity this is selective but it is enough to illustrate what informed the necessary negotiations with local school Heads, local authority partners and university line managers as well as teachers and academic colleagues. More than that, the data facilitates a study of the nature of the struggle to establish this work and embed it as part of a research-informed continuing professional development (CPD) programme for teachers that results in their published work. The concern is to encourage professional knowledge building about poverty and schooling across the pre-service–in-service continuum in order to support teachers and students change their situation in these neoliberal regimes. This is not just for the record because it brings to light the skirmishes and clashes, including the joint efforts of teachers and academic partners to voice concerns in the face of political assaults on local urban schools and the state system.

Thinking strategically

This admission of difficulty for school–university partnership work is disturbing. It suggests threats to the best of what is known and practised about professional development in urban schools (see Lieberman and Miller, 2001, 2008). Of great concern to teacher partners is what they call 'constant fire-fighting', a synonym for the evident reactive crisis management by some School Leadership Teams (SLTs) caught up in a 'crisis politics' (Harvey, 2005): the neoliberal schooling experiment marked by 'failing' schools, damning Ofsted inspection judgements, teachers on 'capability procedures', stress and high pressure and fear of job losses, among other sanctions. This leads to diminished capacity for teachers and academics but also school Heads and staff to participate in professional knowledge building about teaching students disadvantaged by poverty and cumulative multiple deprivation.

This is to suggest that for much of the time, these professionals, under duress, have little or no time to give to critical reflections on the ideas, concepts, theories and doctrines being imposed on urban schools. For example, in primary schools in England, statutory guidelines for National Curriculum prescribe traditional forms of received knowledge like the history of English kings and queens; national-school data, delivered in the form of the 'Reporting and Analysis for Improvement through School Self-Evaluation' (RAISEonline) report, provide reductive directions on work with different student groups like the designated 'free school meals'; Gove's penchant for the 'phonics check' in Year 1 ties teachers to 'teaching to the test' with major consequences for young children learning to read. In high schools in England, further restrictions on modes of delivery and assessment come from schools' selection of Examination Boards[11] to award the General Certificates of Secondary Education (GCSEs). These are tied to government-decreed national benchmarks once described as five A*-C grade GCSEs, now called 'Progress 8 metric', colloquially known as 'Best 8'[12]. Not only are there tight examination regulations but these constantly change, with a consequence that students begin to distrust teachers' competence. For example, in one year in one subject there were three changes to examination specifications and in another there were rule changes on course work going from 50 per cent to 40 per cent to 30 per cent; now it's 20 per cent with the bulk of assessment by end-of-year examination. Further, teachers experience additional pressures with management scrutiny of their marking and feedback on students' work, which occurs once every half term, so six times in the school year.

These problems for practitioners are constructed according to the phenomenon of 'policy as numbers' (Lingard, 2011) and also take effect through Ofsted instructions on using performance data[13] with targeted and intensive support from the Local Authority to meet targets and raise standards. The focus is then on students' performances in tabulated data form to show attainment and progress against key performance indicators, but there is more to it, which has consequences for the marginalization or loss of research-informed professional perspectives. In an effort to explain 'failing' at a glance of underachievement in percentage results against targets, for instance, a typical explanation singles out families in local communities where there are known to be many generations unemployed. Practitioners' analyses are very often limited and rely on a 'deficit' reading of students' families. The ready references to parents with little or no aspirations, or worse, little or no need for schooling, unwittingly buys in to a 'culture of poverty' (see Harvey and Reed, 1996) and myriad interventions, many commercially available. It is as if the neoliberal circle is closed, much like poverty cycles.

This is not to denigrate school Heads and teachers in urban schools but rather acknowledge they work extraordinarily hard to cope with multiple policy and practice dictates from seemingly insatiable politicians, policymakers and powerbrokers. This is almost to the point where practitioner workloads are unsustainable (see MacBeath, 2012), which aligns with public media debates[14], and which is to refute claims about teacher and student underperformance and call into question GERM and the vernacular neoliberal policy ensemble. In my experience working in the north of England, these are highly committed practitioners but they seemingly work altruistically. As one primary school Head put it:

> In an urban environment where there are multiple challenges [you need] the type of school where if you put that determination to make a difference, with good practice, with good team work and all the other aspects of a healthy organization, the potential

is that you could make a massive difference to quite a lot of young lives: if we make a difference between 5 and 11, then maybe that rolls on to 11 to 16, maybe that means that those children will work or they'll go onto even further learning and this will have a whole roll-on effect into society.

The point here is that practitioners in urban schools are forcibly and singularly focused on students' performance and achievement with limited conception of the 'schools can make a difference' message (Thrupp, 1999). While they might want learning experiences to be of benefit to disadvantaged students, short-term target chasing proves counterproductive and precludes necessary improvements in urban schooling. This is dictated by national-school benchmarks, headline measures and Ofsted definitions of 'good' if not 'outstanding' teaching[15] and ignores professional debate over time. For example, what it takes to make a difference (Connell *et al.*, 1982; Thrupp, 2002; Hayes *et al.*, 2006; Beveridge *et al.*, 2005) but also quality teaching (Carr, 1989; Lingard *et al.*, 2003; Hayes *et al.*, 2006) includes professional development to update teachers' knowledge, deepen their understanding and advance their skills as expert practitioners (see BERA-RSA, 2014). A local teacher put it like this:

Teachers tend to derive their teaching from models of practices that are common, internal to the school and parochial, often outdated, yet regurgitated without questioning. We are driven by the school Head's agenda, which is tied to the headline results for school league tables and Ofsted inspections. We are compelled to be 'teaching to the test' and consistently told 'what works'. There is little engagement with in-depth discussion about students/ACORN data, which is used extensively in primary schools, and the RAISEonline categories like 'free school meals'. We certainly never discuss the Index of Multiple Deprivation and social class categories[16].

This highlights grassroots professional concerns in this current vernacular neoliberal regime in England, where research-informed professional activity is ostensibly missing in urban schools and professional knowledge bases are noticeably curtailed. To be sure there are official reports on urban schools and poverty effects, for example, House of Commons Education Committee (2014), *Underachievement in Education by White Working Class Children*[17]. The focus is seemingly fixed on students eligible for free school meals (FSMs) and the impact of so-called economic deprivation on educational performance at all levels. Central place is given to Ofsted's inspection focus on performance gaps for deprived groups and schools' work benchmarked against an 'outstanding' rating with due consideration to data, policies like 'Progress 8 metric' and funding such as 'Pupil Premium' and the Education Endowment Fund 'toolkit'. Test-based accountability aside for the moment, which is to register Lingard's (2009) point about the incongruence of curriculum, pedagogies and assessment, two major silences in the House of Commons report stand out for practitioners: curriculum and the knowledge question (Young, 1998, 2008; Wyse *et al.*, 2013; Wrigley, 2014) and transformative pedagogies (Newmann and Associates, 1996; Hayes *et al.*, 2006). These are both crucial in negotiating the home-knowledge–school-knowledge links (Connell, 2009; Moll *et al.*, 1992). This is required to clarify practitioners' thinking and theorizing around what might engage disadvantaged students in learning and at the same time provide access to 'powerful' knowledge and why.

Academic colleagues are likewise constrained in their participation in professional debates given the rigidity of provision for Qualified Teacher Status (QTS). In university, for example, the faculty was recently totally preoccupied with an Ofsted inspection of provision on phonics. A consequence is a shrinking of time and capacity in teacher education to engage in dialogic professional conversations including theoretical explanations, say, about teaching in urban schools (see Quartz *et al.*, 2003; Frankenburg *et al.*, 2009; Glenny *et al.*, 2013) but also the tensions to do with 'raising achievement' in urban schools as distinct from middle class schools (Ball, 2006). With such tight QTS prescription, student teachers on placement in, say, a local urban high school are ill-prepared on what it means to restructure curriculum much less provide a full and broadly balanced curriculum that takes account of everyday life for students disadvantaged by poverty and multiple cumulative deprivation. Instead they are confronted by the latest Ofsted inspection report, national-school data and headline measures: SATs in primary school and 'Best 8' in high school.

I am advised by another local teacher partner in an urban high school that to reach this 'Best 8' measure the School Leadership Team is always in a panic and engage heavy-handed tactics, which leave little or no opportunities for critical reflections, questioning doctrines and the like but also reviews of other countries' research-informed practices. Anyon's (1997) writing about a similar scenario in North America is instructive for the north of England:

> To really improve ghetto children's chances then, in school and out, we must (in addition to pursuing school-based reforms) increase their social and economic well-being and status before and while they are students. We must ultimately, therefore, eliminate poverty: we must eliminate the ghetto school by eliminating the underlying causes of ghettoization. . . . Unfortunately educational 'small victories' such as the restructuring of a school or the introduction of a new classroom pedagogical technique, no matter how satisfying to the individuals involved, without a long-range strategy to eradicate underlying causes of poverty and racial isolation, cannot add up to large victories in our inner cities with effects that are sustainable over time.

This is a systemic issue for England, which may or may not be addressed by the recently mandated responsibility for research evidence, given the Carter (2015) *Review of Initial Teacher Training* in England apropos the BERA-RSA (2014a, 2014b) Inquiry, *Research and the Teaching Profession*. It remains to be seen what sort of research is favoured (see Pollard and Oancea, 2010; Petersen, Reimer and Qvortrup, 2014), and how long it will take to permeate the so-called school-led system in England (see Husbands, 2013; also Menter, 2013). In any case the system is fragmented:

Schools Direct, Teach First, SCITT, are very often characterized by a shared view of 'teaching as a craft' (Hoskins and Maguire, 2013), underpinned by an apprenticeship model of practice. After years of recycling 'what works' through experience, which is copied and duplicated again and again in decontextualized ways, there is less capacity among teacher-education staff in either schools or universities to think strategically about urban school action plans. This is a worrisome political departure for the profession, which prompts calls for 'rescuing the university project' (Furlong, 2013; Whitty; 2014).

Professional knowledge building

My quest to generate more democratic school–university partnership ways of working in a local network of urban schools – to co-develop professional knowledge about disadvantaged students' learning with teachers, but also with School Leadership Teams and Local Authority School Improvement Advisors in order to show what a 'local' solution looks like in practice – only comes into view with the backstory. This began in Australia where I worked as an academic partner to a few urban schools as part of the Priority Action Schools Program (PASP) and in an inner-city urban high school serving predominantly Aboriginal communities[18] to build a shared vocabulary about how to engage disadvantaged students, families and communities in learning. Groundwater-Smith and Kemmis (n.d.) described PASP, jointly devised by NSW Teachers' Federation and the Department of Education and Training, as knowledge building in the sense that a network of self-identified disadvantaged schools conducted a systematic evaluation of its own work assisted by an academic partner experienced in school-based research. The objectives were to support these schools to build their capacity to:

- improve students' learning outcomes;
- improve students' behaviour and attendance;
- support teachers through mentoring and induction programs;
- support whole school approaches to improved teaching practice;
- reduce high student turnover and increase retention to complete schooling;
- reduce the impacts of socioeconomic disadvantage; and
- maximize interagency and community support.

On my recruitment in 2005 to work in England, more specifically into a university with a long tradition of teacher education, I claimed some knowledge of local urban schools in England. Admittedly this was only through jointly developed critical reviews of literature with Australian teacher partners to help build professional consensus on different ways to approach school improvement (Mortimore and Whitty, 1997/2000; Lupton, 2004a, 2006; Thrupp, 1999, 2005) and to organize curriculum, pedagogies and assessment (Whitty, 1985; Young, 1998). I had also done some intensive doctoral study of the English system to inform my analysis of the introduction of Thatcherism into the NSW schooling system, which I called the 'radical-conservative experiment' (Beckett, 1996)! Plus I had had the privilege of studying at Deakin University where I met Lawrence Stenhouse (1975) and came to consider England as the home of teacher research.

The sort of research-informed partnership work I proposed in the north of England to build theoretical and evidential justification for democratic professional decisions about interventions in urban schools was simultaneously being developed in different parts of the world. Johnson, Finn and Lewis (2005) developed policy initiatives that emphasize democratic collaborations among universities, urban teachers, parents and community members in North America. However, I recognized that work in one location cannot be simply transplanted into another, as Piketty (2014b) rightly points out, 'each country has its own specificities and its own cultural history'. It is one thing to acknowledge vernacular neoliberalism (Cochran-Smith *et al.*, 2013), but again Piketty (2014b) indicates 'national responses to inequality also depend on how the country perceives itself in relation to others'. What I did not anticipate in England's national response to the challenges facing urban schools is the vernacular neoliberal policy construction of 'failing' schools and lack of systemic support for teacher inquiry.

A decade ago it was my hopeful expectation to work with the NUT, at the very least to discuss the possibility of a teacher union–partnership project not unlike the NSW PASP. Indeed I made some early visits to NUT headquarters in London in 2006 to hear NUT General Secretary Steve Sinnot, but with his untimely death I had to step back as a mark of respect for his colleagues and the organization. As it turned out I ended up working with local union-active teacher partners and we went from there. They came to see me as a trustworthy academic partner in a pliable role that allows for support and mentoring and/or acting as a critical friend (Groundwater-Smith and Kemmis, n.d.), which develops as the need arises. Quite early on I made contact with English colleagues Lupton (2003, 2004a, 2004b, 2005, 2006, 2014) and Whitty (1985, 2008, 2014), distinguished for their work on disadvantaged schools. Lupton led a research seminar titled 'Taking School Contexts Seriously: A Challenge for Urban Education' with academic colleagues at the end of my first year, which lent support to efforts to establish school–university partnerships in local networks of urban schools. Whitty's advice early on was brief and to the point: embark on a critical analysis of the possibilities *and* problems of teacher-initiated change to improve student learning outcomes.

My early initiative set in motion a series of pilot studies. These are all elaborated in the chapters that follow, but in this introductory chapter it is enough to provide a thumbnail sketch to make the twin points about the politics of so-called 'failing' schools and teachers' professional knowledge work. It is important to come to grips with vernacular neoliberal policy impositions in order to build a critical understanding of the threats to the profession because Gove's reforms will have repercussions down the twenty-first century, especially where they deny teachers' and teacher educators' professional points of view. The metaphor of 'holding the line', which is the concern of this book, may seem an elusive focus, but professional knowledge of the complex social realities is a bulwark against the 'crisis politics' that dominate teachers' work and grip urban schools reforms as they are not as they could be (see Wrigley, 2006; Apple and Beane, 1999).

The first pilot study came to be recognized as the 'Patterns of Learning' project, the name used in the formal letter of introduction to the school Head, a metaphor that refers to patterns of inequalities that impact on the work of schools, patterns of student learning and school achievement, patterns of pedagogies for a richly rewarding learning experience, and patterns of staff learning. As it was explained, these patterns of staff learning go across the school–university partnership, and across the school/s and system/s, for example academics' learning about urban schools' work, school Head/s' learning about a contextualized school-improvement agenda, teachers' learning about productive pedagogies and systems' learning about forging productive schools. These early efforts to institute a 'local' solution precipitated our local struggle, from a tempering of expectations in a system somewhat hostile to professional knowledge work to mentoring school staff, to develop their inquiry stance (Cochran-Smith and Lytle, 2009).

In many ways this strategic redirection of the thinking behind the school–university partnerships was the first of many instances where recalibrations had to be made to suit the socio-political circumstances. The school Head of this first pilot study school, adept in the educational-political arenas, encouraged my small team of academic partners to scale up the work into the local family of schools to mentor teachers on practitioner research and to seek support from the Local Authority. It happened that the team of academic partners secured funding from the Teacher Development Agency (TDA)[19]. This enabled a second pilot study, named 'Side-by-Side Learning', with the focus more on the processes of practitioner research (see Campbell and Groundwater-Smith, 2010; Campbell and McNamara, 2010) to shore up the teacher inquiry projects. This presented my first opportunity to work with teachers active in the NUT and NASUWT, which led to yet another pilot study, mostly by default, because I continued with one teacher partner in an urban high school on some extension work to continue to develop a more professional response, if not a counter strategy, to rigid performance measures with punitive results. The intention was to explore more elements of productive pedagogies, including efforts to link to students' cultural background knowledge (Hayes et al., 2006; Gallagher and Beckett, 2014). We both took this work to the then school Head with a proposal to institute whole school CPD but this work was seriously thwarted by a political assault that brought me face-to-face with the politics of 'failing' schools.

Systemic difficulties

When I began work at the start of 2006, the Blair New Labour Government was coming to the end of its term, or more accurately, Prime Minister Tony Blair came to be replaced by his Chancellor who formed the Brown New Labour Government. A significant policy announcement by the then-Secretary of State for Education, Ed Balls, was the National Challenge[20] and again I am advised by a teacher partner that his urban high school was included, being ranked in the bottom 10 per cent of schools on headline measures. This attracted national funding to support a Local Authority-appointed School Improvement Advisor to raise standards and boost results in English and Maths. It was all data-driven and results-focused, supportive at one level but the urban high school 'never came out'. As one member of the School Leadership Team (SLT) put it:

> The government is obsessed with targets and attainment at the expense of all the other measures and targets are a very poor indicator of what a school does . . . those particular targets based on pure attainment, are just so, so narrow and unfair [for example] when a student who we thought might have got an F gets a D, that is a great achievement to celebrate yet the government's agenda of just merrily driving on targets is totally, totally wrong.

This thwarted third pilot study presented a different opportunity to work with teacher partners, given their campaigns against school closure in concert with the Anti-Academies Alliance (2013), and again another recalibration was required in the form of tactical work on my part. This began with a reality check; that is, acknowledgement that urban schools operating in this performative system in England are captive to statutory demands held in check by the Local Authority at the Minister's insistence on school performance. This is apparent in this extract from a letter to targeted Local Authorities from former Secretary of State, Ed Balls:

> [T]he performance of some of your primary schools is causing us concern. Our analysis of the 2009 results shows that your authority has one of the highest proportions of primary schools which have been below the floor target for a number of years.

I initiated a collective response from what came to be called 'educationalists'; that is, those on the Board of Governors who worked in the profession as distinct from those outside, such as the group comprised mostly of businessmen, including a lawyer, keen to implement the government's neoliberal agenda in part because of ties to the Liberal Democrats. It was so interesting to be witness to the power plays, political compromises and pragmatic moves on the part of Board of Governors, Local Authority officials and local city councillors as they responded to the campaign against school closure. The educationalists, including union-active teachers, wanted their voices heard and so developed a series of submissions to the public and statutory consultations (see Beckett, 2012a; Gallagher and Beckett, 2014). This provoked yet further tactical work, which arose from a recognition that school Heads and teachers already familiar with extant quantitative national-school data might identify with practitioner research (see Beckett, 2014a).

A note of caution because I am again advised by a teacher partner this quantitative data is liable to cause grief when it is used by School Leadership Teams as a tool of crude comparative analyses to highlight student groups identified by official categorizations in disaggregated data. Teacher partners are quizzed on the performance and achievement of boys and girls but there is no sensitivity to social markers like gender, race and social class much less their intersectionality. It follows teachers are also grilled on particular ethnic groups but only as far as the official categorizations including white British, then students with 'special educational needs' (SEN) and non-SEN students with English as an additional language (EAL) and non-EAL (see Wrigley, 2000). Teachers are also scrutinized about students with low socioeconomic status termed 'free school meals' (FSMs) along with 'looked-after children' (LAC) and students perceived to be 'gifted and talented' (G&T). This presents some conflict for teachers in regards 'policy by numbers' when it goes against their better professional judgement.

One local teacher partner put this question: Does it matter if there is a difference in the performance and achievement in and between these [officially categorized] groups? The answer is derived from local urban school practice, where crude comparative analyses are done over three-year blocks to identify trends in order to inform select mandated interventions colloquially called 'a rollercoaster'. For example, a School Leadership Team concerned with a group of girls and trends over time could result in a 6–12-week focus on girl-friendly teaching, after-school clubs and the like, but then the concern shifts to another group, other trends and foci. This anecdotal evidence suggests some proof that urban schools are using extant quantitative data on instruction from Ofsted for the purposes of quick-fix interventions that satisfy tick-a-box criteria for 'Pupil Premium' funding, inspections and standardized school improvement. I am told it is easy to demonstrate great flurries of activity around national-school data and school-generated data but it is always marked by 'crisis politics', not necessarily democratic professional deliberations.

The final pilot study in a forced academy provided insights into this way of operating but our joint work required yet another recalibration. When presented with School Leadership Team concerns about performance data on white British students, we set out to do some practitioner research activities to get to the stories behind the data by reading international research literature, critical questioning, developing pen portraits of students and focus group interviews. Slowly we began to build a practice-focused ethnographic case study (Hammersley and Atkinson, 2007; Warren and Hackney, 2000) until it was disrupted by curious power plays orchestrated by the school Head. For teacher partners keen on professional decision making, it proved helpful to identify and name the dominant ideological message. As another urban high school Head put it:

> *The concern for all of us working in urban schools is that the data set is the first thing that Ofsted look at and that will drive the hypothesis about the quality of the school and the experience of urban Heads is that Ofsted come forward with that hypothesis and then look for evidence to prove it or disprove it. It can be very difficult for schools that might be working very hard.*

It is the argument of this book that teacher inquiry, done with the support of academic partners well versed in sociology of education, among other professional knowledge bases, enables would-be research-active teachers to name their concerns with particular samples of students beyond 'the numbers game'; develop some investigations into some identified complexities and nuances; and marshal the evidence, which should come in the form of extant data but also 'other' data (see Johnson, 2002; Johnson and La Salle, 2010). The aim is to engage in critical analyses in order to highlight the unrealistic policy and time pressures in urban schools (see Beckett, 2013a, 2013b). This requires empowering forms of practitioner research (see Cochran-Smith and Lytle, 2009; Hulme and Livingstone, 2013), which equips teacher partners to describe the social determinants of disadvantaged students' learning in accurate terms and document the case against the derisory charge of 'failing' school and by implication demonization. As Piketty (2014b) said, we need the right tools to represent inequality, which then becomes a way to re-focus attention on those responsible for the social and economic fallout in local urban school communities in Austerity Britain. This takes a cue from Anyon (2009), something I shared with teacher partners:

> We know, however, that even theoretically informed scholarship is not always politically progressive. Theory has been used to conserve an unequal social status quo as well as to challenge social inequities . . . we employ theory in ways we believe will encourage our own and each others' action against injustice.

The way it happened in the north of England, I had to find a way to link theory, research, analyses and action, and eventually recruited a small team of academic partners to work on contextually sensitive and locally responsive yet semi-structured CPD programmes to support teacher inquiry. These teacher educators were keen to engage with theory about 'teaching to the test', pedagogies of poverty (Haberman, 1991) and alternatives such as productive pedagogies (Lingard et al., 2003; Hayes et al., 2006), and we went from there in the face of enormous constraints. They could see strength in the argument that research-active teachers have the wherewithal to hone their professional voice not only about the complexities of teaching in different urban school contexts but also about what it takes to work in exemplary ways with students who experience poverty and cumulative multiple deprivation (see Munns et al., 2013). These teachers are then in a better position to inform urban school action plans in the classroom, but also policy advocacy for contextualized school improvement as well as the pre-service–in-service continuum of teacher education. The agreed task is to SPEAK TRUTH TO POWER[21].

Insisting on school democracy

Following the pilot studies, a challenge was to convince school Heads and teacher partners that the focus of our school–university partnership is for long-term sustained CPD to support and mentor teachers to be better qualified to work in urban schools. This is a description from the marketing flier:

> *The 'Leading Learning' project is school-based (not top-down or centralized); it is about local solutions (but not parochial because it brings international perspectives to bear); and it is about working collaboratively and cooperatively (holding an informed conversation, constructing a refreshed vision of teaching and teacher education). The timing of the partnership work is right as schools need to build support networks across the city and meet increased demands of expectations and accountability.*

I made a promise that the team of academic partners would study the 2010 *Schools White Paper* and the 2011 *Education Bill* as well as other reports along with national, regional and local urban school data to help mediate demands and work with teacher partners to develop a research perspective on practice. Inevitably this meant more recalibrations had to be made. For instance, a school Head would only approve a teacher partner's participation given the stipulation from one of their School Improvement Advisors that the teacher inquiry focus on closing the achievement gap in English from the beginning of Year 7 (see Gallagher and Beckett, 2014). This effectively inhibits any sustained practitioner research activity on the social determinants of students' learning, but we made a start. Once academic partners got underway working with a cohort called Trailblazers (see Beckett, 2014a), it eventually got to the point where teacher partners came to diagnose the nature of the calls to 'raise achievement' and 'close the gap' as something of an illusion on a couple of counts. First, urban school inspections are apparently made with pre-formed ideas of national-school comparative data so that inspectors are ever ready to ignore contextual considerations and castigate if not condemn teachers' work. This is captured by a high school Head sharing his views on Ofsted:

> *I would question the rigidity of [Ofsted inspection judgments] and the fact that the urban school context [is named and all but ignored]. I would absolutely go along with the fact that I am held accountable, as Head, I'm accountable for results. . . . The difficulty is that the judgments are very finite at the moment and the snapshot of what you see [is] unable to take into account all those additional factors. So I think that pressure is very much on urban schools in areas where there is wider challenge [and] that's very difficult.*

Second, since the urban school context is not necessarily given full consideration, even in view of local area data and the IMD, the onus is on the school Head to make the case for 'mitigating circumstances' (Arthurs, 2012, 2013) and furnish evidence to deflect any hint of defective teaching practices and the like. This may or may not include analytic findings useful to more professionally determined courses of exemplary action, but under the circumstances, it is crucial for practitioners to initiate some sort of constructive dialogue to deepen inspectors' understandings before any damning judgements are made. This was reiterated by a primary school Head, when he shared his experiences and views of urban school inspections and the need to garner the evidence to put their case:

16 A 'choreography of policy conflict'

> *We have to make sure [of] our case for the defense. If there is a hypothesis that our school 'requires improvement' or needs to be better in some respect, or in our case to show that our practice is 'outstanding', we have to make sure that we can put [evidence] on the table as and when it's required. The concern is that if we can't put it on the table at the moment of inspection to justify or to explain why something is as it is, the data argument will come thundering in on top of it and [inspectors will] say 'ah, you've got nothing to show us that contradicts or challenges what the [official national-school comparative] data is saying'.*

This recognition that there is more to it than meets the eye prompted me to turn to the French sociologist Alain Touraine's (1977) *The Voice and the Eye*. His recognition of mistrust in society [read the teaching profession] to shape the choice of its future through its social battles and internal political mechanisms speaks to our efforts in the north of England to engineer school–university partnership ways of working. Touraine's own construction of a sociology of action and the research methods to fit these orientations is useful to help the development of democratic 'local' solutions as practical actions. His insistence on reflexive accounts of social movements interconnects with Whitty's early advice, this time about how our work with research-active teachers might articulate with other interventions and wider social movements. My professorial inclination is to link with the Strategic Forum for Research in Education (Pollard and Oancea, 2010) and the BERA-RSA (2014a, 2014b) *Inquiry into Research in Teacher Education* to ensure practitioner research activities reverberate across the profession so that teachers, student teachers and teacher educators can draw on loops of feedback learning[22]. This has possibilities for acting in the interests of disadvantaged students and reaching out to school communities wracked by inequalities. An urban high school Head gave voice to the situation:

> *We met the Year 7 students joining us and their experiences of vulnerabilities are etched into their faces. These are children with massive, massive personal challenges. Certainly they come with a lot of learning needs but an awful lot more because of their social circumstances and not just material poverty [given] their family background, their own experiences.*

So what began for me as a work brief to initiate school–university partnerships in networks of urban schools has now become a quest to wrest back professional control from authoritarian education politicians like Gove and his replacement Morgan, who took office towards the end of the previous Cameron-Clegg Coalition Government's term and held it after Cameron led the Conservatives to an election victory in May, 2015. The urgent necessity to at least articulate some meaningful sense of democracy in teaching and teacher-education faculties sits well with collective action to engage in policy advocacy and teacher agency, which is not to ignore counter resistance (see Compton and Weiner, 2008; Little, 2015). That said, I take to heart a comment made by a local urban primary school Head:

We're not sat around trying to push forward an agenda within the classroom of any particular type; no one's interested, no one's got the time for all that. All we're interested in is how we develop the core aspects [of schooling] for the children so they've got a greater opportunity to go on and be successful, either later in their learning or later in their life in terms of their work and family.

The twin points here are that *there is* a neoliberal agenda that works in favour of a powerful business elite and the profession needs to reclaim its stake in teaching and teacher education. It needs to engage in professional knowledge building in order to state the case, marshal the research evidence and make some collective urban school-wide professional decisions about appropriate interventions with transformative potential. The trial 'Leading Learning' project in this northern city of England only came to fruition through the perseverance of some very determined teachers and academic partners, who helped fashion a model of CPD for urban schools that is locally sensitive and contextually responsive (see Beckett, 2014a). These practitioners can see the necessity – in the face of politically motivated charges of 'failing' schools – to network, develop their own accounts of their day-to-day struggles, pool their collective intelligence and ultimately 'go public' with their findings. This is about democratic control of urban schooling in the north of England.

Conclusion

Sennett captured the spirit of this sort of book in his Foreword to Touraine's *The Voice and the Eye*, where the great emphasis on conflict as a means of 'gluing' social life together may be best described as a *'choreography of policy conflict'*. Two things spring to mind, derived from Whitty's concern about external linkages and oppositional politics registered in his classic publication (Whitty, 1985):

Interventions within education can be effectively radical only when they have potential to be linked with particular struggles elsewhere to produce transformative effects.

The profession may balk at the term 'radical', which is something to broach, and maybe it comes down to the teacher unions to organize the professional concerns of teachers and academic partners in urban schools. Collectively it is better to orchestrate a *choreography of urban schools policy conflict*. In an effort to link with the NUT, I invited General Secretary Christine Blower to deliver the 2015 Winifred Mercier public lecture[23] and share the details of the NUT manifesto[24] for the election. Imagine my delight when she framed the work of teachers in terms of social movement trade unionism and when in turn I was invited to the 2015 NUT conference. There I witnessed a call to fight back *against* GERM and the managerialist-performative dictates but also a call *for* teachers' CPD. I can only hope our small modest local efforts in the north of England contribute to deliberations by the NUT and other teacher unions the world over.

18 A 'choreography of policy conflict'

There needs to be a LOUD collective teacher voice in reply to criticisms of teachers' work in urban schools but particularly the urban schools' derision and demonization. The last word derives from working class history in England, poetically provided by E.P. Thompson (in Winslow, 2014), who lived and worked in Yorkshire:

> This way of struggle, against class rule above, and between competing moralities . . . has never been a blind, spontaneous reflex to objective economic conditions. It has been a conscious struggle of ideas and values all the way.

By Arrangement with the Licensor, Tohby Riddle, c/- Curtis Brown (Aust.) Pty Ltd.

Notes

1 See www.westyorkshireobservatory.org
2 The 'Pupil Premium' grant was an initiative of the Liberal Democrats, enshrined in their 2010 election manifesto and instituted not long after entering the Cameron-Clegg Coalition Government with the Conservatives in May, 2010. It is allocated to schools

on the basis of the number of children on 'free school meals' within the last 6 years and the number of 'looked after' children. At the time of writing, the grant is £1325 per student according to a report on the expenditure of the grant tabled by an urban primary school Head at a local Board of Governor's meeting. There are departmental guidelines and schools are subject to the usual accountability: see www.gov.uk/pupil-premium-information-for-schools-and-alternative-provision-settings. Anecdotal evidence suggests urban school Heads deploy the grant to meet demands of school budgets in Austerity Britain, which is in keeping with public media debate, as this editorial in *The Guardian* shows: www.theguardian.com/commentisfree/2015/apr/06/guardian-view-on-education-system-in-flux

3 In my experience working with school Heads and teacher partners there is ready identification of disadvantaged students but these are according to official designations of FSM, 'looked after children' and now 'Pupil Premium'. They are proxy indicators of poverty and deprivation, which are also the subject of public media debate. For example, journalist Zoe Williams takes issue with the effects in an article 'Child rearing is far too important to be left to the market' in *The Guardian*: www.theguardian.com/commentisfree/2015/mar/15/child-rearing-early-years-market-society-public-sector-monetise

4 For more detail on the Bradford ILP, see www.independentlabour.org.uk/main/history/

5 Undated letter with explanation of spending decisions from Gove to Rt Hon. Ed Balls, MP in House of Commons immediately after the Cameron-Clegg Coalition Government took office in May, 2010.

6 It is not surprising to see Grace (2007) cite Thrupp's (1999) call for the profession's public rejection of the politics of polarization and blame, which hold urban schools individually responsible for supposed 'failure', and so become advocates for the students and others in disadvantaged urban school communities.

7 See www.gov.uk/government/publications/school-inspection-handbook

8 Teacher partners typify the profession's worries about students whose priorities lie elsewhere, from caring responsibilities for siblings, parents who are sick/dependent, to showing a mindset for survival without adequate coping strategies.

9 See www.lrb.co.uk/v36/n20/owen-hatherley/who-will-stop-them

10 Murdoch's intention to get a foothold in Britain's schools was twice reported in newsprint: by journalist David Leigh in 'The Schools Crusade That Links Michael Gove to Rupert Murdoch' in *The Guardian* on 27 February, 2012, which noted his intention to engage his media companies in online education; and by Andy Beckett in his review of McKnight's book, *Murdoch's Politics: How One Man's Thirst for Wealth and Power Shapes our World*, in *The Guardian Review* on 23 February, 2013, which noted a long battle for England's schools as Murdoch's *Times* columnist from 1983–89 David Hart consistently called for the privatization of all state education.

11 The choices open to schools are the Oxford, Cambridge and RSA examinations (OCR); the Assessment and Qualifications Alliance (AQA); Pearson's Education and Excellence (Edexcel); and in Wales the Welsh Joint Education Committee (WJEC).

12 For the subjects and calculations, see: www.calcul-8.co.uk/progress8.htm

13 See www.gov.uk/government/organisations/ofsted/about/statistics also http://dashboard.ofsted.gov.uk/

14 See http://download.ei-ie.org/Docs/WebDepot/EI%20Study%20on%20the%20Future%20of%20Teaching%20Profession.pdf, also Sally Weale's article dated 31 March, 2015, on the exodus of new teachers in *The Guardian*: www.theguardian.com/education/2015/mar/31/four-in-10-new-teachers-quit-within-a-year

15 See the official Ofsted criteria: www.gov.uk/government/uploads/system/uploads/attachment_data/file/391531/School_inspection_handbook.pdf

16 This derives from the BBC social class survey: www.bbc.co.uk/news/magazine-22000973

17 See www.publications.parliament.uk/pa/cm201415/cmselect/cmeduc/142/142.pdf

18 Here I must acknowledge Dr Chris Evans again, given our work together as academic partners in inner-city Sydney and how much I learnt from her about such work with these communities.
19 Following her appointment to the university, Professor Anne Campbell took the idea of scaling up our 'Leading Learning' project and married it to her idea to secure funding from the TDA 'CPD for schools in challenging circumstances'. We negotiated the foci and named the funded project: *Side-by-Side Learning: An Innovative Approach to Leading the Learning of All Staff in a Cluster Group of Schools in [this northern city]*.
20 This is different to the London Challenge and Manchester Challenge.
21 Note on the history: see www.independent.co.uk/life-style/the-reith-lectures-speaking-truth-to-power-in-his-penultimate-reith-lecture-edward-said-considers-the-basic-question-for-the-intellectual-how-does-one-speak-the-truth-this-is-an-edited-text-of-last-nights-radio-4-broadcast-1486359.html
22 This more or less sits well with the terms of the Carter (2015) Review of Initial Teacher Training (sic) in England, which seemingly gives university faculties with responsibility for teacher education the authority to shift towards embedding a research focus. This is mainly derived from work with Ofsted 3- & 4-grade schools, not necessarily urban schools: see www.gov.uk/government/publications/carter-review-of-initial-teacher-training
23 Every year, in the week of International Women's Day, I organize a public lecture to commemorate the life and work of Winifred Mercier, first woman Vice Principal 1913–16 at City of Leeds Training College, who coincidentally resigned in protest over lack of women's voice on the nascent policies for these new institutions apropos the 1902 Balfour Education Act.
24 See www.teachers.org.uk/manifesto

2
'LOCAL' SOLUTIONS TO 'FAILING' SCHOOLS

Introduction

I came to England 10 years ago to set up networks of school–university partnerships firm in the view that teachers' professional knowledge about the interconnections between disadvantaged students' lives, learning and schooling experiences is the key to work in local urban schools. The task, given my professorial appointment, was to set up a structure for a professional knowledge-building programme about local school communities in difficult circumstances. Academic partners would support and mentor teachers to engage in empowering forms of practitioner research to investigate and develop 'local' solutions. I was convinced teacher inquiry projects would build capacity for consideration of theories of poverty and schooling and entrenched social and educational disadvantage (Connell *et al.*, 1991; Lupton, 2003, 2004a, 2004b, 2005; Thrupp, 1999; Mortimore and Whitty, 1997/2000).

I began with a modest aim of an initial pilot study called 'Patterns of Learning' in a small local community primary school that might set up a reciprocal relationship to learn about what it takes to 'make a difference' to disadvantaged students' learning and life chances, assisted by an equally small team of academic partners with experience in school-based research. In the event, there needs to be a way into school-based investigations through teacher inquiry projects that takes some account of students' particular family and social circumstances, including intergenerational poverty. One pedagogical strategy is to encourage school staff to self-consciously engage in professional conversations about social disadvantage particularly the inequalities experienced by students with a view to their urban schooling experiences. Another is for teachers and academic partners to build a school learning portfolio, characterized by school documentation and professional literature but also written evidence of professional learning activities focused on classroom practices and transformative interventions.

At the end of the first year on the school Head's recommendation this pilot study was scaled up into its family of schools as the 'Side-by-Side' project. The project leaders, myself included, secured TDA funding for 'CPD in schools in challenging circumstances' to develop capacity in practitioner research[1]. When the funding ran out, there was no follow-through to embed the work so I again approached the Local Authority for funding support. Senior leaders indicated in-kind support but not the funding to sponsor the project citing a severe budget settlement that required extraordinary savings, which was characteristic of Austerity Britain. I envisaged that ongoing pilot studies in my new setting in the north of England would be a trial way to learn how 'local' solutions to problems arising in local urban school communities could be reconfigured as a 'Leading Learning' project. This took a cue from Lingard et al. (2003) to focus on urban school improvement through professional practice, particularly dispersed leadership to enhance disadvantaged students' academic and social learning outcomes. At the time what ultimately took precedence under the auspices of the then-new Brown New Labour Government was a new policy initiative, National Challenge. It provided funding for School Improvement Advisors to support urban schools but performance indicators meant short-term target chasing to improve disadvantaged students' learning outcomes. It was all driven by punitive sanctions against so-called 'failing' schools issued with notices on 'structural' solutions by politicians and Local Authority officials to close and reopen as sponsored academies.

New to England, this came as a jolt to my professional sensibilities and penchant for 'local' solutions: the NSW Priority Action Schools Program, co-designed by the teachers' union and departmental officials was a model cooperative initiative as part of a commitment to urban schools but also public education more generally (Groundwater-Smith and Kemmis, n.d.). I was more shocked to experience harsh alternatives to knowledge-building programmes albeit as an academic partner and governor in local urban schools. It seemed everyone was locked into tight prescriptions of urban school performance with punishing sanctions if/when national targets are not met. It made no practical sense, but I came to see it tied neatly to consecutive neoliberal governments' policy agendas. Forced academization typifies Harvey's (2005) twin concerns about the use of force to secure the proper functioning of markets and the state's role to create and preserve an institutional framework appropriate to neoliberal political-economic practices around free markets and free trade. This dovetails with academic analyses of the hegemonic nature of the neoliberal precepts and the ways they fundamentally change educational governance and school practices (Rizvi and Lingard, 2010). With the benefit of hindsight, given the global networks of philanthropy, business and governments come together in new sites of policy development (Ball, 2012), it was a wonder the pilot studies ever began.

In this chapter I continue to share extracts of the teachers' voice, which were recorded in initial briefing meetings, CPD sessions and focus group interviews in order to build collective intelligence. Over time, the different teams of teachers and academic partners engaged in practitioner research activities to develop arguments about the challenges they confront in this local network of urban schools, which take seriously local context, neighborhoods and communities (see Lupton, 2003). Eventually this led to critical discussions of extant government policy dictates on ever higher standards through national targets, which enable participants to draw on their evidence, hone their professional voice and 'go public' in modest ways. At first this is in-house in their urban schools, with each other but also with a view to contextualized school improvement, plugging into urban School Development Plans, but in time in conference presentations and publications[2]. None of this is to guarantee research-informed teaching and teacher education in urban schools in England, given increasing policy and time pressures and threats of sanctions. This requires close attention to home in on what it means to improve student learning outcomes under duress, and what it could mean when professional knowledge building takes into account social determinants coupled with a consciousness of social and educational inequalities. This might sound vague but again political wit to the fore given Whitty's early advice on a critical analysis of the possibilities *and* problems of teacher-initiated change because his concern is that an overreliance on teachers' consciousness raising, without any effort to articulate with wider social movements, amounts to 'naïve possibilitariansim' (see Whitty, 1974, 1985).

Forewarned is forearmed

At first, when I began working in the north of England, the meaning and significance of Mortimore and Whitty's (1997/2000) claims made some time ago were not readily apparent:

> *Despite the Thatcher and Major governments' refusal to acknowledge the importance of the relationship between social disadvantage and educational achievement, stark differences in the lives of [students] with different family backgrounds have not gone away, nor have the problems of knowing how to best deal with them. . . . The Blair government have shown an alarming tendency to perpetuate such attitudes . . .*

I bought into naïve possibilitarianism assuming that urban schools might want to buy-into a co-developed professional knowledge-building programme with academic partners and jointly learn about the relative effectiveness of different elements of the package of strategies they tried, which was my experience in Australia. Groundwater-Smith and Kemmis (n.d.) had eloquently articulated some major issues, from social geography, which identified the reproduction of poverty and deprivation effects in urban school communities but also the distribution across postcode areas to urban school reform packages of support. The most successful strategies included a shift towards transformative pedagogical practices, but also whole school vision and culture building, leadership and risk taking, challenging orthodoxies in the form of 'challenging current knowledge about good educational practice' and new forms of accountability for allocated funds expended. This was underpinned by a whole-of-government approach to problems of entrenched disadvantage experienced by urban school communities, but this was in another system.

Initially I learned much from a study of the history of ideas on poverty and schooling in England[3]. The Educational Priority Area programmes of the 1960s and 1970s featured extra payments made to urban schools with high proportions of disadvantaged students (see Halsey, 1972; Smith, 1987 cited by Mortimore and Whitty, 1997/2000). Mortimore and Whitty (1997/2000) summarized the remedies adopted in trying to change the patterns of disadvantage: equalizing opportunities through choice and competition; compensatory measures for students from low income families such as 'free school meals' and uniform grants; intervention projects like 'Reading Recovery'. I also learned from their outline of a two-pronged approach to school improvement based on research into school effectiveness but also the broader social and cultural context in which education takes place. This included a government program of Education Action Zones (Department for Education and Employment, 1997), which had as its centre a forum of local parents and representatives from local business and community interests in which action plans and targets were formulated, implemented and monitored.

By the time I arrived in this northern city there was no mention of these sorts of initiatives[4], but there was a palpable sense of government-enforced responsibility onto urban schools, including governors, to accommodate if not override social disadvantage and simply 'close the gap' (see Perry and Francis, 2010; House of Commons Education Committee, 2014). I took to heart Grace's advice about 'producing naïve school-centred solutions with no sense of the structural, the political and the historical as constraints' (Grace, 1984, cited by Mortimore and Whitty, 1997/2000) as well as Grace, Menter and Maguire's (2006) acknowledgement of the need to relate school-based analysis to wider theoretical, historical, cultural and socio-political analysis.

I saw merit in being an academic partner who could assist in teacher inquiry, urban school self-evaluation and reporting but also as a critical friend (Groundwater-Smith and Kemmis, n.d.) identifying, gathering and interpreting appropriate evidence and providing advice on curriculum construction and pedagogical strategies (Beveridge et al., 2005). This role evolved, given the task to co-develop the school–university partnership, which aligns with Touraine's (1977) efforts to set out the principles and methods of a sociology of action concerned with social movements. In the case of the co-developed 'Leading Learning' CPD twin-pack for this local network of urban schools, it is the academic partner's responsibility to bring out the conflicts around the 'crisis politics' in urban schools structured by neoliberal precepts simultaneous to improve professional knowledge and actions. Eventually academic partners are akin to Apple's (2009) secretaries for socially critical educators to make public their stories[5].

The challenges in building school–university partnerships tie very closely to the challenges that confront school Heads and teachers. As one urban primary school Head described them:

There are loads of challenges. [The overarching one] is the difficulty for our children who struggle to achieve or struggle to make the progress that we would like them to make. They have got very chaotic home lives. The challenge is how do we try and bring some order and develop some trust, some resilience and capacity so they can engage and learn when they might be hungry, sleepy, distressed. They might have missed learning, but they might have witnessed all sorts of things. They might be growing up a whole lot sooner than we would like, and they might be using language or not using language. [Now] it's how we support teachers in the classroom in terms of enabling them to meet the children's learning needs, first of all getting that child into school and support them. These issues are very real.

This data is telling, but it requires a second reading. The focus on achievement and progress in students' learning is tinged by the dominant systemic policy agenda and echoes the push to be 'raising achievement' and 'closing the gap', which is all-encompassing in teachers' work. The challenges are named in relation to disadvantaged students' capacity to learn, and the provision of urban schooling experiences is more or less unquestionably assumed to be fair. The support to be provided is singularly the staff responsibility to compensate for what is happening in the students' home life. The intention of the 'Leading Learning' pilot study was to provide opportunities to question the expectations on urban schools to take these actions and tailor their practices to students' experiences of poverty and cumulative multiple deprivation. It is to make the point that this way of thinking upholds deficit views as if this is the fault of the victim while other more advantaged students are privileged and the school system in England upholds this.

The 'complex hope' is that the profession, overloaded with so many centrally imposed responsibilities, would come to see the structural and historical difficulties (see Grace, 1994, 2007; also Thrupp and Tomlinson, 2005) and would come to consider different courses of action to include rather than exclude students in poverty. The practitioner research activities are constructed to support school Heads and teachers identify and name the complexities, to embrace these students' lived experiences, interests, abilities and aspirations, and to bridge with the goals in urban School Development Plans. This is to go further than Ofsted inspectors' judgements[6], confined to overall effectiveness and grade descriptors on particular foci of attention such as school leadership and management, behaviour and safety of students, quality of teaching and student achievement. Rather, practitioner research is to look out into the school community. This is how one school Head (cited in Mortimore and Whitty, 1997/2000) described the inner-city setting:

This is where the worst problems are found in Britain. High density living is not, in itself, a bad thing . . . but it tends to mean living in greater proximity to crime and drugs and it frequently means living in poor quality housing.

This resonated for me on arrival in this northern city, where there are cohorts of white British students but also students from different and diverse minority ethnic backgrounds, including black and Asian. Some students' families have experiences of poverty and cumulative multiple deprivation, unemployment and 'worklessness', and limited social mobility, while others have experiences of immigration, low socioeconomic status, and cultural barriers to negotiate.

Getting started: getting through

Strategically the place to start is with local area data tabulated to include information on the latest census, children, citywide communities, crime and safety, deprivation, economy, environment, health and well-being, housing, population and so it goes in alphabetical order[7]. Also the city's Neighborhood Indices provide interesting information that feature a narrative description and map, then statistical tables with the main one 'domain summary' on economic activity, low income, housing, health, environment, education, community safety, for example. These are accompanied by different graphs to provide pictorial representations.

This is complimented by government reports, notably an early Ofsted (1993) report, which apparently gave recommendations for 'closing the gap' on the educational achievements of children from rich and poor backgrounds in the English education system, and which painted a bleak picture of the quality of education received by the majority of children and young people at the time[8]. This was followed by *Access and Achievement in Urban Education: 10 Years On*[9] (Ofsted, 2003), *Aiming High: Raising the Achievement of Minority Ethnic Pupils* (Department for Education and Skills, 2003), *Deprivation and Education: The Evidence of Pupils in England, Foundation Stage to Key Stage 4* (Department for Communities, Schools and Families, 2009), plus *Access and Achievement: 20 Years On* (Ofsted, 2013)[10]. Of significance are practitioners' experiences/views of Ofsted emphases, especially the way inspectors arrive at judgements:

> *An inspector may not bring the level of understanding about what is required to work with children in urban schools like ours; there are very few of them who understand the complexities, especially if they have had no experience of it themselves.*
>
> *It's curious isn't it because in a way you're reliant on somebody else making the judgment about your work, with or without personal experience [of poverty and deprivation], with or without teaching experience, with or without inside knowledge. Yet your own judgment somehow is lost in all of this. It's like you relinquish your own right, your responsibility to be making a professional judgment.*

The message on inspectors' lack of understanding echoes concerns expressed by social commentators like Toynbee (2011) that people have lost their bearings on social class [and incomes]: the mega-wealthy are clueless; the poor are misled; aspiration and social mobility are a useful mirage, laying blame squarely with individuals, instead of seeking great fairness for all (see also Wilkinson and Pickett, 2010; Jones, 2011, 2014; Piketty, 2014a, 2014b; Dorling, 2011, 2014). This sort of scenario in urban schools provokes some professional disquiet (see Beckett, 2014a;

Connell *et al.*, 1991). One urban primary school Head was forthcoming about disquiet:

> Well a major disquiet is that every day we are the only profession that is a news item. . . . Every day there is something else that urban schools need to do better, improve on, change, or take a step back in time to, or some sort of comment. Often, whether it's [Her Majesty's Chief Inspector] or it's [the Secretary of State for Education] it will be tempered by 'more schools are rated good' or 'we value our teachers', you know, sound bites [for the media] but the over-riding message that's coming over to the profession is that we're not good enough, things need to get better and there's lots of different aspects that urban schools need to do better. It's unrelenting.

These concerns resonated with the urban primary school Head who responded to the request to do the first pilot study though she required some convincing given the role of the Chair of the Board of Governors. He reported that an Australian wanted to work in a 'failing' school, which was something of a misrepresentation. In the phone conversation, in trying to explain the intentions of this proposed school–university partnership, I indicated an interest in the relationship between poverty and disadvantaged schools. I wanted to learn what this disadvantaged urban primary school is doing, and what it might do, to enhance provision. I also indicated it was a reciprocal partnership where we would learn from each other. To provide clarification, I innocently equated the work in PASP schools in Australia with 'failing' schools in England.

The school Head not only balked at the label 'disadvantaged' school[11] (Connell *et al.*, 1991; Halsey, 1972), preferring the description of a 'challenging' or 'interesting' school. She then flatly refused to negotiate on the idea that her urban primary school is a 'failing' school and academics wanted to study it! I could only applaud, but of course the task was to convince the school Head I subscribed to a commitment to equity and social justice in and through schooling (see Connell, 1993; Sturman, 1997; Smyth *et al.*, 1998; Gale and Densmore, 2000; Thrupp and Lupton, 2006). Moreover I knew urban schools in low socioeconomic status communities as disadvantaged schools in the international research literature (see Lupton, 2006; Connell *et al.*, 1991). While one had to respect the school Head's point of view, it was a job to further convince the school Head the most successful strategy for supporting urban schools is to establish professional learning communities that lead to authentic changes in teaching practice and improved student learning outcomes (Lieberman and Miller, 2008).

The first trial

The school Head agreed to the school–university partnership with two provisos: it was to be an expression of goodwill with in-kind support from both parties because no funding was available. Second, it was not to be 'quick-and-dirty' but meaningful, long-term and sustained, with CPD sessions provided for ALL staff, until they withdrew and academic partners were not to peddle accreditation programs such as MA degrees. This was described as the university's agenda, which was something of a censure against what was realistically expected from academic partners but she may have wanted to call our bluff. In any event, it was crucial to go into the school prepared to acknowledge and respect the demands of the school Head given this urban primary school's work in the face of multiple challenges.

The academic partners' preparatory work was then geared to articulating a theory of non-accredited CPD drawing on Lingard et al. (2003), Hayes et al. (2006) and Loughran (2006) but also Lieberman and Miller (2008), Cochran-Smith and Lytle (2001, 2009), Lingard and Renshaw (2010), and Menter and Murray (2011). It happened academic partners had to recalibrate their intentions at almost every step to take into account the staff learning readiness for professional knowledge building and teacher inquiry. Two pedagogical strategies are noteworthy. One was to provide select professional readings accompanied by a series of tailored 'homework activities' as they were known. Here is a sample that followed the very first interactive workshop session:

1. A short statement on what you make of the book title, *Teachers and Schooling Making a Difference* (see Hayes et al., 2006).
2. A story about your classroom work, prompted by a sample of students' work.
3. A story about your concerns, prompted by an artefact from your classroom.
4. A note on your favourite part of Ruth Lupton's six-page article, 'Understanding local contexts for schooling and their implications for school processes and quality', in *BERA Research Intelligence,* Number 89, November 2004.

These were used in the follow-up session to focus attention on professional conversations and develop some graphic accounts of teachers' work in this urban primary school, which was shared via a school–university newsletter. This pedagogical strategy followed every session and enabled a continuation of honest talk about myriad issues that came up in face-to-face conversations, connecting to précised academic literature to familiarize staff with ideas, concepts and theories in wider arenas. It also allowed academic partners to build a different relationship to knowledge with a chance to alert staff to different ways of thinking and talking, at the same time as it is intended to stimulate learning and build capacity for knowledge work. For example, this is the newsletter report on staff discussions in reply to the professional learning activity cited above:

> *'Making a Difference' can happen with individual students and/or the whole class, mindful of access to learning, engagement and active participation, all often easier said than done. Staff efforts ranged across every conceivable demand on their time, from teaching and learning and accommodating routine expectations, to addressing social exclusion, whatever its form, and attending to different crises. . . . The BIG questions are HOW to make a difference, and HOW do we know we are making a difference?*

> *This sits well with Maguire, Woolridge and Pratt-Adams' (2006) view about theorising the urban setting and urban education, where urban education policy-making often starts with problem(s) rather than an appreciation, and theoretical analysis, of urban settings. As they put it, it might seem that standing back and theorizing about urban schools misses the point because what is needed is action. Urban primary schools face many – and we would add urgent – problems, but how these are understood have a powerful bearing on what practical outcomes are recommended.*

Each of the newsletters also included a cartoon, reproduced throughout this book, to literally illustrate the critical edge to practitioner theorizing[12]. Teacher partners ultimately came to identify some inquiry projects: for example, student needs in the inter-school Learning Support Unit; creative curriculum with particular reference to ethnic minorities; race as an educational issue; white working-class underachievement; student confidence and motivation; reading student quietness; and student health and well-being (see Beckett, 2009). The major complaint was that they struggled to find enough time to develop their projects beyond an activity to be completed, which was evident in what could be called mainstream problematizing of professional concerns and light-weight analysis of the effects of poverty and cumulative multiple deprivation. For example, one teacher inquiry project was guided by the question: How does the creative curriculum[13] provide an enriching learning experience which is accessible to all children? The concern was for students who do not make the same progress in reading and writing and whose levels of progress are lower than national average. When pressed on recurrent equity considerations like poverty, here is a response, which includes an indication of the analysis:

> *Yes poverty does have an impact. Nationally there is a concern about children [mainly boys] on 'free school meals' underperforming. However at [this urban primary school] they are making accelerated (value-added) progress. . . . The creative curriculum, immersed learning, personalized learning [interventions] give more opportunity for [these boys] to identify their preferred learning styles and find their own strengths. 'Talk for writing' really supports those who find it difficult to write as they can share their ideas, record their work on a microphone or camcorder, role play or story-board their ideas.*

The data shows a preoccupation with the performative agenda, free school meals as a proxy indicator of poverty, and named interventions as part of standardized school improvement practices apropos neoliberal government policy announcements and/or commercial packages. The team of teachers and academic partners were hard pressed to explore alternatives beyond the sort of feedback learning compiled in newsletters for the school learning portfolio, which is yet another pedagogical strategy suggested by one of the architects of the PASP in NSW. Groundwater-Smith (2007a, 2007b) visited this urban primary school and worked with us, which coincided with her 2007 BERA keynote address.

The school Head would not allocate any additional time beyond the two back-to-back CPD sessions one day once every half term, with arrangements for the school staff including teaching assistants to cover timetable. The difficulties in orchestrating a 'local' solution that derived from professional knowledge-building activities became more and more apparent. As one teacher partner put it after some professional learning activities around the different dimensions of 'productive pedagogies': intellectual quality, connectedness, supportive school environment, and recognition and valuing of difference (Lingard et al., 2003; Hayes et al., 2006):

> *All of us teachers had to do university so we recognize a lot of the words but no longer really use them. I could still go and look and remember them. Like I remember the 'higher order thinking' straightaway but I just think is there a need for it? We don't normally talk using these words in our day-to-day work. I could understand if you were talking to academics then yes, it would be very useful.*

This data echoes the view of most teachers that theory and research are considered irrelevant if not useless (see Lieberman and Miller, 2008). It is a stark reminder of the impact of vernacular forms of GERM (Sahlberg, 2011) that see a diminished scope for professional influence on teaching practice apropos the increased influence of central regulation and marketization (Gewirtz et al., 2009). The time and inclination for teachers' intellectual engagement soon came to light in an interview:

> *Sometimes you do read short [newspaper] articles in the Times Ed or is it the TES? I don't even look at the titles but if there's an interesting article I might read it although I don't take notes on it. I don't necessarily think about it but then it does come into everything it kind of becomes part of what you do. You don't really think that I've read that article and therefore I'll do this, it just comes up as an idea at the appropriate time. I don't read books on it to be honest.*

This is a worrying development for the profession. The teachers' experiences of deskilling and reskilling, which have come to replace more substantive conceptions of what it means to operate professionally in culturally, socially and educationally critical ways (Apple, 2009), should come as no surprise. I was dumbstruck by a presentation delivered by the then-Chief Executive of the not-for-profit company that ran the education department of the local city council[14]. She used 'brilliant schools, brilliant teaching and brilliant learning' jingoism with an audience of practitioners. The ideological assemblage for marketing purposes signalled a shrinking of the ability to theoretically engage in professional knowledge building (see Goodlad's Foreword in Cochran-Smith, 2006).

Over time in this first pilot study some teachers in the Learning Support Unit along with other staff notably teaching assistants and nursery nurses withdrew citing intensified work demands, and those remaining juggled time pressures and centralized mandates to improve school performances and provide measured 'value-added' experiences for students. It ran over 4 years, 2006–10, and it was apparent they were keen to learn from each other and hear what academic partners had to offer. There was assurance staff learned much and saw great value in the 'Patterns of Learning' project. The deputy school Head, who was eventually promoted to a school Head's position[15], had this to say:

> I have thoroughly enjoyed the work and the experience of working with you [and the team of academic partners] as well as a group of great [teacher] colleagues. I have learnt a great deal, and I would like to thank you so much for inviting me to be a part of this amazing learning journey as a teacher partner and practitioner researcher. I hope to sometime in the future be able to continue what we've started [in my new school].

The challenge was to capitalize on these good working relationships. When the team of academic partners hosted an invitational seminar it was billed to share expertise on pedagogies, promote research-informed teaching and build a co-developed research culture between the Local Authority, schools and the university. Invitees included Lingard and Mills, authors of *Leading Learning* and architects of productive pedagogies (see Lingard *et al.*, 2003; Hayes *et al.*, 2006). The host urban primary school Head did a presentation, 'Productive pedagogies and educational research making a difference'. It was a breakthrough to showcase some practitioner theorizing but also strategically welcome. The school Head was keen to promote the first pilot study as an exemplary project and made it known the teachers' joint work with academic partners to develop evidence-informed practice was a significant factor in it being ranked '1st most improved school in this northern city of England', fourth in county and twentieth nationally in 2008 (see Beckett and Wood, 2012). On her recommendation, this was scaled up into the local family of urban schools at the end of the first year.

Scaling up

The 'Side-by-Side' project proposal to the TDA kick-started a second pilot study, best described as a capacity-building programme. This was to support teacher inquiry projects with mentoring in practitioner research but also to enhance their sense of agency. It recognized the urban schools in challenging circumstances, but also the experiences of disadvantaged students, families and local communities. It drew on 'inside' knowledge of urban schools about its school community to assist them develop 'local' solutions (see Groundwater-Smith and Kemmis, n.d.). The project is described in this extract from the submission for funding:

> *What is distinctive about this provision is:*
> - *The emphasis on learning from each other through investigation of practice*
> - *Support in situ for the critique and development of practice and changing the curriculum partnership between primary and secondary schools and HE*

- *Piloting new models of professional learning with teachers and support staff with an emphasis on leading professional learning in schools*
- *Research based evaluation of the venture re impact and effectiveness*

This second pilot study sat well with the 'Leading Learning' motif because it aimed to work with leadership teams and groups of staff in and across the family of urban schools to create a vision for professional learning that places it at the very heart of quality school improvement plans. With the allocation of funding, the two project directors, myself included, joined a team of academic partners to work with teacher partners from five urban primary schools and two urban high schools. The sequence of sessions designed to mentor participants on practitioner research followed directions already published by one of the project directors (see Campbell and Groundwater-Smith, 2010; Campbell and McNamarra, 2010):

> *Practitioner research, located in the larger field of practice-based and applied research, is distinguished by its focus on research done by practitioners themselves, usually an investigation of practice with a view to evaluation or improvement. . . . We are focusing on teachers as practitioners. . . . We turn to Stenhouse (1975), Elliott (1985, 1991), Cochran-Smith and Lytle (1993, 2007) and Ziechner and Noffke (2001) and their work which promoted curriculum reform and teachers as researchers of the curriculum and the practice of teaching. They foreground:*
>
> - *teachers' work and teachers themselves as a basis for research;*
> - *critical reflection and systematic study of practice;*
> - *practitioner control and ownership of research.*

The emphasis on practitioner-research processes could be considered a 'master stroke' in regards the scaling up of the school–university partnerships, to a degree. Here is a sample of the titles devised to guide the teacher inquiry projects:

- *Emotional Intelligence within [an urban high school]*
- *On Your Marks. . . . Set 4 . . . the race to [GCSE results: A study of productive pedagogies]*
- *Incorporating stakeholders' views in what contributes to a successful school*
- *Student views on making the transition from primary to high school*
- *A school-community homework project*
- *New to English students and the impact of their induction [to school]*

The findings from these teacher inquiry projects were presented by teacher partners at the conclusion of the TDA-funded project, which was some achievement given the period allocated had been truncated. Unexpectedly, before the end of the year-long period of the TDA national funding contract, we were advised the timeline was to be curtailed and we were requested to furnish an immediate project report. For the most part the 'Side-by-Side Learning' project was a success. The school Head who had hosted the first pilot study in her urban primary school had joined the cohort and constructed a head teacher inquiry project called 'What's the point'. As she reported:

> There was a recognition our children come to school and go through the motions of the National Curriculum but for most of them it's whizzing well over the top of their heads. They're not engaged with it. They're not interested. Behaviour is not good then they think 'Well what's the point?' That was the thing that came back from children [in interviews/informal talks]: 'Well what's the point?' [of learning]. We decided, which was brave of us, [to review] National Curriculum. If you actually look at the statutory orders it's this thick, given all the hoo-ha that comes with it. You know, 'if you teach this scheme of work you'll have met this requirement'. That's what we were embroiled in [until we] realized actually we have to teach it, so we decided to make this change with our curriculum. The staff then felt in a position where they were really in control of letting go [of national prescription] . . . and the children now feel that they are in control of their learning.

It was fortuitous the school Head had the confidence to voice concerns, augmented by practitioner research activities including data gathering like student interviews and data analyses. This homed in on boys' attitudes to learning, self-belief and aspirations. While it might appear that local context and larger social and economic structures are being overlooked in these discussions, it is not to ignore the deeply ingrained hierarchical class structure which remains one of the hallmarks of British social life (Sveinsson, 2009). The school Head identified working class role models; the poor concentration, attention and engagement of boys who meet the deprivation criteria like free school meals; feelings of hopelessness, lack of aspiration or positive image of the future and productive role in society; parents' lack of aspirations for their sons; and the connectedness between education and home and a partnership between schools and parents (see Beckett and Wood, 2012).

In the event, this bore witness to the salience of academic partners' pedagogical strategy of returning newsletters after CPD sessions, which proved a successful 'method of intervention' as triggers for professional knowledge work, including critical thinking. Teacher partners acknowledged this was the first time since pre-service that they took an interest in professional reading outside prescribed reading of circulated policies and material updates. Joint discussions about the literature give us all an opportunity to construct knowledge and a shared vocabulary and reclaim the profession's place as a driving force in educational activity. Only one newsletter was produced for this TDA-funded 'Side-by-Side Learning' project, which was more a medium to share organizational details. It happened the newsletters could not be sustained without significant funding for academic partners to employ a designated research assistant.

Again with the benefit of hindsight, had the resources been available, a follow-up final newsletter could have reported on a meta-evaluation. Groundwater-Smith and Kemmis (n.d.) had posed the following sample questions of the NSW PASP:

- *To what extent was the program an adequate response to the circumstances of students, families, teachers and schools in communities with deep needs?*
- *To what extent did 'local' solutions, devised by schools to meet local problems and concerns, turn out to be adequate in addressing the actual needs of students, families, teachers and schools in these communities?*

The project directors' reflections on the TDA-funded second pilot study should have embraced similar evaluative questions. They should have reflected on their theorizations and conclusions say about schools in challenging circumstances (see MacBeath *et al.*, 2007). This ties into a critical discussion about different conceptualizations of poverty and cumulative multiple deprivation, including practitioners' reliance on 'poverty of culture' explanations (see Thrupp, 2005; Lingard, 2009), for example. The project directors should have taken the time to revisit ideas, concepts, theories and doctrines being imposed on urban schools, say, decontextualized school improvement that ignores 'school mix' or social class composition (Thrupp, 1999). With the collapse of this TDA-funded project there was no further system support for such a capacity-building programme, as this email advice shows:

[We are] unable to offer funding for your project as it does not fit with our current remit – our funding is currently tied up in particular programs and projects which do not offer us the scope to fund independent research like yours.

The politics of failing schools

The Local Authority, itself hard hit in Austerity Britain, suffered major staff reductions in its School Improvement team of advisors who are greatly valued by urban schools. Still it seemed opportune to again broach local support this time with a case to the then-city council Children's Services Director[16] on the worth of knowledge building in the citywide network of urban schools. This is an extract from a memo dated June, 2009:

The 'Leading Learning' project in [local urban schools] would involve:

- *Agreement in principle from [local] Children's Services & [this university] Faculty to proceed with the plans for coordinating professional learning communities in urban schools and the university;*
- *A tailored program for teachers' professional learning and development co-developed with representative teacher partners for commencement in the 2009–2010 school year*

This Children's Services Director allegedly allocated considerable funding, a move that recognized the synergy between the Local Authority's local urban schools and the university in terms of common aspirations to secure quality work in respective

'Local' solutions to 'failing' schools 35

institutions. The commitment was to guarantee a professional workforce at the cutting edge of research and practice improving the learning experience of staff and students in urban schools and the university, including initial teacher education. However, before the agreement was signed off, the Director was forced to resign following a negative Ofsted inspection report on the Local Authority's capacity for safeguarding children[17]. This proved to be a setback to our citywide school–university project work, but there were two things of significance: academic partners continued a series of meetings with the then-Deputy Chief Executive of the not-for-profit company engaged by city council, the School Improvement team and local urban school Heads. Second, there was noticeable ongoing commitment to our pilot studies from participating teacher partners and school Heads[18]. An urban primary school Head had this to say:

> The big benefit from the university is the work that [the academic partners] did with staff in practitioner research. . . . They work incredibly hard [in the classroom], but it empowered them. That is the word that I would use; it empowered them and reminded them [of their professional knowledge] . . . and it didn't change because [the academic partners] were coming in and saying; 'Right, we're all going to talk like academics now'. It wasn't like that. It was this growth in their own awareness of how much they knew, realizing that actually what they do know is really worth something.

The significant point here is that this school Head sees the necessity to draw attention to teachers' professional knowledge, which suggests it is not at the forefront of their work. This raises questions about what counts as legitimate knowledge and legitimate teaching and the dominance of managerial emphases (Apple, 2009). I hasten to add none of these negotiations are easy especially when the task is to support teachers' critical engagement with practice (see Menter's Foreword in Philpott, 2014). Moreover, teachers' knowledge work in urban schools is circumscribed by ever intensifying policy and time demands to respond to centralized mandates to improve school performances. There is precious little opportunity for teachers to engage professional conversations much less contextual considerations, beyond intermittent meetings with parents if not local communities. Yet these are crucial because the origins of the challenges experienced in the classroom very often lay outside the urban school.

Any wonder there is reticence to work with academic partners. It is simply unrealistic in the current conjuncture, where academic contributions, particularly professional reading even in book publications much less practitioner research, are not necessarily valued[19]. As one of the school Heads interviewed after the pilot study indicated:

> I think it's a balancing act. Long term [practitioner] research is hard where there are staffing issues because we don't have lots of spare bodies. Staff don't have free periods in primary schools as they may have in high schools. So it becomes another plate to spin but the benefits outweigh the pressures that it can put on you.

Little did we know at the time the pressures would be magnified in the brewing educational-political storm, which was to bring the full force of the performative policy construction of 'failing' schools in the National Challenge. On a first reading, the additional funding that enabled the allocation of School Improvement Advisors might sound like valuable systemic support for urban school teachers. The insistence on urban school closures when they failed to meet floor targets was another matter altogether. I soon came to learn that the sort of system support put in place heralded a contradictory role for the Local Authority. By then it had been reconstituted apropos further budget cuts but exerted considerable political influence implementing enforced 'structural' solutions where urban schools are required to come under the jurisdiction of a corporate sponsor and be cut adrift from the Local Authority. In effect its own political activities result in its own diminished capacity, plus National Challenge apparently had no democratic mandate at least at the local school-community level.

Forced academization

The National Challenge policy initiative heralded punitive results for two of our partner urban high schools, who were confronted by closure notices, which serves to show just how much policy pressure was being brought to bear on this network (see Beckett, 2012a). From my own personal perspective I found it extremely annoying that the work that had continued after the 'Side-by-Side' pilot study to support my teacher partner was yet again curtailed. The budding 'local' solution of transformative teaching had the support of the then-school Head keen to engage the whole school staff, but it came to a grinding halt, which was not without union-active teachers voicing their disquiet. As one made it known about the proposed 'structural' solution:

> *The inadequacy of this measure is acute in the case of [this urban] High School which in addition to a core British-born White and Asian student body educates children from a hugely diverse range of cultures and ethnicities (over 70 languages are spoken in this school of, currently, under 600 students).*

These teachers swung into action and developed campaigns against school closure to galvanize the local communities. It was an extraordinary display of teachers' politicization (see Ghale and Beckett, 2013) to show the National Challenge policy emphasis seemingly spurned recovering the context of school improvement (see Maguire *et al.*, 2006) and teachers' sociological analyses of poverty and urban schooling. This echoes Touraine's (1977) concerns about the post-industrial programmed society (read national targets, Ofsted inspections) and the data-processing apparatus (read government policy dictates, national-school data banks), which is ensuring the often monopolistic control of the supply and processing of a certain type of data (read termly and yearly students' attainment and progress summaries) as a way of organizing social (school life).

Again the union-active teachers voiced their support for the work done by teachers and academic partners. Here is an extract from their counter-solution:

> The [local] area currently served by [this urban] High School is recognised as one of vulnerability, deprivation, reduced social equity and cultural diversity. Whatever the benefits, suggested by some, of the school's closure the costs to this community are too high.
> We propose working with our five [feeder] primary school partners through a Co-operative Trust . . . [and] with extended services partners to become a learning community offering inclusive through-schooling from 0–19 years. . . . We will plan specific interventions for meeting the challenges of the 'Raising the Participation Age' agenda. . . . We will build on a successful TDA-funded project to create a mutually beneficial school-university partnership.

My tactical response was to follow suit and galvanize the educationalists with an agreed written response to public consultation. I put the case:

> Disadvantaged schools are well recognized in the international research literature, which documents the complexities of urban education: the learning needs of disadvantaged students and the impact of poverty on the schools' work, for example, additional learning needs, material poverty, the emotional climate and disturbed behavior, and reluctant participation (see Lupton, 2006).
> [The] City Council has an opportunity to determine the fate of [these two urban high schools] but it needs to do so with integrity, taking into account the empirical evidence, including longitudinal evidence, and arguments put by stakeholders and the educational community writ large across the city.
> When coupled with Ofsted reports, the schools' self-evaluations and school improvement plans, this all paints a comprehensive picture of the schools' work, including the complexities and contextual considerations.

This urban high school ultimately won the battle to remain open, but there were costs. Inexplicably, the Local Authority maintained its '[this urban high school] closed' sign on its website, which in effect meant parents reneged on sending students, numbers fell, budgets streamlined, and battles continued (see Beckett, 2012a; Gallagher and Beckett, 2014). As a member of the SLT put it:

> Money came into school but the money for National Challenge wasn't as big as it was made out and there were certain [attainment] conditions to it, but it was new money. . . . So it's wrong to paint everything as 'doom and gloom' as we've been able to get lots and while we always want more we got lots of things that we weren't getting [ten years ago]. For me the frustrating thing is the disproportionate effect that chasing narrow attainment targets means . . . and fending off the sort of blunt weapon approach from Ofsted.

Given these circumstances, the school–university partnership work being trialed in the pilot studies deserves consideration. This takes a cue from Cochran-Smith and Lytle (2001), who have done extensive work on school–university partnerships in North America. Their idea about local knowledge foregrounds the processes of constructing knowledge, not the products. They see teachers' knowledge expressed and integrated in the daily life of schools and classrooms, which is seemingly overshadowed in the north of England. Again Touraine's (1977) point on resistance to domination by the data apparatus proves insightful. These are truly social struggles which bring a social relation into question because they are no longer able to support a profession. When translated into the urban school setting for CPD, it has to do with teacher partners' insistence on professional knowledge work that includes some critical self-evaluation when it comes to poverty and urban schooling. To continue with Touraine's (1977) second point on reconciling these two orders of behaviour, we have to acknowledge the policy and time pressures in a performative system BUT still trigger professional self-determination.

Conclusion

Once underway in the north of England with the first pilot study called 'Patterns of Learning', I soon got the impression that efforts to build a professional learning community were contrary to standardized practices. It was an unusual request for academic partners to come in to an urban primary school and its family of schools to support teachers to deepen their sociological thinking and theorizing and develop 'local' solutions to plug into contextualized school action plans. Although there is recognition at local urban school level about students on free school meals, none of their lived experiences of poverty and cumulative multiple deprivation is self-consciously named and identified as such. There is little or no evidence of any critical understandings as they relate to students' readiness for learning, or teachers' attitudes and values and the ways these influence urban school practices much less present a challenge to inequalities. Piketty (2014a) lays out the role for research and calls for patiently searching for facts and patterns, which accords with our 'Patterns of Learning', analyzing the economic, social and political mechanisms that might explain them. As he said, it can inform democratic debate and focus attention on the right questions. That there is resistance to this sort of work harks back to what Mortimore and Whitty (1997/2000) said, which proved prescient:

> [O]ur society [in England] appears to be deeply confused about the relationship of disadvantage to patterns of achievement. In particular there is confusion over how much underachievement is due to the actions of individuals and how much to the influence of the school or the attitudes of the wider society.

'Local' solutions to 'failing' schools **39**

© Chris Slane. Reproduced by permission of Cartoon Stock. www.CartoonStock.com (Image ID: csan29).

Notes

1 As noted in the previous chapter, Campbell and Beckett gave this next pilot study its full title in the funding application to the TDA: *Side-by-Side Learning: An Innovative Approach to Leading the Learning of All Staff in a Cluster Group of Schools in [this northern city]*.
2 This book is geared to the special collection of *Urban Review* 2014, 46, 5, a showcase of the teachers' voice in journal articles authored by the Trailblazers, that is the teacher partners who signed up as the first cohort of the 'Leading Learning' CPD twin-pack. This teacher learning and development programme, which resulted in the publication with the support of their academic partners, is detailed in the chapters that follow.
3 See some sites devoted to this sort of work: www.poverty.org.uk/19/index.shtml; www.historylearningsite.co.uk/poverty_schools.htm
4 For information on poverty see www.jrf.org.uk/publications/monitoring-poverty-2012
5 In the absence of system-wide support, this work is in part reliant on sources of self-funding through entrepreneurial activities and bids for research grants. The team of academic partners have mostly worked in urban schools as an expression of goodwill because the funding bids are incredibly difficult to secure. In my experience, many grants are tied to dominant political agendas: see the Education Endowment Fund earmarked to build the 'toolkit' at https://educationendowmentfoundation.org.uk/toolkit/
6 See www.gov.uk/government/publications/school-inspection-handbook
7 I have purposefully de-identified the following internet location to maintain anonymity of this northern city: http://observatory.xxxx.gov.uk/dataviews/
8 Citation taken from www.gov.uk/government/news/major-review-of-access-and-achievement-in-education
9 See HMCI David Bell's speech at the time: www.theguardian.com/education/2003/nov/20/schools.uk3

10 See www.education.gov.uk/consultations/downloadableDocs/213_1.pdf; www.the guardian.com/education/2003/nov/20/schools.uk3; also www.gov.uk/government/publications/unseen-children-access-and-achievement-20-years-on
11 A continuing issue of contention with the school Head and indeed the team of academic partners has been the term 'disadvantaged' school: check Harridge *et al.* (2014).
12 Here I must acknowledge the contribution of Dr Jon Tan, who furnished every school–university newsletter with a cartoon.
13 This mention of the creative curriculum no doubt derives from a landmark 2007 report from the National College for School Leadership (NCSL) called *Lifting the Lid on the Creative Curriculum*.
14 Erroneously I had always assumed that this was the Local Authority, given earlier formal introductions, but then I did not have the benefit of local historical knowledge about local educational politics: some 15 years ago its education department received a very poor Ofsted report which led to the setting up of a wholly owned city council not-for-profit company. This operated as a public–private partnership with a group that provides business process management and professional support. Interestingly in time the then Chief Executive received an education excellence award in recognition of her work as one of the most successful education leaders in the country and attracted recognition as a 'Times 100 Best Company' a few years later. It is noteworthy that *The Times* is part of the Murdoch group of companies, which has some interest in schools and universities in England being open to private providers (see Beckett, 2013a).
15 It is important to mention that three of our teacher partners were promoted to school head positions and others to assistant head, heads of department while some required transfers and one felt forced out of the profession.
16 By this time the city council's partnership with the not-for-profit company that ran the local education department had ended, although the Chief Executive remained until Labour regained overall control of the council and abolished the not-for-profit company, merging its remit with a Children's Services Directorate.
17 The educational politics was something to negotiate: the unfavourable Ofsted report ultimately led to the replacement of the not-for-profit company, which took effect on 31 March.
18 For example, two instances of 'going public' with conference presentations and publications proved significant: I was accompanied by the school Head who had hosted the first pilot study to Sydney for my 2009 keynote and we were then invited by Groundwater-Smith to talk to colleagues at the University of Sydney who were seemingly keen to hear the details of our north of England-based school–university partnerships work.
19 My experience with the National Teacher Research Panel (NTRP) and the Centre for the Use of Research and Evidence in Education (CUREE) was interesting to say the least: teachers may be encouraged to undertake practitioner research but there is seemingly a distinct lack of critical social analyses. One cannot help but conclude that this sort of practitioner research, supported by a private provider, is the preferred version to funded and rolled out.

3
CRITICAL DEMOCRATIC WORK

Introduction

The termination of the TDA-funded 'CPD in schools in challenging circumstances' at the national level made no practical sense, but significantly, I became aware that local educational politics in the north of England is more complicated than I ever imagined. The launch of the then-Brown New Labour Government's National Challenge policy came to bring the full force of 'failing' school closures, forced academization and corporate sponsors into local urban high schools. The campaigns against school closure brought school communities into view, and ran right up to and past the 2010 election of the then-new Cameron-Clegg Coalition Government [and indeed the 2015 election of the Cameron Conservative Government]. This showed continuity in the neoliberal reform agenda across governments comprised of different mainstream parties, which differed only in degree. While one battle was lost another was successful, but then I witnessed the most startling display of anti-democratic ways of working in my capacity as an academic partner but also as school governor.

The Board of Governors of the urban high school that won its campaign was summoned by the Local Authority to an extraordinary meeting to precede the regular meeting in an hour's time. Two options were put: the Board of Governors could vote to dissolve itself and save the urban high school any political embarrassment in the public media, or it would be dissolved. Either way, with the approval of the then-Conservative Secretary of State for Education Michael Gove, a new Interim Executive Board (IEB) was to be put in its place to oversee managed staff reduction, or MSR, as it was called. This included the replacement of the school Head with an Acting school Head, himself an Ofsted inspector. I was aghast at the advice that, given staff anxieties and tears about job loss, family and mortgage responsibilities, only governors 'who have the stomach for it' would be considered.

In the time available the Board took the first option, cognizant of the fallout of any further publicity about the school, in an effort to protect student enrolments and budget income.

The ultimatum from the Local Authority showed political manoeuvring at its worst and sowed the seeds of my rejection of the term 'failing' schools, which I came to see as a nasty example of derisory discourse (Ball, 1990/2012) and demonization of teachers of disadvantaged students (see Jones, 2011). Again the historian E.P. Thompson (in Winslow, 2014) proves insightful as he described what is at issue for working people when they get bound up in one way or another with political organization, cease to be victims of their environment (read neoliberal schools policy regime) and achieve the dignity of actors in the making of their own history. A major pedagogical task for academic partners in urban schools is to support and mentor teachers to develop a critical consciousness of the profession including knowledge of its potential strength. It is crucial for urban schools, not to forget governors, to see their problems within some historical frame of reference and in the context of struggle.

The school Head, union-active teacher partners, governors and other stakeholders involved in the political activities around school closure certainly had a sense of the struggle (see Beckett, 2012a). They made numerous submissions during the public then the statutory consultation periods, which are testimony to the unanimity in the school community in its opposition to closure and the loss of secondary provision in [this] city but also their political organization in the preparation of an agreed action plan. The then-school Head led a coalition and presented a proposal to close the current provision and reopen as a newly configured twenty-first-century school that is locally owned and professionally operated by the school community in the form of a collaborative Trust. The vision was to actively involve twenty-first-century school partners in a professional learning community to improve the quality of schooling and educational provision, that is, inclusive through-schooling from 0–19 years and beyond, given the university's 'widening participation' initiative. The Local Authority's officials acted as civil servants in compliance with national government policy dictates but also presented as powerbrokers. The whole thing might not be so worrisome if it did not ignore the local democratic mandate and then uphold the dominant ideological message about academies and corporate sponsors taking responsibility for urban schools. As it was described by a teacher partner:

> *Unfortunately just saying 'educate children' doesn't work when you're faced with the sort of challenges [this urban school] is faced with. We have 600 students speaking 74 different languages, so the remit should be to enable those students first and foremost to communicate with each other, with the staff, and with the world around them. Then they start to learn, but until we've actually managed to bring them in, make them feel comfortable and happy, there's no way you can progress with them. It's taken an awful long time to come to grips with [the fact] this not is not a factory that just produces students with qualifications. Some of these children haven't even had a*

year of study in English before they're taking those [GCSE] exams. So in the first place, [this urban high school] is a place that cares for the young and brings them back into valuing the people and the world around them, and [afterwards] it settles them back into their communities.

This data can be read as indicative of a considered professional response from a teacher who knew what the local urban school needed to do to provide for white British but also minority ethnic students, all with complex learning needs. This included constant vigilance against the whole range of attitudes that come with the 'failing' schools agenda. Another union-active teacher put it bluntly:

I think the attitude of the Local Authority is determined largely by statistics and urban schools like [ours] do not fit nicely into that lovely bell curve. These people don't look beyond the end of their nose. They don't look at the real school and the real children and the real people in the communities the school serves.

This mirrors Lingard's (2011) concern about 'policy as numbers' and Apple's (2001) concern with the realities of real schools and real classrooms, real teachers and real schools. Where he expressed reservations about naïveté in regards to the economic and social conditions of parents and communities in North America, it is important to note teacher partners' sophistication in these urban schools under threat of sanctions in the north of England. They readily engage in practical-politicized dialogue that reflects contextual understanding and they have a good sense of quality teaching (see Darling-Hammond and Lieberman, 2012; BERA-RSA, 2014a, 2014b; Philpott, 2014) beyond Ofsted's inspection criteria. These teacher partners recognize disadvantaged students' learning is a more serious matter than the numbers game and that official decrees prove inadequate to the task of improving their academic and social learning outcomes. That these arguments are not necessarily theoretically-informed and well formulated is in itself an argument to build the 'Leading Learning' project as a co-developed knowledge-building programme to support and mentor teachers to deepen their sociological thinking and theorizing.

This chapter continues to give voice to school Heads and teacher partners who engaged the offer of school–university partnerships to build critical democratic work in urban schools. It is a long-term project given the neoliberal settlement with its unrelenting focus on 'raising achievement' by way of standardized school improvement is entrenched, and the authoritarian political action is all pervading. This has incalculable effects on efforts to co-develop research-informed teacher education to improve quality teaching. It happened academic partners were requested to formalize a series of ongoing sustained CPD activities to facilitate collective thinking and theorizing. Concerns were expressed about whose knowledge of teaching drives the school's work (see Apple, 2001) and teacher partners wanted some guidance on *knowledge of practice* (Cochran-Smith and Lytle, 2001).

Social and political realities

The efforts to formalize the 'Leading Learning' CPD programme were a struggle on two fronts, beginning with professional self-determination. Here I take a cue from a union-active teacher partner, who played a central role in one of the campaigns against urban high school closure. She equates my rationale to engage teachers in co-developing programs of professional learning with the union argument that teachers' professional responsibilities are linked to the struggle to reclaim the right to make professional decisions (see Gallagher and Beckett, 2014). A good place to start is to find the points of leverage for teachers and academic partners, particularly co-developing their reflexive yet constructive accounts of *what needs to be done* in classrooms and school action plans to secure improved outcomes for students affected by poverty and cumulative multiple deprivation. A second front is more democratic forms of transformative practices and exemplary work (Munns et al., 2013). This is aligned to the challenge confronting teachers and academic partners to identify and name the professional concerns and disquiet being played out in local urban schools.

In the final pilot study reported here, academic partners had to work out how to negotiate the tensions and challenges of tightly prescribed ways of working with attendant policy and time pressures, and how to restate quality teaching along more democratic lines. It happened the previous Deputy Chief Executive of the not-for-profit company answerable to the city council had been open and amenable to the school–university partnership and meetings to discuss possibilities for operationalizing plans. Academic partners relied on this sort of local political support to smooth the way forward for the 'Leading Learning' CPD programme, at one point suggested to be rolled out into the 14 National Challenge urban high schools and feeder primary schools across the city. This led to some apparently genuine meetings with the School Improvement team and urban school Heads.

The irony was the requests for more formalized CPD that came from two sources, operating independently. The first was a school Head of a forced academy but who had resigned in protest. This is my reading of the situation only because he was in post for less than 12 months and clearly not happy with the directions for the school and the system, and because he would not divulge the circumstances of his resignation except to say he had signed a confidentiality agreement. It was enough for him to urge me to co-develop a CPD programme that was critical of extant school policies in its neoliberal orientation (see Wrigley and Kalambouka, n.d.). The second request came from one of the school improvement consultants lucky enough to find a job after the MSR in the Local Authority, which had been reduced to 25 per cent capacity.

I read these requests to be recognition of the need for academic input into urban school teachers' professional learning and development. Both these practitioners were concerned about the need for a CPD programme that could equip teachers with the wherewithal to prepare the evidence in the case for the defence against charges of 'failing' schools. Again Touraine's (1977) argument about 'the great resistance' has salience: the new adversary (read politicians, policymakers and powerbrokers including corporate sponsors) has not yet become clearly delineated; but in the face of an undefined threat, a community (of professionals) turns back on its past [urban school closures], not in order to defend its former leaders, but in order to salvage a collective existence threatened with disintegration. This threat is real given moves towards unqualified teachers and trends to shift teacher education out of universities into schools (see Beckett, 2013a; Furlong, 2013; Whitty, 2014). I certainly got the sense that this local request for professional knowledge work was a step towards new collective action by the profession.

There is a fine line to tread in co-developing this sort of school–university partnership work: satisfying urban schools' needs in the face of national targets, school inspections and threats of sanctions; a much reduced Local Authority compelled to respond to centralized political agendas and supply low-cost, quick-fix solutions to urban schools at high risk of not achieving floor targets; and university requirements to promote its teaching and research. While all these institutions embrace performative policies, my perception is local schools and the university prefer 'local' solutions, but I take Ball's (1993, 2006) point about the complexity and scope of policy analysis given the workings of the state to a concern with the contexts of practice and the distributional outcomes of policy. The task is to find the organic link, which requires theoretical and practical explorations and some tenacity to work around the profoundly anti-democratic nature of vernacular forms of GERM rolled out nationally and locally. Academic partners opted to continue to work tactically with the performance agenda and consistently focus on student underachievement, but yet again we had to recalibrate our thinking at every step to take into account the shifting political terrain.

The change of government in 2010 to the Cameron-Clegg Coalition presented both challenges and opportunities given its educational reform package boasted a commitment to better qualified teachers, high standards and 'closing the gap' between rich and poor and help for disadvantaged students[1]. Political rhetoric notwithstanding, this was precisely the focus of our school–university partnership. In an early promotional flier it was noted academic partners are guided by a practical question: How can we support good teaching in order to narrow the gap in achievement (see Connell, 2009)? The tentative answer on the flier drew attention to good teachers who make some difference to improving student learning outcomes (see Hayes et al., 2006) with an accompanying quote from Cochran-Smith and Lytle (2001):

> [I]t is assumed that the knowledge teachers need to teach well is generated when teachers treat their own classrooms and schools as sites for intentional investigation at the same time as they treat the knowledge and theory produced by others as generative material for interrogation and interpretation.

Academic partners are under no illusion their work is different to the usual university involvement in schools via student teachers' placements for Qualified

Teacher Status (QTS), or indeed formally funded research projects. The proposed 'Leading Learning' CPD requires logistical support, not easy to come by in Austerity Britain. My records of briefing notes to the previous Deputy Chief Executive of the not-for-profit company show she remained interested in proposals to develop citywide research-informed understandings of curriculum, pedagogies, white British students' underachievement, black ethnic minority (BME) students' underachievement, student health and well-being, and critical interpretations of school data. Two events worked in our favour.

The first was a visit to the university and a local urban primary school by Gove's newly named Department for Education's Research Dissemination Manager in the School Improvement Division of the School Standards Group[2]. The meeting was to respectively discuss facilitating the school–university partnership and research-engaged schools. Some good advice followed: that the team of academic partners makes enquiries about expressions of interest then being called for the Education Endowment Fund. Second, we were invited to submit research summaries to the Department for Education, no doubt an intelligence-gathering exercise. This was followed sometime later with an invitation to attend departmental-sponsored events in London. The emphases was on partnership work to develop school-generated data strategies to close the achievement gap, an ideologically driven intervention to improve performance that contrasted markedly to a 'local' solution forged through teacher inquiry into the social determinants of disadvantaged students' learning. Two teacher partners accompanied me to London on this occasion.

The second event that worked in our favour was the official launch of the 'Leading Learning' CPD project, which had been 5 years in the making in trial partner urban schools in this northern city of England. Just as many years had been spent in negotiations with Local Authority officials and local politicians on the city council, simultaneous to arbitrations on our work in the university. Drawing on local co-developed knowledge about teachers' work in urban schools, academic partners continued to try and plug practitioner research findings and sociological insights into QTS though it is more likely in Education Studies and Masters' provision. The launch was co-sponsored with the British Educational Research Association (BERA) Practitioner Research Special Interest Group and featured Lupton (2003, 2004a, 2004b, 2006), whom we came to call a consultant academic partner. Her abstract titled 'Understanding the Challenges for Disadvantaged Schools' on the promotional flier touted the plans for our professional knowledge work:

> The challenges faced by schools in disadvantaged settings often go unacknowledged in official policy discourses and are inadequately reflected in systems for teacher training and development, school funding, accountability and inspection. External performance pressures and the need to avoid 'excuse-making' can even make it hard for staff working in these contexts to articulate the impact of local context on student learning and school organisation, sometimes blocking the way to shared professional understandings and the development of tailored interventions in curriculum, pedagogy and management.

Critical democratic work 47

Yet in a new world of rising poverty, local funding cuts and potentially increasing school autonomy, the need for schools and local partners to analyse and respond to socially disadvantaged contexts will become increasingly pressing.

Lupton's presentation was extremely well received given she examined what research shows about the effects of socioeconomically disadvantaged contexts on schools, including the nuances of particular local settings. She highlighted some of the analytical and conceptual tools that we could use to make sense of context, and the ways these could contribute to knowledge sharing and action among teachers, school leaders, academic partners, school governors, politicians and other stakeholders in this northern city. Foremost is the 'spider web' for illustrating school context graphically, using data from publically available sources (see Thrupp and Lupton, 2011). The idea is to produce a simple profile of the urban school, informed theoretically by the inclusion of three distinct sets of measures that are thought to impact on individual and school-level performance:

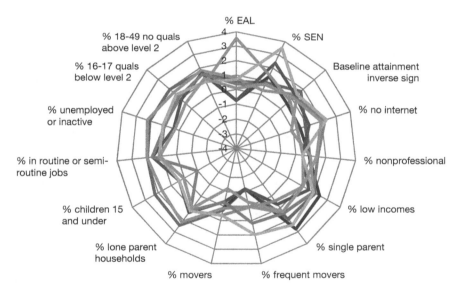

Reprinted with kind permission of the Centre for Analysis of Social Exclusion, London School of Economics, from *The Impact of School Context: What Headteachers Say*, Martin Thrupp and Ruth Lupton (2011), p. 49.

Teachers' nascent politicization

It was to be another 6 months before we recruited a cohort. The lack of momentum came as no surprise as urban schools struggled to come to terms with the release of a plethora of new education policy initiatives under then-new Secretary of State for Education Michael Gove. The proposal for the 'Leading Learning' CPD met with various responses. Some school Heads were prepared to fund teacher partners to work with us because we had agreement about the politics of education. As one urban high school Head put it:

> Children have got one chance and that is with us here and now. So I think from that point of view, if an urban school is [in 'special measures'] and needs to move forward it does. But it's how it's [forced] managed that worries me because it is such a damning judgment [of the school], which has an impact on the education of those children and the community. That is a real issue around the Ofsted [inspection] framework.

There was evidently only a minority of school Heads prepared to give voice to these sorts of concerns, reflected in the silence following what seemed to be genuine meetings with the school Heads' fora, the city council, and school Heads negotiating corporate sponsors. In the meantime, academic partners took it upon themselves to engage in their own professional learning and development. For example, I had meetings with Local Authority truancy staff, who were to prove extremely helpful with advice for ongoing work in the final pilot study in an urban high school. Second, two academics attended a series of workshops on RAISEonline, which was run by a newly appointed urban high school Head. Then a Local Authority School Improvement Advisor accepted an invitation to come to the university to brief academic colleagues on it, which prepared academic colleagues to co-develop critical understandings with teacher partners of local students' achievement data.

I was increasingly exasperated by the lack of response to my questions about the terms of the analyses of different cohorts of students' underperformance, given the emphasis on national benchmarks, targets and progress. This could be read as a lack of professional knowledge and/or reticence to consider social determinants but I came to learn the exercise is depersonalized to the extent students are anonymized, counted as numbers only. I also noticed a disinclination to challenge dominant readings of RAISEonline, and again I came to learn any explanations by teachers are seen as 'making excuses' for students' underperformance. The status quo is dominant because it connects to a politics of fear (Ghale and Beckett, 2013; Beckett, 2015) not least of the threat of sanctions but also the history of so-called 'managed staff reductions' in the Local Authority and local urban schools. However, this does not altogether drown out the oppositional voice because it happens the practitioners in our school–university partnership networks are wont to declare their professional values and commitments. This not only calls into play an ethical argument (see Groundwater-Smith and Mockler, 2007) but also demonstrates some firm beliefs in work to be done in urban schools. As an urban primary school Head put it:

> A lot of what we say about our children having one chance and it's with us [relates] to our moral purpose to make sure that we do the very best for them. If you look at the students' opportunities and life chances and our efforts moving them on, there is

massively positive work being done by a range of teachers in classrooms every day. They are trying to do that extra bit to compensate for all those things that we've identified in students' lives that are not there, for example, high school readiness. Then somewhere along the line, their motivation develops. So while they may not have 'the wrap round' and the back up at home, we've got a teacher who says 'not on my watch'. I will not let that child slip through!

That compensatory efforts are named again reveals an assumption that the urban school is there to provide what is perceived to be lacking in students' home environment. While this calls into question the premise about poverty as the fault of the victim and any likely deficit views of disadvantaged students, there is a practical reality. The school Head and staff in urban schools have virtually little option under threat of sanctions but to insist on students' learning, which is no bad thing except high stakes testing and examinations risk negative results (see Blacker, 2013). That they recognize students' capacity to become motivated by learning, even in the face of failure and alienation, shows a commitment to students living in poverty. The 'not on my watch' comment also hints at some expressive and extensive discontent about the performative system, but as Harvey (2005) put it, the big question is how might this discontent be handled.

Of course some practitioners are more politically active and some take quite a hard line, as I discovered to my detriment. There were further local education-political developments in the urban high school that had won its campaign to remain open, but at some cost. Even after the Interim Executive Board (IEB) had been installed along with the Acting school Head who had experience as an Ofsted inspector, the student numbers did not improve and the school had been starved of funds. A process was begun to convert to academy status and a corporate sponsor was mooted, this time in the form of a local further education institution that could provide a broad curriculum offering to students who may want to pursue vocational education pathways. Professional debates about knowledge stratification to the side (Young, 1998, 2008), the 'old' Board of Governors was invited to contribute to the deliberations or at least that is what we were led to believe. Perhaps it was another effort to contain any likely public media coverage that might again bring unwelcome attention on this urban high school.

My preferred path, rightly or wrongly at the time, was to join a group of former governors who pragmatically agreed to support the Acting school Head's decision on academy conversion, which coincidentally had the support of the remaining school staff including union-active teachers. This effort to negotiate the conflict came up against negative criticisms from a somewhat militant former governor who stood firm with the stance put forward by the Anti-Academies Alliance (2013). This is no bad thing but the situation called for compromise, which should not be read as a 'cop out' because it was simply an effort to acknowledge the harsh realities of teachers' survival in the face of a difficult punitive sets of measures that pervade urban schools, which differ from place to place. In any event, the local school community wanted to retain this local urban high school and accommodate local students.

The group of educationalists, which previously came together and enthusiastically supported the campaign against school closure, simply had to concede. It had lost its long-standing campaign for a newly configured twenty-first-century school to be locally owned and professionally operated by a collaborative Trust. It was overruled and the quasi-marketization of this urban high proceeded piecemeal until it was legitimized. It had much to do with the Acting school Head asserting control over a fractious 'old' Board of Governors as it did with overseeing the implementation of national policy dictates from the then-Cameron-Clegg Coalition Government as well as directives from Local Authority powerbrokers. Teachers' fears and insecurities not to mention former governors' anxieties were successfully channelled into the decision to embark on academy conversion under the auspices of a local further education college. Again, this sort of political manoeuvring does not quell oppositional voices. As one high school Head put it:

> *One of the difficulties in the current climate of [inspection] judgments either being 'good' or 'requires improvement', is that we all know it really isn't anything like that. Yes it's very challenging for schools because we have students [for example] who've come to us with reading ages not commensurate with their actual age. We've have a high number of students in the 'free school meals' category, well over a third. We have anything up to 40 per cent, normally, of our postcodes in the lowest 10 to 15 per cent in the Index of Multiple Deprivation. We have 27 countries and 30 languages represented, so we have got challenges. Those aren't excuses in any way but the finite Ofsted judgments are more challenging . . . and all kinds of people acknowledge [it].*

The admission that Ofsted inspection categories do not command professional respect is suggestive of a dysfunctional system that is anti-democratic. In the event, teacher partners who had worked on the TDA-funded pilot study and beyond still made it known they wanted some directions on critical and constructive engagement with the research and policy agendas. This signals that outwardly there is compliance with hegemonic school leadership but inwardly it is being challenged. This too can be harnessed[3]. Oddly enough, after the campaigns against school closure, the final pilot study took place in the other urban high school that had been unsuccessful in its campaign, lost and immediately went through the process of closure to reopen as an academy with a corporate sponsor.

At the time, I bought into naïve possibilitarianism (Whitty, 1974, 1985) because at the conclusion of the campaign I took it upon myself to lobby the corporate sponsor's national school project manager on the 'Leading Learning' CPD and the support required for a 'local' solution now that a 'structural' solution had been affected. I had visions this might be rolled out nationally at least in the network of urban schools with this corporate sponsor willing to sponsor it! As it happened nothing came of it at that level, but at local level I was approached by a member of the new Senior Leadership Team. I must declare my scepticism, shared by the small team of academic partners, although it was important to lend support and without funding this was gratis, an expression of goodwill on the part of the university. I still felt some ideological tension because at the back of my mind was the sense a neoliberal point needed to be proved in that academy conversion was the answer to urban schools' so-called underperformance. It was more likely academic partners invited to work in this forced academy were being co-opted. I take heed of Touraine's (1977) advice about the probability of assimilation as an element in the ideology of the ruling elite.

Teachers' own accounts

The small team of teacher partners had concerns about white British students who composed approximately 30 per cent in the census, with half registered for free school meals (FSMs), making them almost the largest single cohort. This group's achievement, therefore, was a key determinant in meeting the then-national target of 30 per cent A★-C including English and Maths. The white British students were understandably a group of particular interest and once some sort of trust was established the work began with teachers' professional concerns:

> If you look at the [named] family, not trying to paint them in the worst light possible but the elder brothers took nothing from [this urban high school]. [Boy 1] certainly took nothing from school; he basically came for the day, caused chaos and then left. Not an unpleasant character. [Boy 2] again came, caused a few problems, was put into [an intervention program], did relatively well but very low literacy skills and again, left with not much. Whereas [Boy 3] was in year 7 when I first started. He was one of the first students I taught and he showed promise. He was in transition and within two months of teaching him, this kid's through the roof: did an exam paper and got a level 6A in year 7! The rest of the cohort were getting 3s.

There were multiple starting points. It began with discussion of the purposes of teacher learning and agreement that academic partners should explore ways to equip them to forge their own accounts of their day-to-day struggles to achieve equitable learning outcomes. It was crucial to find the common ground or third space between teachers' practical knowledge and academic knowledge (see Mockler and Sachs, 2011) so that we could build what Cochran-Smith and Lytle (2001, 2009) called *knowledge of practice*. It was also crucial to identify and name some terms and assumptions, particularly what I perceived as teacher partners' 'deficit' perspective of white British students and their families (Mortimore and Whitty, 1997/2000). This is often consistent with policy findings that white British students fail to do as well as they should and lack motivation, which seemingly ignores the fact that these students can be alienated by the current education system. A first task for the team was to read policy documents[4] and strategies in conjunction with this urban school's Ofsted report, which noted that many of its students came from poor backgrounds.

These teacher partners were certainly amenable to practitioner research activities and teacher inquiry with the intention to build evidence banks in reply to charges of 'failing' school now a forced academy. An early pedagogical strategy was to orient teacher partners to reading and reporting, which helped develop a critical understanding of the situation for white British students. For example, Lupton's (2006) work on schools in disadvantaged areas looked at low attainment and the 'quality problem' and what additional learning needs, the emotional climate and disturbed behaviour, and reluctant participation mean for the urban school's working environment. In a related edited collection aptly titled *Who Cares about the White Working Class?* (see Sveinsson, 2009) it is argued class inequality is making its way back onto the political agenda because there are legitimate issues and grievances to be discussed and debated. In the same volume, Reay (2009) focuses on white working class educational underachievement, noting it has always been an issue with moral outcries but what is new about the current concern is the emphasis on whiteness. This calls into play concerns about an ethnic minority married to a cultural reading that disregards wider structural aspects of inequalities, which distorts and misinforms just as other more familiar efforts to blame teachers for educational failure.

The agreed primary aim with teacher partners was to develop a critical understanding of attainment data of students from low income backgrounds, which shows that white British FSM GCSE performance was low in comparison to non-FSM cohorts. At the time, the gap between FSM and non-FSM (5+ A*-C) was 32 per cent (37 per cent to 69 per cent respectively, the biggest of any ethnic group). The secondary aim was to investigate the white British students' urban schooling experiences, as this extract from a teacher partner's case story shows:

> *Philip was selected for monitoring [at the end of the first year of high school] because he is a white British student with poor attendance, standing at just 64 per cent at the end of the year. Philip comes from a difficult home life: he has lived at three different addresses during the 11 months, all of which were located in extremely deprived areas of the city. . . . His 'sleuth' report, which documents any negative incidents relating to him that occur in school, shows a total of 55 incidents were recorded . . . disruption; serious defiance; dangerous behaviour; leaving the lesson; truancy; aggression and inappropriate language.*

The teachers and academic partners came together in regular sessions at mutually convenient times, invariably in school, often in school time but mostly in twilight sessions depending on teachers' timetable demands. Here is a sample of some follow-up questions to support teacher partners' intellectual engagement:

- How would you describe a preliminary analysis of this data?
- What are the major considerations when it comes to underachievement?
- What is a proposed course of action?

One teacher partner's preliminary analysis at classroom level led him to believe that, in general (and there are exceptions), those who are supported the most at home, and who come from families who value education, are more successful at school than those who do not come from such an environment. He qualified this by saying that one simply cannot believe that if their families do not value education then teachers have no chance with them. This is how he described some of the major considerations:

> Here we are blaming the parents for having low expectations but have they got low expectations? [Maybe] over the years they've been led to believe that [this urban high school] isn't going to produce the results . . . that just got me thinking. We're blaming them, we're blaming the parents but [while] some of them obviously do have low expectations for a whole multitude of reasons but it just got me thinking about this cultural capital and the expectations from the middle classes and the upper classes that their sons and daughters are going to do well and it's imbued from a very early age. . . . [Maybe] we think our students are not going to do very well. We expect them not to do very well, though we do try. I'm not trying to sell the staff short because it's a very difficult job here. I enjoy working here and we're looking to how to improve the lot of our kids.

This data shows teacher partners' growing capacity to embark on contextual analysis and look to the literature for examples to guide their own practitioner thinking and theorizing. On this occasion, teacher partners move beyond the 'blame game' and investigate the contextual influence of white British student's family/social background. They agreed on a course of action to look at their extant school-generated data (see Johnson and La Salle, 2010), which includes students' inclusion profiles, primary performance and attendance data, and demographic charts. The team followed through with student interviews, surveys, informal conversations with parents, classroom observations using the productive pedagogies coding sheet, and analyses of teaching programs and student work samples. Most importantly, these teacher partners embraced critical reviews of literature (see Perry and Francis, 2010; Sveinsson, 2009). This is how one described a proposed way forward:

> I found the article on the [RSA] area-based curriculum resonated very nicely with the work of Lupton with regards contextual school improvement. Using the local environment to bring the curriculum to life seems an excellent way to realize the government's agenda in [our local context]. Also, Lupton cites a lack of aspiration as an issue facing many white British students. The area-based curriculum could offer, in part, a solution to this problem, in that it could open students eyes into what's on offer to them in their own area, linking it to what they learn in school.

This shows the beginnings of a more realistic picture of both the problems and possibilities of teacher-initiated change, which connects with Whitty's early advice. Yet another pedagogical strategy on my part was to devise a template for an Annual Report, partly to marshal the records of our joint work into some order but also to focus attention on the significance of what we had done. The draft copy went back and forth between us and eventually the senior teacher partner, acting as a Coordinator, was happy with its written form. It could be presented to the school Head and other members of the School Leadership Team plus the Board of Governors and corporate sponsor at the end of the first year[5]. Here is a sample of the jointly co-authored conclusions and recommendations:

- That [a team of research-active teachers] be supported to work regularly with white British students to understand their cultural heritage and produce resources that will engage them in teaching and learning.
- That [a team of research-active teachers] focus on the knowledge needs of white British students and a review of curriculum to reflect on provision that is both creditable (in terms of mandatory requirements for test results) and relevant (that is, inclusive, community-based and experiential), and that broadens horizons.
- That [a team of research-active teachers] work to support [another colleague's] work on student voice. Questions for consideration might include: How does staff take into account student voice? How does staff show all students that we are actually listening to them? Is there a place for a student teaching and learning group?
- That the school considers activating white British parent involvement, and [a team of research-active teachers] conducting a focus group interview. Many parents think it is the school and only the school's role to educate their children and many of the parents are young and have had poor experiences of school. We need a concerted effort to build good relationships with parents.

It took more than a school year to arrive at this point, but it showed what had been achieved. The intention was to proceed into another school year and engage another round of reading and review of literature, considered important to keep the momentum building *knowledge of practice* (Cochran-Smith, and Lytle, 2009) about white British students' underachievement. It was important to impress upon the school Head and other powerbrokers that the teacher partners who engaged with practitioner research activities made great strides in their capacity to embark on teacher inquiry and a determination to learn about how it is done. It must be reiterated again and again it is not always easy to engage the processes of research-informed teaching and teacher education in a performative system given ultra-busy and demanding work schedules not to forget local educational politics.

Teacher inquiry work co-opted

I took every opportunity to brief the school Head and Board of Governors, for example in a half-yearly report titled 'FSM Data & Poverty: A CPD Matter'. This included an update on the teacher inquiry that evolved from the previous year's work where the emphasis was on developing a teacher-research perspective on white British students:

Critical democratic work 55

- Teachers, teaching and understanding 'from the inside out' are central to our school improvement and school development efforts.
- Professional readings are crucial to teachers' conceptualizations of their concerns and problems, e.g. Lupton, Groundwater-Smith, Wrigley and the first annual progress report provided to the school Head.
- Data analysis is a first step, e.g. school GCSE results and disaggregation of data by social groupings like FSM, poverty, ethnicity, gender, etc.
- Data collection is invariably necessary, e.g. student and parent interviews, school surveys, lesson studies, classroom observations, teacher interviews, longitudinal pupil data.
- Equally valuable are teachers' logs, field-notes, reflections, formulations and reformulations about school and classroom work as well as the school learning portfolio.
- Critical analysis of the findings, including the 'nitty gritty', is the hallmark of teacher research, and this informs action plans that are cyclical.

One of the teacher partners also passed on her MSc dissertation, titled 'Raising white British students' achievement: teachers' expectations and students' aspirations', to the school Head. It was a case study in the urban high school of the possible causes of student underachievement, including the impact of social disadvantage on students' performance and attainment. This teacher partner coined the term 'mitigating circumstances' in this dissertation and it was probably the most significant instance throughout all the pilot studies of a research-active teacher SPEAKING TRUTH TO POWER[6]. These reports and the dissertation consistently met with non-replies from the school Head, and it was as if he was determined not to engage with the teachers' professional knowledge work much less academic debate. In fact not once did the school Head accept an invitation to any of our workshop sessions, whether university- or school-based. This experience connects with Ball's (1993, 2006) analysis of power, where he discusses agency and constraint in relation to policy – this is not a zero-sum game. This requires not an understanding based on constraint *or* agency but on the changing relationships between constraint *and* agency and their interpenetration.

Not surprisingly, the only time the school Head engaged was when the local Member of Parliament came for a school visit, which was requested after one of our visits to London. It was only on the teacher partners' insistence that I received an invitation to the meeting, given the school Head had stepped in to take over proceedings and invite the corporate sponsor's national school project manager and assistant. On the day, it was amusing to find the school Head somewhat anxious, perhaps in anticipation of what I might say, but I simply introduced our co-developed knowledge-building programme. I had hoped the corporate sponsor's staff might see the worth of this sort of school–university partnership project and consider its national roll-out!

It was a proud moment to listen to research-active teachers put their case about the effects of poverty and cumulative multiple deprivation and offer their 'local' solution that derived from practitioner research activities including talks with parents and the school's Pastoral Support Team. It was as if these teacher partners had taken heed of Ozga's (1990; cited by Ball, 1993, 2006) advice about policy sociology to 'bring together structural macro-level analysis of education systems and education policies and micro level investigation, especially that which takes account of people's perceptions and experiences'. Then came the reply from the corporate sponsor's national schools project manager: 'that's all very well, but what counts is targets'. The politician remained aloof and the school Head said nothing.

This reaction from powerbrokers, who effectively rejected much less refuted these research-active teachers' report, required some analysis of policy effects. As Ball (1993, 2006) said, these are the outcome of conflict and struggle between 'interests' in context. It was galling on two counts. First, teacher partners had made time for reading more widely and for critical reflections not only on their teaching but on disadvantaged students' learning and lived experiences. They had also made time for 'other' data collection and analyses, which included recommendations for classroom practice and contextualized school improvement. The expectation was for some sort of acknowledgement of their findings and then some negotiation.

Second, we were well underway with the preparation of a paper from the teacher partners to be included in an American Educational Research Association (AERA) symposium titled 'Mobilising teachers' knowledge: school improvement in [this city], UK'. This followed an earlier visit to England by Professor Ann Lieberman (Stanford), who came to one of the pilot study schools as well as university and my first attendance at an AERA annual meeting the year before [7]. I went ahead with the submission for this next annual meeting, erroneously as it turned out. I did this on the basis of conversations with the school Head, who seemingly provided approval at every step of the process, including reading the paper abstracts, which had to accommodate numerous revisions. It happened the one teacher partner who was able to go was prepared to self-fund and come in the Easter holidays, but ultimately her request for two days leave was refused by the school Head, who made it very clear teacher partners were not allowed out of school during term time under any circumstances. Imagine the frustration and the perception of such a 'short-sighted' decision, but in the end I had to withdraw the symposium abstract!

It could be said the politician, corporate sponsor's staff and school Head are somewhat constrained by ignorance of these teacher partners' professional knowledge work, white British students' experiences of extreme inequalities, and how this plays out in classrooms. As Ball (1993, 2006) indicated, analysis must achieve insight into both overall and localized outcomes of policy. There are power games seemingly at play, given two further developments. The first came with notice from one of the Assistant school Heads to change the focus of the teacher inquiry project, initially given to the senior teacher partner–Coordinator, who passed it onto teacher partners and then to me. On the first occasion, the direction was to focus on persistent absentees. Again I met with Local Authority truancy staff to get another briefing on policy documents and I did a preliminary review of literature. Teacher partners set about reading and re-drafting research questions, deciding on methods for collecting data, and considering social determinants, then notice came to change focus again to literacy and students' self-esteem. Then it was on to social and emotional health, and every notice meant a new topic, a new review of literature, new teacher inquiry questions, different practitioner research methods, and so on.

It is worthwhile sharing the details of the notice that research-active teachers focus on students' social and emotional health: they were required to co-construct another action inquiry to support a tailored teaching program with a class teacher working with disaffected students in Personal, Social and Health Education (PSHE). The team with my support gave it some consideration, drew on a critical review of Young's (1998) concerns about curriculum priorities to help the class teacher conceptualize what is on offer in the face of students' material poverty, cultural capital, and not just aspirations. The class teacher and her supervisor agreed a major task was to begin with the students' feedback that PSHE was boring, devise a lesson study (Groundwater-Smith, 2007a), and work on developing some responsive productive pedagogies. In the process an independent decision was made to bring in external partners who delivered sessions on art and poetry, in line with the 'retail model of schooling' (Ball, 2012). The teacher inquiry foundered and the teacher left suddenly, but it eventually came to light it was all engineered to form part of the judgement for this teacher on 'capability procedures'[8].

The second development came in the form of an email exchange with the school Head, who wrote to tell me about the forced academy's improved performance and that the 'Leading Learning' CPD programme had not made a difference to the school and that no findings from the teachers' inquiry projects were being reported to him and the SLT. It seemed a stalemate that required a response and further critical analyses to ascertain what it all means for democratic school–university partnerships. I indicated the constant redirections for teacher inquiry seriously impacted on the process and progress of practitioner research. I offered to meet the school Head and the SLT along with teacher partners, a hallmark of the operation of the trial 'Leading Learning' CPD programme to keep open the channels of communication between academic partners and school staff. Teacher partners were bemused but not daunted and maintained a determined focus on white British students' underachievement. They wanted an emphasis on improving learning outcomes and success criteria in regards curriculum and transformative pedagogies. They are to be congratulated on their work, their learning portfolios, 'practice' practitioner research activities, and intellectual engagement as well as their publication[9] (see Arthurs *et al.*, 2014) and one's Master's dissertation (Arthurs, 2012). It happened two teacher partners were summoned to brief SLT on their progress and I reissued a standing invitation to the school Head and the Senior Leadership Team to come along to our citywide sessions and also to the university research day at the end of that year. Other than teacher partners, no one came.

It could be these research-active teachers and their academic partners are all rendered incapable of standing up against the policy ensembles described by Ball (1993, 2006) to include the market, management, appraisal and performativity as 'regimes of truth' through which the school Head and the corporate sponsor's staff govern themselves and others. However, this is not to dwell on the negative and the problems of teacher-initiated change. Ball suggests it may only be possible to conceive of a possibility of response in and through the language, concepts and vocabulary which the policy discourse makes available. This harks back to our 'Leading Learning' CPD tactical foci on student achievement, making a difference, quality teaching and the like. Ball says Offe (1984) might be right in stressing that struggle, dispute, conflict and adjustment takes place over a pre-established terrain. So it is for teachers and academic partners in this network of urban schools in the north of England as they come to grips with GERM, including conservative reform of teacher training with less emphasis on theory and academic study (see Beckett, 2013a).

Conclusion

This chapter provided a good indication of a rationale for practitioners and other stakeholders to participate in CPD so they can actively co-construct professional knowledge about urban schooling in the interests of all students. This includes those who are disaffected, given practitioner research on ways to chart provision and 'go public' to generate some sort of collective action. The educational politics at the micro level, which interconnected with the macro level, serve to galvanize our team of teachers and academic partners to become involved in what Touraine (1977) called an anti-technocratic battle: here social movements are capable of directing their own actions, of managing themselves, instead of being merely a transmission or relay station in the service of political forces. Coincidentally he also noted this calls in a more reformist way for an enlargement of industrial democracy, or school democracy in our parlance. Teachers and academic partners take it up as a struggle on the grounds of technocratic management through school data.

Before turning to practitioners' requests for even more formalized school–university partnership work which calls into play a democratic agenda for urban school teaching, it must be said I am comforted by teacher partners' appreciation. Perhaps academic partners are few 'outsiders' to recognize what it takes to meet the needs of students and families living and learning in difficult social circumstances and the complexities of teaching in different urban school contexts. As one urban primary school Head put it:

> *After coming along to some of the [workshop sessions] and presentations that you and your colleagues have done, what we often reflect on is that it explains what we do and feel. We can actually energize that process because sometimes we do need to be reminded or we do need to understand why we're doing something, or we need to be challenged about why we're doing something. So the benefit of investing in [the 'Leading*

Learning' CPD] and broadening our thinking and having that time [is great]. . . . That's pretty much how it feels in [urban] schools, whether it's me as the Head or somebody else in the classroom. If you can just have that opportunity to step back: do a bit of reading, a bit of listening, a bit of thinking.

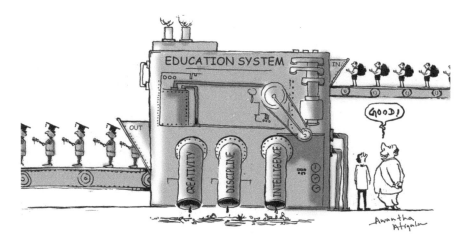

© Awantha Artigala. Reproduced with permission.

Notes

1   This eventually came in the form of 'Pupil Premium'.
2   I had met this civil servant at a BERA conference and I was subsequently engaged to the DCSF (Department of Communities, Schols and Families) gender agenda.
3   See the University and College Union (UCU) campaign briefing 'Teacher education under attack': www.ucu.org.uk/index.cfm?articleid=7025#.VTdtViFViko
4   At the time the Department for Communities, Schools and Families (2009) report proved valuable because it articulated deprivation and why it mattered. It looked at deprivation and measurement, demographics, the impact on student attainment and other outcomes, and analyzes why deprived students can fall behind. It also looks at school effects, poses further questions and highlights evidence gaps.
5   There were two written in as many years, but the team of teacher partners were very particular about what was said and how it was said. Their political sensitivities were to the fore.
6   This phrase originated with the Quakers in a 1955 pamphlet (Speak Truth to Power: A Quaker Search for an Alternative to Violence) promoting pacifism, in the belief that love can overcome hatred. It has come to mean 'speaking out to those in authority' and is now used in politics and human rights activism. Reference: www.urbandictionary.com/define.php?term=speak%20truth%20to%20power
7   Professor Ann Lieberman (Stanford) delivered a keynote at the 2009 BERA conference in Manchester, and in my capacity as Chair of the BERA Practitioner Research Special Interest Group (SIG), I not only gave the vote of thanks but asked her to visit my university and see our pilot study in operation in another northern city. In due course, Lieberman provided invaluable advice and following our visit to Cambridge a suggestion that

60 Critical democratic work

UK colleagues submit an abstract for a joint symposium at the 2011 AERA conference in New Orleans (see Baumfield *et al.*, 2011). It was there that Lieberman issued another invitation to me to bring teacher partners to the 2012 AERA conference in Vancouver.
8 The team of research-active teachers had to regroup, and potential publications are focus of further conversations with teacher partners
9 This is discussed more fully in the next chapter.

4
ACADEMIC PARTNERS AND THE 'UNIVERSITY PROJECT'

Introduction

In the last of the pilot studies, academic partners acted as critical friends (Groundwater-Smith and Kemmis, n.d.; Beveridge *et al.*, 2005) but also secretaries (Apple, 2009) to support and mentor teacher partners to undertake school-based investigations and find their voice. Their nascent teacher inquiries into white British students' attainment data and their urban schooling experiences helped to build critical understandings about local context, the twin concerns of whiteness and poverty, students' families on low incomes and urban school 'failure' but also ways to make significant progress. The practitioners' decision at the beginning of the second year to focus on curriculum and quality teaching or productive pedagogies showed an embrace of transformative classroom practices. This was overtaken by management directions to shift attention and re-focus on persistent absentees, then literacy and self-esteem, then social and emotional health, which all stymied sustained efforts in practitioner research.

The teacher partners were determined to continue, and academic partners made a commitment to publicize research-active teachers' work, including their conclusions and recommendations to be shared modestly at first with each other, then the school Head and School Leadership Teams but also Boards of Governors, the Local Authority and/or corporate sponsors. A template for an Annual Report proved a good pedagogical strategy to engage the team of research-active teachers and their Coordinator in co-writing a description of what they do over the course of a school year. Here is an extract from a report in the urban high school, a forced academy:

- *Teacher inquiry offers powerful insights into the nature of teaching and learning, particularly for disadvantaged students, and the conditions of such teaching and learning.*

- *Teacher inquiry projects, like the ones developed in [the final pilot study], contribute to knowledge building and critical understandings of the socio-cultural world of the urban high school in its local community context.*
- *The task is to support research-active teachers, together with the school Head, staff, Governors, parents/carers/ and students, to know and understand this world, informed by insights from practice and research.*
- *The findings from teachers' CPD and their teacher inquiry projects do deliver recommendations about what it is that the school needs in regards redesign and regeneration of teachers' work in urban schools.*

The silence in reply to this form of local modest policy advocacy for contextualized school improvement was deafening, which again requires Ball's (1993/2006) insights, especially the point about needing more than one good theory to construct one half-decent explanation or account. In a discussion about policy effects, he argues policies from 'above' are not the only constraints and influences on institutional practices. In the last chapter I showed the power games at play in the last of the pilot studies in a forced academy, which is something that may need to be unmasked. This connects to Touraine's (1977) point that only by locating and recognizing power sources can one define and predict the areas of dispute and fields of conflict. There was seemingly a blanket determination between and among the School Leadership Team in regards neoliberal governments' policy directions on school performance where the control over professional decision making was all pervading, particularly around standardized school improvement.

I am advised by an urban primary teacher partner of the need to follow all policy directions, especially when the Local Authority subjects these local urban schools to constant scrutiny on attainment targets. Likewise an urban high school teacher partner indicated the constant flow of external policy directives are taken 'as gospel', not questioned at all. This left staff compulsorily changing ways of working in the classroom all throughout the teaching year, which pays no heed to disadvantaged students who find comfort in routines and who struggle with change. Staff who raise concerns are not seen as a 'team player', which leads to a resentment of the School Leadership Team and a 'them-against-us' attitude permeates throughout. The policy directions to improve performance take precedence, as Gove's letter dated 1 March, 2011, and headed 'Improving Underperforming Schools' indicates:

> As a minister, I cannot allow underperforming schools where children are not receiving the education they deserve to carry on, unreformed. . . . That is why I am determined that, together, we can raise standards in our underperforming schools . . . we need to take a tougher approach . . . the floor standard will have to rise further over time. Other nations are rapidly improving their own education systems and we cannot allow our children to be left behind in the global race to the top.

This obsession with improving standards in view of international competition was accompanied by the call to Local Authorities to draw up plans for all schools excluding Academies below the floor: for primary schools it was raised to 60 per cent of students to basic level (Level 4) in reading, writing and maths at the end of primary school Key Stage 2; and for high schools 35 per cent of students to get five GCSEs at grades A★-C, including English and Mathematics (now termed 'Best 8'). This might focus attention on disadvantaged students' learning but it is a particular type of learning expounded by politicians, policymakers and powerbrokers. There are practical political questions to be asked at local level about classroom work focused on performance in tests and examinations as well as results, which is anathema to professionally valued ways of teaching and learning about culturally valued knowledge and skills.

In the course of the pilot studies I could not help but think there is a form of planned anti-intellectualism in operation, a consequence of short-term target chasing that proves counterproductive. I saw this with the school Head of the forced academy loathe to engage in professional conversations with research-active teachers, which limits opportunities to develop research-informed ways of working. One teacher partner (Arthurs, 2013) coined the phrase 'Stepford wives' to describe the mindless cloning of teachers who refrain from asking questions, though I am reminded the consequences are dire. Yet the apparent effort to quell professional knowledge work about the effects of poverty and cumulative multiple deprivation and silence the practitioner voice only spurs them on. Here it is important to acknowledge evident professional concerns to find ways to generate a professional and politicized dialogue about teaching in urban schools (Ghale and Beckett, 2013; also Arthurs, 2013).

This chapter homes in on what came to be called the CPD twin-pack: a non-accredited teacher learning programme, which stuck with the name 'Leading Learning' and which had to go through the university's QA process. Second, the allied Masters' program to provide accreditation for teacher inquiry work came to be called the allied MA 'Achievement in City Schools', which likewise had to go through the university's validation procedures[1]. Taken together, these professional learning and development experiences show how in-depth critical understandings are both possible and necessary in order to improve education in urban schools. Although a fine example of research-informed teacher education, the 'Leading Learning' CPD twin-pack hinged on continuing to find the points of leverage for teachers and academic partners to develop research-informed and evidence-based practices, and this chapter concludes with summary notes to this effect. In many ways these local efforts pre-empted the BERA-RSA (2014a, 2014b) *Inquiry* and published concerns about 'the university project' (Furlong, 2013; Whitty, 2014).

Support for teachers' intellectual work

A teacher partner's observations, registered in a reflective journal, of the white British students on free school meals in an urban high school provide prototypical professional concerns about disadvantaged students' achievement. The focus of attention was on small groups of white British boys' and Asian boys' approaches to learning, noting the cultural differences between the two ethnic groups. At the same time, both groups' attendance and behaviour were monitored throughout the period of observations to provide some insights into their longer-term aspirations. Attendance of the white British boys was poor, and the attitude of one in particular was very poor. The Asian boys' attendance was good but their behaviour around school was not. The staff managed conversations with the Asian boys about work and their future, but the white British boys mostly refused to engage in such talk. The conclusion for the teacher partner was that parents played a role here. Asian parents were more in control; but white British parents were at a loss in regards what to do, which was linked to the social circumstances of the communities in poverty.

While this data might suggest a premature professional recognition of the social class gap in educational achievement and how it is complicated by other factors, such as gender and ethnicity (see Perry and Francis, 2010; also Milner, 2013a), these research-active teachers are keen to co-investigate the social determinants of disadvantaged students' learning:

> *A survey carried out [in this urban high school] asked what makes white British students different from other ethnic groups of students. 13 respondents replied and gave a picture of what they believed a typical student might be like. Firstly, they have poor social skills particularly the boys. They have difficulty engaging with people of other cultures and building relationships with others. Their sense of neglect and lack of identity makes them feel inferior, producing low self-esteem and low aspirations, making them feel that they are unable to achieve.*

The twin point here is that teacher partners' effort to understand disadvantaged students, their family and social backgrounds and local circumstances, however imperfect, is fundamentally important to engaging these students in urban schooling and facilitating success. It is important to find ways of reaching a deeper professional understanding in order to bring positive gains for disadvantaged students and local school communities. These teacher partners took direction from the Runnymede Trust report, *Who Cares about the White Working Class?* (Sveinsson, 2009). As Gavron in the Foreword noted, we need to be aware of what is really happening to minority communities but also the white majority, especially white working class communities:

> *What we learn here is that life chances of today's children are overwhelming linked to parental income, occupations and educational qualifications – in other words, class. The poor white working class share many more problems with the poor from minority ethnic communities than some of them recognize. All the most disadvantaged groups must be helped to improve their joint lot. Competition between them, real or imagined, is just a distraction.*

This lends itself to practitioners' more theoretically informed arguments not only about 'school mix' or social class intakes (Thrupp, 1999) but also the strategies in place to 'close the gap' in educational achievement. A DfE press release[2] headed 'New Approach to School Improvement' springs to mind. This announced Gove's letter to Directors of Children's Services, as noted earlier, to outline how departmental officials will work with Local Authorities to develop a so-called robust school improvement plan for those schools below floor target. Political manoeuvring to conceptualize and orchestrate school improvement to one side, the naïve hope is that these plans would contain more nuanced structural accounts and creative interventions that seek to genuinely engage with and value the lived experiences of disadvantaged students, families and communities (see Perry and Francis, 2010). As one teacher partner identified:

> *[Students] achieving often means moving out of their comfort zone and potentially looking foolish, something they are averse to doing. Consequently, they form negative attitudes towards school, education and work in general. They often have no extended family and/or there is a high prevalence of single parent families which reinforces rather than breaks this cycle of hopelessness. And because the plight of the poorer white British student is masked by the achievement of this group as a whole, there is little external support to counter this from government.*

There is seemingly just 'more of the same' from neoliberal governments with consistent foci on improved performance. Interestingly, some alternative came into view towards the conclusion of the TDA-funded pilot study when one of the school Heads accompanied me to Sydney (see Beckett, 2009). There we co-presented to different audiences on what we then had to do in our local professional learning and development sessions, continuing our professional conversations, discussing and debating crucial issues. Here is an extract from my field-notes:

- *naming challenging or interesting schools as urban schools who serve disadvantaged students, families and communities;*
- *more open discussion and debate about poverty and deprivation and the combination and concentration of social and economic disadvantage experienced in this inner northern city;*
- *whether this automatically means impoverishment for children given the number of aspirational families;*
- *changes to the 'school mix' over the last 20 years, from predominantly white British working class to a culturally diverse school population that remains fluid;*
- *sustained work on practitioner research to go past crisis management and quick-fix solutions to thoughtful and considered work in situ that can contribute to knowledge building and theory development;*
- *the opportunities that are presented by our budding relationships with colleagues in wider education circles, including Local Authority civil servants, to build contextualized school improvement plans.*

It is gratifying to know that practitioners in urban schools want to work with academic partners, up to a point. The request for the formalized CPD twin-pack means I take the long view and map the current research and policy terrain in order to connect with school Head's and teachers' anxieties about students' performance and achievement. As one urban primary school Head pointed out:

> *Actual improvement in these [urban] schools is rarely [achieved in] one short term, unless there's genuine slacking and a complete systemic break down. If you believe that improvement is around school culture and people and developing over time and layering up and building community links, these things take time and there's no short-termism about them. So if that is your belief, actually it could be stripped away from you [simply] because one year [SATs results] went a bit off, or a cohort came through that didn't do as well, or a cohort makes your data not look so good, or things have slipped, or data suggests that there's a pattern of underachievement in [a particular] group of children. [An inspection judgment is most likely that] that's a result of your leadership [and] that would be tough.*

The nervousness over school leadership is real, given public statements on leadership in reply to Gove's letter titled 'Improving Underperforming Schools'. In the Local Authority's School Improvement Plan 2011–2015 termed *The [northern city] Education Challenge*, under the heading of 'Underperforming schools and vulnerable schools: Actions for schools causing concern' mention is made:

> *. . . about the approach to pursue when a school is demonstrating an 'emerging concern' i.e. barriers to progress, or requires additional capacity to ensure continued school improvement. . . . In the event there are concerns about the [school Head's] leadership, these will be shared with the head as appropriate and a program of support agreed. . . . If over a period of time, evidence shared indicates that the barrier to progress is the underperformance of the head, this will be discussed in advance of any discussion with the chair of governors. The school may be issued with a warning.*

Such a punitive approach to leadership is in marked contrast to leadership characterized in our pilot studies of 'local' solutions in this northern city of England, which took a cue from Lingard et al.'s (2003) conceptualization of dispersed leadership. Of course this is open to critical interpretation, given the DfE's cascade of doctrinaire instructions[3] to the Local Authority School Improvement team and into local urban schools. However, 'Leading Learning' sits well with academic partners whose task is to equip teacher partners to identify their professional concerns about, say, particular disadvantaged students and groups of students and channel these into teacher inquiry projects. On the strength of their practitioner research activities, they are armed to report back to school Heads with recommendations for preferred chosen strategies as responses to local needs and social circumstances. The moot point is that this takes time and energy with whole school staff to develop more nuanced structural accounts and creative interventions and to self-critically interpret ideas, concepts and theories.

The QA process

This request for the non-accredited course had to go to Faculty Leadership Team in the first instance. I came to learn it is out of the ordinary and contrary to contemporary school–university practices in England. It is not consistent with QTs, which extends into programmes for newly qualified teachers (NQTs) and recently qualified teachers (RQTs) but also middle managers and those looking for qualifications for school Headships[4]. I put the argument that Faculty should be responsive to requests from potential urban school partners, not just 'outstanding' school partners, which is the tendency in view of Ofsted inspections of initial teacher education (ITE). In developing the case, I drew on international experiences and professional learning in the pilot studies but also joint critical reflections on the necessary negotiations with local urban school Heads, Local Authority civil servants and most importantly teacher partners. I was keen to get university leadership and line managers to approve this work with teacher partners, which was forthcoming given a first proviso in that this was to be a commercial venture[5].

The next step was a formal procedure through the university's QA process to secure so-called Operational Approval, which began with a justification:

> *The 'Leading Learning' CPD program consists of a series of scaffolded activities over three years, conducted year-on-year, to support teacher learning and practitioner research for the purposes of school improvement with a particular emphasis on the needs of disadvantaged students and their urban schools.*
>
> *. . . Urban schools and the Local Authority are extremely conscious of government pressures to raise achievement and are searching for quality CPD support which relates to their needs and contexts. This program will help participants to develop grounded knowledge and evaluate current practice, and to access relevant knowledge from wider sources to find new solutions to problems of student under-achievement.*

The case for Operational Approval also relied on so-called market research and an indication of proposed teacher partner numbers to assess the financial viability. Again I put the argument that practitioner research, encompassing teacher inquiry, is a well-established form of teacher learning that supports urban school development and facilitates the critical study of classroom and urban school practices for the purposes of improving disadvantaged students' achievement and life chances. Following the successes of the 'Leading Learning' pilot studies in different combinations of urban primary and high schools, the programme's reputation is cemented and interest across the city has grown. Clusters of schools indicated a willingness to join a citywide network of school–university partnerships led by the university, which is best placed to ally their work with larger intellectual networks across the world working for school improvement and social justice (Cochran-Smith and Lytle, 2001, 2009; Connell, 1993; Sturman, 1997; Smyth, Hattam and Lawson, 1998; Gale and Densmore, 2000; Thrupp and Lupton, 2006).

A key part of the argument for Operational Approval was the university's unique contribution: academic partners, carefully chosen for their knowledge and experience relating to urban school teachers' needs for CPD. It happened some on the team had already been involved in the pilot studies and attended the series of associated campus-based research seminars for staff. These academic partners take a central role in orchestrating practitioner research activities such as critical analyses of school data and classroom observations, and suggesting professional readings to stimulate discussion and introduce methods of enquiry. Visiting Professor Terry Wrigley was generous with his contribution to the 'Leading Learning' CPD twin-pack via the MAACS, and visiting academics such as Professor Bob Lingard (University of Queensland) and Professor Ruth Lupton (University of Manchester, formerly London School of Economics) agreed to act in a consultancy role. There was always the intention to have an Advisory Group consisting of stakeholders, which harks back to Lieberman's advice during her visit to this northern city: associated academic partners, school Heads, teachers, and Local Authority officials, notably members of their primary and secondary School Improvement teams.

The Faculty QA committee wanted to know about support and guidance to teacher partners, so note was made this will be provided by the programme director and by associated academic partners. Because costings are based on contact time and there is no assessment requirement, it is envisaged that time spent with teacher partners in their urban schools to support their selected practitioner research activities is to be negotiated and overseen by the programme director to ensure quality assurance. Selective use will also be made of parts of the distance learning resource being developed for the allied MAACS 6x20 credit modules, plus teacher partners will have university library access and the use of interactive ICT to communicate within or between groups.

The Operational Approval was forthcoming, but only after I was invited to the Faculty QA committee to defend the proposal and respond to some members' concerns. Not surprisingly there was likely opposition to the non-accredited component no doubt given ideologically dominant policy and practice dictates. I am advised by an urban primary school teacher partner that CPD is usually focused on improving results and quick fixes to immediate problems like lack of progress towards attainment targets, and provided by the Local Authority or external consultants. An urban high school teacher partner opined school-based CPD is assigned around school priorities, very prescriptive and closely monitored while externally provided opportunities are seen as expensive and unnecessary. Any requests are usually rejected.

This is not to denigrate Faculty QA committee members' concerns about the non-accredited component, but the tone and tenor about unusual CPD practices was again a reminder of the sense of standardization in teaching except this time in teacher education. This is not to criticize teachers and academic colleagues so much as note the harsh demands made of them in this performative policy regime and doctrinaire instructions on school improvement. This brings me back to Ball's (1993, 2006) concern to distinguish between the generalities and specifics of policy effects. The policy and time pressures on academic colleagues in teacher education are indicative of the harsh social and political realities of QTS, including Ofsted inspections and judgements. There are specific regulated forms of school–university partnerships for student placement but also CPD for school staff. Worryingly, academic staff like teacher partners have little time for intellectual engagement and lose their own professional identity in the process (see Gewirtz et al., 2009; Furlong, 2013; Whitty, 2014) at the same time as they too suffer from exhaustion[6]. In the end, the Operational Approval was responsive to practitioners' request for the university to provide them with intellectual-practical system support to teach in local urban schools.

Research-informed teacher education

The task in developing the more formalized responsive, semi-structured yet non-accredited 'Leading Learning' CPD programme requires academic partners to distil their own professional learning from the series of pilot studies working in a network of urban schools in this northern city. It is always the case academic partners are guided by a practical question worth mentioning: how can we support good teaching in order to close the gap in achievement? The more informed answer to the question is to be found by practitioners working together, finding the common ground, conjoining practice and research intelligence. Different conceptualizations of quality teaching (see Groundwater-Smith and Kemmis, n.d.; Lingard et al., 2003; Hayes et al., 2006; Lieberman and Miller, 2008; Lieberman and Darling-Hammond, 2012; Munns et al., 2013) are mined to show different articulations to suit the contextual setting of local urban schools. These contrast to Gove's dominant idea of teaching as a craft[7] (see Lieberman and Miller, 2008; Hoskins and Maguire, 2013; Philpott, 2014) and the 'one-size-fits-all' Ofsted specification of quality teaching to be graded in Ofsted inspections but also mock inspections. The contrast is writ large in inspection specifications for judging quality in the colour-coded sheet, provided to me by an urban high school teacher partner who previewed this book: see Figure 4.1.

The grid indicates mostly atheoretical directions so academic partners responded accordingly. The three proposed component parts of the non-accredited component of the 'Leading Learning' CPD to run over three years consist of:

1. knowledge building about the importance of local context and the impact of the socioeconomic and cultural characteristics of the [northern city] on the school's work;
2. teachers' action inquiries on self-identified concerns peculiar to school; and
3. what a contextualized School Improvement Plan might look like.

Note has already been made of academic partners' studies of local area data, the city's Neighborhood Indices, and numerous government reports that stemmed from an early Ofsted (1993) report, which apparently gave recommendations for 'closing the gap' on the educational achievements of children from rich and poor backgrounds in the English education system[8]. The focus now is on extant national-

Outstanding 1
- Almost all pupils currently on roll in the school, including disabled pupils, those who have special educational needs and those for whom the pupil premium provides support, are making rapid and sustained progress.
- All teachers have consistently high expectations of all pupils. They plan and teach lessons that enable pupils to learn exceptionally well across the curriculum.
- Teachers systematically and effectively check pupils' understanding throughout lessons, anticipating where they may need to intervene and doing so with notable impact on the quality of learning.
- The teaching of reading, writing, communication and mathematics is highly effective and cohesively planned and implemented across the curriculum.
- Teachers and other adults generate high levels of engagement and commitment to learning across the whole school.
- Consistently high quality marking and constructive feedback from teachers ensure that pupils make rapid gains.
- Teachers use well-judged and often inspirational teaching strategies, including setting appropriate homework that, together with sharply focused and timely support and intervention, match individual needs accurately. Consequently, pupils learn exceptionally well across the curriculum.
Good 2
- Most pupils and groups of pupils currently on roll in the school, including disabled pupils, those who have special educational needs, and those for whom the pupil premium provides support, make **good progress** and **achieve well over time**.
- Teachers have high expectations.
- Teachers plan and teach lessons that deepen pupils' knowledge and understanding and enable them to develop a range of skills across the curriculum.
- Teachers listen to, carefully observe and skillfully question pupils during lessons in order to reshape tasks and explanations to improve learning.
- Reading, writing, communication and mathematics are taught effectively.
- Teachers and other adults create a positive climate for learning in their lessons and pupils are interested and engaged.
- Teachers assess pupils' learning and progress regularly and accurately. They ensure that pupils know how well they have done and what they need to do to improve.
- Effective teaching strategies, including setting appropriate homework, and appropriately targeted support and intervention are matched well to most pupils' individual needs, including those most and least able, so that pupils learn well in lessons.
Requires Improvement 3
- Not good so requires improvement.
Inadequate 4
- Pupils or particular groups of pupils including disabled pupils, those who have special educational needs, and those for whom the pupil premium provides support, are making inadequate progress.
- Pupils cannot communicate, read, write, or apply mathematics as well as they should.
- Teachers do not have sufficiently high expectations and teaching over time fails to engage or interest particular groups of pupils, including disabled pupils and those who have special educational needs.
- Learning activities are not sufficiently well matched to the needs of pupils.

FIGURE 4.1 Judging the quality of teaching and learning

school data called RAISEonline, and again note has been made of academic partners' professional learning and development led by a local urban school Head and a Local Authority School Improvement Advisor. There was pause for concern about the terms of national-school data analyses given different cohorts of students' underperformance which included the official categories of students on 'free school meals' (see Tan, 2013). The focus now shifts to the mapping supplied by the Department of Communities, Schools and Families (DCSF) in the then-national Blair New Labour Government (see Figure 4.2).

This pictorial representation of departmental intelligence on GCSE floor targets shows the 'hot spots' across England, particularly the areas of low achievement according to then-national benchmarks. This sort of mapping is used by department officers in the schools division of the DfE but also Ofsted, Local Authorities, school Heads and other stakeholders in considerations of forward planning with due consideration to predictions/targets, resourcing, funding and staffing[9]. I am advised by both primary and high school teacher partners there are 'standardized' ways of reading the 'map' data, mostly to confirm the school's status/location in indicated 'hot spots'. The emphasis is more on using league tables and other data like ACORN[10] but only to make comparisons with like schools, which informs decisions about student targets and rates of progress. In one urban high school, the forced academy, the Student Information Management System (SIMS) was amended halfway through the school year so targets were intensified from three to four levels of progress. There were no directions on what it might take to get students there, yet teachers are constantly reminded they are in a 'failing' school in a hot spot and they require constant scrutiny.

There are many points of contention, not least politicians, policymakers and powerbrokers' assumptions that insistence on students' better test results and constant surveillance of teachers would somehow work in 'raising achievement' and 'closing the gap'. However, it is teachers' practical knowledge about the challenges to improving disadvantaged students' learning that proves to be of particular interest to help shape shared professional learning. These practitioners' perspectives need to be drawn out in supportive and trustworthy settings so that together with academic partners they can critically interpret national-school data and other criteria used in judgement, investigate social determinants, and develop more nuanced structural accounts as noted earlier. Once again in the planning for the 'Leading Learning' CPD academic partners had to mine their records for pedagogical strategies purposefully honed for the pilot studies: in the school-university newsletters, the school learning portfolios and the Annual Reports to the urban School Leadership Teams. Here is an extract from one of these reports, co-authored with teacher partners:

> *A major dilemma presented itself [to research-active teachers], under pressure to ensure the school achieves to the increased Cameron-Clegg Coalition Government benchmark of 50 per cent 5 A*-C grade GCSEs, given the majority of these white British students have not yet reached the C/D borderline:*

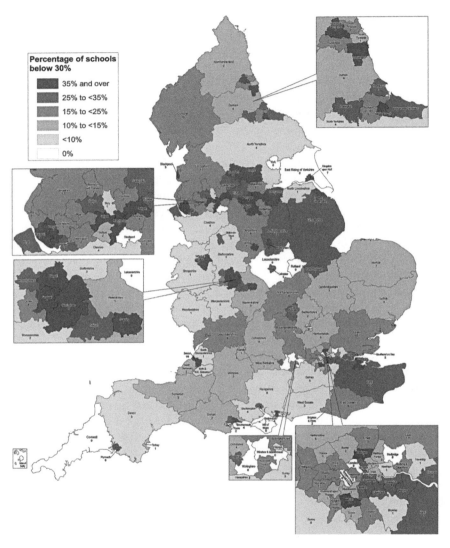

FIGURE 4.2 Schools with <30% of pupils achieving 5+ A★ − C GCSE including English and Mathematics, 2007

Contains public sector information licensed under the Open Government License v3.0

- *How much teacher time should be allocated to raising these white British students' achievement and improving their performance when the chances of success, given the revised 50 per cent benchmark decreed by current policy agenda, are so slim?*

This involved reading the assigned literature in order to develop research-active teachers' ideas and conceptualizations of social poverty, material poverty, cultural capital and their effects on schooling, and government policy emphases on students' aspirations and social mobility. The team learnt from the readings, professional conversations and shared views that the school's community context is not necessarily taken into consideration, which presented a second dilemma:

- *How can education policy recognize the achievements of schools in low socioeconomic communities, when they are currently judged in exactly the same way as schools in affluent areas?*

An initial challenge was to analyze the extant school data, e.g. the Student Information Management System (SIMS), and try to identify the reasons for white British students' underachievement. One concern for the team of [research-active teachers] was that the peculiar social circumstances and the specific educational needs of these students are not automatically seen as an issue because the overall achievement of the whole cohort masks the problems. However there is recognition of underachievement for students on FSM, the school's main indicator of poverty and deprivation.

These sorts of critical understandings/structural accounts, co-developed by teachers and academic partners in the pilot studies, then fed into the Module Aims in the non-accredited Module outline:

The program provides teachers with the opportunity to work in partnership with associated [university] staff (academic partners) in professional learning communities to build grounded knowledge about achievement in the local school setting to bring about change for improvement. The focus is on teachers and school leaders as practitioners developing 'insider' accounts of the achievement gap through inquiries into the factors that impact on student learning, from local context and circumstances, to influences on 'making a difference'. The CPD sessions are designed to support practitioners share and enhance their ideas and field-based understandings of why and how different and diverse students 'succeed' and/or 'fail'. In doing so practitioners increase their knowledge to improve student achievement and develop action plans to change the patterns of learning in the school and its communities.

This was followed by a set of 'Learning Outcomes' in the non-accredited Module outline:

On completion of this program the teachers will be able to:

- *identify and critically comment upon the different ways of knowing about achievement in [city] schools, with special emphasis on under-achievement;*

- *conduct practitioner research to build research-informed knowledge about teaching practices and student learning to improve achievement;*
- *develop joint analyses with other teachers and associated [university] staff (academic partners) to inform their judgement about enabling meaningful change in classroom and school practices;*
- *utilise collective knowledge to inform school-wide discussion about the school's performance, review, debate, evaluation and ultimate improvement; and*
- *contribute to discussions and debates about evidence-informed policy and practice.*

With this non-accredited Module outline in hand, I continued to try and recruit a cohort. I engaged a former school Head, who coincidentally had been sacked from another urban high school also a forced academy and replaced by a corporate sponsor, to organize urban school visits and accompany me on these promotional talks. The exercise of recruiting a cohort enabled the two of us to simultaneously canvass urban schools' needs, namely as much advice as possible on 'what works' in 'raising achievement' and 'closing the gap' with little demand for creative interventions. A few are willing to lend time and effort to experiment with teacher inquiry and different constructions of curriculum and pedagogies (see Young, 1998; also Leitch, 2013; Hulme and Livingston, 2013). By every indication, including the pilot studies, the 'Leading Learning' CPD work to be done around quality teaching was best grouped under five umbrella areas:

- curriculum,
- pedagogies,
- white British students' underachievement,
- black minority ethnic students' underachievement,
- student health and well-being, and
- interpretations of school data.

Operational points of leverage

This all fed into a brief required by the university for marketing purposes, the language and discourse of 'retail schooling' notwithstanding (see Ball, 2012), which in effect became the advertising flier. It benefitted from the inclusion of the city council's logo, itself a mark of Local Authority support. The flier was strategically headed 'Raising Achievement' and 'Closing the gap' and it began with an opening paragraph:

> Leading Learning is a CPD program for sustainable school improvement, developed in consultation with [the local] City Council and local schools. It will draw on teachers' [practical] knowledge and the best of international research. It is designed to build a better understanding of successful learning and teaching by engaging teachers in investigations in their community, school and classroom.

These pointers became the operational points of leverage between teachers and academic partners: *sustainable school improvement* (Thrupp, 1999, 2005), *teachers' [practical] knowledge* (Lieberman and Miller, 2008), *successful learning and teaching* (Cochran-Smith and Lytle, 2001, 2009), and *teachers' investigations* (Groundwater-Smith and Kemmis, n.d.; Menter et al., 2011). This is how it was presented in the flier:

> 'Leading Learning' will strengthen school leadership by working closely with teachers in a local cluster of schools. This might involve, for example, a group of 5–6 teachers from a high school and 1 or 2 from each neighboring primary school. Each cluster will have a designated academic partner to support knowledge-building, plan classroom based inquiries, and stimulate school development. It will also connect teachers with other teachers, school Heads, Local Authority officials and academic partners in a city-wide professional learning community. It is locally designed to enhance the quality of teaching, curriculum and assessment for all, but with a particular focus on the learning and achievement of disadvantaged and 'harder to reach' students.
>
> 'Leading Learning' will relate teachers' knowledge building and practitioner research to school improvement, in connection with the best international knowledge of teaching, social justice and school change.

Academic partners are keen to draw on teaching, social justice and school change (Connell, 1993; Sturman, 1997; Smyth et al., 1998; Gale and Densmore, 2000; Thrupp and Lupton, 2006; Arshad et al., 2012; Wrigley, Thomson and Lingard, 2012). Of particular interest are Thrupp and Lupton's (2006) ideas about a range of social justice rationales for taking school contexts into better account, and the challenges contextualization currently poses for practice and for policy. This provides some direction to embark on practitioner research to better consider urban school contexts in this city in the north of England, in order to provide a stronger underpinning for contextualized school improvement marked by nuanced structural accounts with transformative practices. Accordingly, it was important to alert the new cohort of teacher partners about ways to critically interpret national-school data and other criteria used in judgement; invite them to identify and name their professional concerns; and show the ways to embark on teacher inquiry and investigate social determinants of disadvantaged students' learning. These multiple foci are captured in the 'Leading Learning' flier:

- *How can we engage more students in active learning?*
- *What do we know about students who underachieve?*
- *In what ways do poverty and deprivation impact on schooling?*
- *How can education be improved for disadvantaged students?*
- *What can we learn from official data?*
- *What are the issues of concern specific to local schools?*
- *What are the best ways to help white British FSM students or bilingual students?*
- *Which teaching strategies enhance thinking and cognitive ability?*

- What kinds of differentiation avoid stigma?
- Which approaches to literacy can improve learning?
- What are 'productive pedagogies'?
- What are effective ways to influence school improvement?

Significantly, the city council had named the 'Leading Learning' project in its School Improvement Plan 2011–2015, termed *The [northern city] Education Challenge*, in reply to Gove's letter titled 'Improving Underperforming Schools'. Perhaps naïvely, I could only assume there was some recognition of *a challenge* for educationalists in this northern city and the 'Leading Learning' CPD twin-pack had something to offer. I asked teacher partners to comment on the idea of a challenge, which is reminiscent of our second pilot study with TDA funding for 'CPD for schools in challenging circumstances' (see also MacBeath *et al.*, 2007). These are their replies:

> Teacher in an urban primary school: *Every day is a challenge, but everything is harder and it is more and more difficult to get expected results. That there is no recognition of the challenges is demoralizing.*

> Teacher in an urban high school: *The idea there might be recognition of the challenges and complexities, after years of none, is exciting and reassuring.*

This points to the effort required to bring some alignment between policy, research, theory and practice in urban schools supposedly 'failing', which is a daunting task for academic partners in the current neoliberal regime battling moves to undermine university-based teacher education. In planning the non-accredited component of the 'Leading Learning' CPD twin-pack, it was interesting to consult the Local Authority's School Improvement Plan 2011–2015 and note its conceptualizations of the challenges in local urban schools. At the very least it reflects some contextual data such as city profiling, the Neighborhood Indices and IMD to provide a 'desktop picture' but also to ascertain priorities, determine planning, and design services[11]. However, from the outset the emphasis is on school accountability with mention of common purpose to tackle challenges and accelerate progress. The challenges, pertinent to all local schools but especially local urban schools, are listed:

- Maintaining and accelerating performance;
- Delivering significant improvements in the key performance indicators, in particular 'closing the gap';
- Supporting and challenging strong clusters of schools given the Coalition Government's white paper, *The Importance of Teaching*;
- Responding to increased demand for school places and services arising from increases in the birthrate in the city; and
- Narrowing persistent health inequalities against a background of complex changes to health services.

It is also curious to look back and see the original flier for the 'Leading Learning' CPD twin-pack and its banner heading: '["Leading Learning"] is ideal to meet the challenge of the [northern city] education challenge!' At the time, I felt the liaison with the Local Authority leadership team and the school improvement partners was genuine. I certainly did not feel any ideological tension because I sincerely believed they were concerned to develop packages of strategies designed as 'local' solutions to local problems and issues. With hindsight perhaps it was another instance of naïve possibilitarianism on my part as if the political rhetoric held promise. For example, a DfE press release dated 1 March, 2011 categorically stated:

> *The Secretary of State is also urging Local Authorities to consider the use of national and local leaders of education and teaching schools to drive improvement.*

It happened I was invited to numerous strategy meetings, suggestive of some positive joint activity. As formal agenda notes for a meeting organized by one of the School Improvement Advisors (SIA) indicates:

> *Arrange for Lori to meet with primary SIA team and possibly to meet with external [school improvement partners] 'SIPs' if appropriate, so they are aware of and understand 'Leading Learning'.*
>
> *Set up a group to share knowledge of school improvement issues which would then inform practice and help develop effective strategies. The group would comprise representatives from: [the university], Local Authority School Improvement team, Advanced Skills Teachers (AST) team, school Senior Leaders.*

This suggests at least some heed of Lieberman's early advice about a Reference Group. I attended a series of meetings with the ASTs, which was part of the Local Authority's own 'Learning Partnerships' project, a commercially viable partnership package with a £3k cost to schools. It secures consultancy services from the School Improvement team previously available for free. An additional cost buys the 'Partnership Plus' package, which secures consultancy services from the team of accredited ASTs. This consisted of so-called strategic support, as noted, plus training and development:

> *Advice, support and guidance on key local and national developments through:*
>
> - *Helpline Service*
> - *Electronic UPDATES*
> - *Briefing papers*
> - *Curriculum updates/access to online subject-specific support*
>
> *Sharing and developing outstanding practice [across the city] through:*
>
> - *Online CPD modules and support materials*
> - *Online forums*
> - *Area-based and citywide networks*

This partnerships package is a reflection of the Local Authority's School Improvement Plan 2011–2015, the reply to Gove's letter, and different to the 'Leading Learning' CPD twin-pack. However, at the very least I was invited to talk to the ASTs about the worth of teacher inquiry and professional knowledge work, which was ongoing for a short while. Again, naïvely I thought they might be potential teacher partners. My field-notes show a draft briefing paper with a proposal to extend the commercial 'Learning Partnerships' on offer:

> Colloquially the 'Leading Learning' project is known as the 'Partnership Plus One' package, and for £1k per teacher p.a. schools secure participation in a long term sustained program of CPD geared towards addressing the needs of disadvantaged students and the effects of poverty on schooling and education.

In the end, nothing came of the meetings with the School Improvement Advisors/Partners and the Advanced Skills Teachers. By this stage, after huge time investment, I could sense some continuity with the previous experience of academic partners invited to work but in some sort of co-opted way. It was as if the Local Authority's twin initiatives, *The [northern city] Education Challenge* and the 'Learning Partnerships', echoed academic partners' briefings over many years about ways to support schools to build their capacity to address quality teaching. It must be asked if/how the school–university partnership model that we had devised, co-developing 'local' solutions, did not garner the support from these local constituents. An Advanced Skills Teacher, now named a Lead Professional, suggested it is like a conflict of interest between the Local Authority's paid offer to provide targeted support determined by local school Heads in accordance with policy and practice dictates and what academic partners have to offer.

The most frustrating aspect of all this is that academic partners could work in so many different ways with the Local Authority to jointly co-develop research-informed and evidence-based knowledge of the local context and the immense policy and time pressures on urban schools. The point of work with teacher partners as part of the 'university project' (Furlong, 2013; Whitty, 2014) as it is conceived in this book is very simple: to facilitate professional knowledge work that brings to the fore urban school teachers' perspectives and professional concerns about working in urban schools, help them co-develop their contextual understandings, marshal their collective intelligence and find their voice. I take a cue from Groundwater-Smith and Kemmis (n.d.) about

> developing a more measured sense that schools are highly agentic forces in the lives of students, their families and communities, while not being solely responsible for the outcomes they achieved. This is to be contrasted with the impression given by [others] which seem to suggest that schools and teachers have the kind of primary responsibility for student learning outcomes that reflect entirely on the competence of the staff.

All the while academic partners are prepared to share what they learned from the pilot studies, especially about social determinants of students' learning and contextualized school improvement. There is much to be picked up from academic partners who had trialed a new kind of support to urban schools and who brought new ways of thinking about teaching disadvantaged students and improving student learning outcomes. They can tap a wealth of experience working collaboratively in this network of local urban schools in the north of England, from the initial community primary school on 'Patterns of Learning'; through the 'Side-by-Side Learning' in the family of urban schools doing teacher inquiry projects of different sorts; and into two high schools (one a forced academy and one a converter academy) both interested in future curriculum and transformative pedagogies.

It is telling the 'Leading Learning' CPD twin-pack consistently maintains school Heads' and teacher partners' interest given the academic input on poverty and cumulative multiple disadvantage made available to them. It is seemingly a lost opportunity that the Local Authority does not see fit to work with the team of academic partners so that organizationally they could work together in mutually respectful and trustworthy ways. This should come as no surprise given the doctrinaire results-driven, one-size-fits-all approach to school improvement (check Angus, 1993; Thrupp, 1999, 2005) in contrast to research-informed teaching and teacher education. These are no doubt professional and political challenges to negotiate. While politicians, policymakers and powerbrokers insist on urban schools' performative practices then hold teachers to account for matters beyond their control, it is as if there is a tinkering at the margins while establishment ways of working hold sway. The dominant ideological message in this neoliberal regime seemingly has such a grip on school Heads' and teachers' thinking (see Ball, 2013), but thankfully not everyone!

Knowledge-building partnerships

The team of academic partners are lucky to have begun with a cohort of 17 teachers who became known as the Trailblazers[12]. This small group painstakingly recruited for the 'Leading Learning' CPD twin-pack wanted to become research active, obviously attracted by the offer to learn key skills registered in the formally approved non-accredited Module outline:

Practitioner research is the key to:

- *Reading and reflection;*
- *Knowledge-building and inquiry;*
- *Data collection and analysis;*
- *Strategic thinking about application;*
- *Debate and action plans;*
- *Purposes and principles;*
- *Review and evaluation.*

I came to learn later one cluster of four teacher partners signed up on the strength of meetings with two members of an urban high school's leadership team where

I was accompanied by my sacked school Head teacher partner. In turn the two deputy school Heads went to their school Head, who gave her approval to circulate an internal memo, which spells out a convincing argument:

> **PROGRESS FOR ALL** – *Tackling underachievement at [this urban high school]*
>
> *With lack of progress and poor value added data, we at [this urban high school] have to address this as a matter of urgent priority. Good work has started already but there is a crucial requirement to embed, sustain and create a culture of achievement across the range of abilities, cohorts and gender at [this urban high school] and at the same time offer CPD opportunities to our workforce who will relish addressing these challenges and making sure that this school becomes one of the most improved schools in England.*
>
> *With this fundamental yet necessary vision we would like to present an unprecedented opportunity that will put [this urban high school] at the forefront of educational reform and make real impact on our underachieving students . . .*
>
> - *An opportunity to forge a family/cluster of our main feeder primary schools and engage them in tackling underachievement and lack of progress in our school;*
> - *CPD that is sustainable and produces real impact;*
> - *Taking control of our whole school development and improvement.*

These teacher partners' sign-up to the formalized yet non-accredited component no doubt had practical value, given the utility of the focus on student underachievement with an acknowledgement of the professional and political challenges. It also showed potential to put the urban school at the forefront to improve its work with disadvantaged students. It showed promise of collaborations across a citywide network of other urban primary and high schools and making real impact. Finally the 'Leading Learning' CPD twin-pack opportunity spoke to a democratically determined professional response derived from joint work knowledge building and building a practitioner research evidence bank.

More realistically, it must be acknowledged that this particular cohort of four teacher partners and a senior colleague with responsibility for teachers' CPD came to work with us on the strength of their internal school memo which broadcast:

> **WHAT WILL WE GET OUT OF THIS PARTNERSHIP?**
>
> - *Each teacher will receive an invitation to attend six seminar workshops; once per half term in two hourly twilight sessions;*
> - *An academic partner with designated intra and inter school groups on teacher action inquiries;*
> - *Publication and distribution of a school-university newsletter;*
> - *Attendance at a yearly 'Leading Learning' conference;*
> - *Opportunities for staff to engage authored publications nationally and internationally;*

- *Optional accreditation for Graduate Certificate in year one, in year two Diploma and Master's degree three leading to educational doctorates;*
- *Access to [the university] library;*
- *Program of support [from the university] for 'Widening Participation' for disadvantaged children into FE and/or university.*

The team of academic partners dared hope the CPD twin-pack would provide an opportunity for the revival of critical social explanations (Anyon, 2009) in the construction of the urban school's 'case for the defense' (Arthurs, 2012; Gorton et al., 2014). Anyon (2009) is worth quoting in full: 'critical social theory can be a powerful tool with which to make links between educational "inside" and "outside", between past, present, and future, and between research design and larger social meanings'. At the same time, academic partners had to be sensitive to the urgency of policy demands on local urban schools. As an urban school Head reminded us:

The difficulty with the 'closing the gaps' [agenda] is the gaps change [on instruction from government]. Four or 5 years ago the focus nationally was on Pakistani boys. Now our Pakistani boys do extremely well, but you turn round and suddenly another gap is thrown at you. Last week it was very clearly going to be about achievement of white working class boys, particularly able white working class boys. It's almost suggested we haven't spotted that and we're not doing something already. That is difficult [to take when] . . . not a stone is left unturned [yet] the Government is saying 'while you're looking at that, can you look at these 3 other things as well'.

This data, which suggests 'shifting goal posts' in England's performative system, typifies the struggle to establish professional learning communities of teachers and academic partners to focus on poverty and cumulative multiple deprivation. Yet again Touraine (1977) provides some insight into thinking on the present historical moment that explains why the main aim is to establish a link between the theory and the practice of collective action, though for academic partners it is an alignment between policy, research, theory and practice. To quote in full: '*Our most urgent need is to learn how to name and analyze the new social practices and the new forms of collective action which are shaping the societies [read urban schools] of today and tomorrow.*'

Conclusion

Just as we came to the processes to secure the formal approval for the non-accredited component of the 'Leading Learning' CPD twin-pack, which in effect authorized the 'university project' (Furlong, 2013; Whitty, 2014), there was a curious development with the urban high school Head of the forced academy. He had hijacked the politician's visit, dismissed research-active teacher partner's findings, sat silently as the corporate sponsor insisted on targets, then ignored our efforts to engage intellectually, redirected the teacher inquiry projects, and complained that the practitioner research findings are not plugged into the school's improved performance. He gave approval for four teacher partners' formal participation in the 'Leading Learning' CPD project, which required endorsement and financial support, e.g. four/five teachers p.a. over 3 years. This was no small outlay: as a commercial venture, the cost to this urban high school was considerable given their CPD budget[13].

While this urban school Head's approval is most welcome, perhaps the change of mind on external provision was because the 'Leading Learning' CPD programme was so cheap compared to other external commercial packages. It could satisfy Ofsted inspection tick-a-box requirements. It may bring some kudos to the forced academy via support for teacher learning, invitations to London, [foiled] opportunity to attend the 2012 AERA annual meeting in Vancouver, visiting academics including Lupton (2003, 2004a, 2004b), and meetings with international visitors. I like to think it was triggered by my proposal to the Board of Governors to win support for teacher partners' practitioner research:

1. That the teacher researchers be supported with teacher time allocated for their work;
2. That the teacher researchers liaise with feeder Primary school colleagues, notably to begin their longitudinal study in grades 5 and 6 and forge a network to share intelligence;
3. These opportunities for joint learning require regular timetabling at Board of Governors and staff meetings;
4. The school's formal participation in the 'Leading Learning' project requires endorsement and financial support, e.g. 4/5 teachers p.a. to sign up to teachers' CPD; and
5. The teachers' optional accreditation for a Grad Cert, Masters, PhD or EdD requires encouragement and financial support.

It happened there was nothing beyond the school Head's formal approval to enrol the teacher partners, but this is coterminous with the way local educational politics are played out and again this is part of the struggle. It must be said teacher partners are happy to work with us in twilight hours for the non-accredited component and at weekends on the accredited MAACS, but it needs to be underlined *they need a time allocation* to engage in practitioner research activities in order to really develop their teacher inquiry projects so it plugs into contextualized school improvement. As one of them said to me, this time is crucial for professional conversations with others in the team, planning the teacher inquiries, going through the processes, and writing up. Teacher time is a major consideration in more ways than one in this neoliberal regime, especially when it is so tightly controlled.

Academic partners and the 'university project' 83

© Randy Glasbergen, Glasbergen Cartoon Service. www.glasbergen.com. Reproduced with permission.

Notes

1 Professor Meg Maguire (Kings College London) was the external on the MAACS validation committee, which awarded two commendations
2 This was a DfE press release 'LA update' dated 1 March, 2011: http://education.gov.uk/childrenandyoungpeople/strategy/laupdates/a0074707/new-approach-to-school-improvement
3 Ibid.
4 See www.leedsbeckett.ac.uk/cpd/education/#cll
5 The second proviso, which came about following ongoing negotiations with potential school partners reporting back to Faculty leaders and managers, who suggested a two-for-one on costs, still a commercial venture in keeping with current higher educational policy. This is in reply to teacher partners who ultimately asked for accreditation and because the university needed business. It was agreed: the costs to each urban school for each participating teacher is £1k p.a = £3k over three years + it is suggested teachers meet the costs of an additional £500 p.a if they sign up for optional accreditation in the MA 'Achievement in City Schools' (MAACS) = £4500.
6 I have no doubt of the need for some critical gender analyses of this scenario, something I take up in the concluding chapter and again in a paper presentation at the 2015 Gender and Education Association conference (see Beckett, 2015).
7 This is contained in the 2010 *Schools White Paper*: www.gov.uk/government/uploads/system/uploads/attachment_data/file/175429/CM-7980.pdf
8 Menter (2013) draws attention to concerns about the conceptual difficulties if not flaws with this phrase 'closing the gap', which is taken up in the next chapter.

84 Academic partners and the 'university project'

9 Here I should acknowledge critical conversations about this data with my colleague, Dr Doug Martin at Leeds Beckett University. I learned much about such mapping in England.
10 This is a commercial package purchased by local urban schools to provide detailed demographic data about the local area: http://acorn.caci.co.uk/
11 Again I should acknowledge critical conversations about this data with my colleague, Dr Doug Martin at Leeds Beckett University. I learned much about Local Authority planning.
12 See story in Beckett (2014a) editorial.
13 See endnote 5 on the 'two-for-one' costings.

5
MAKING COMMON CAUSE

Introduction

My early vision for the 'Leading Learning' project to generate 'local' solutions in reply to the challenges of teaching in urban schools was to mentor and support teacher partners to identify and name professional concerns about the social determinants of disadvantaged students' learning. I could see the need to supplement this professional knowledge work with an effort to develop and strengthen their researcher-oriented disposition (Gale, 2010; Lingard and Renshaw, 2010). This was crucial to underpin teacher inquiry projects into the effects of poverty and cumulative multiple deprivation in this northern city. I had hoped there would be enough buy-in across the local network from school Heads and teacher partners with common interests in, say, the umbrella areas of curriculum, pedagogies, white British students' underachievement, black minority ethnic students' underachievement and student health and well-being. I envisaged 'going public' with their practitioner research evidence and there would be some response to this collective intelligence. I thought Local Authority School Improvement Advisors/Partners would work with us and other teacher partners would follow suit to focus on professional concerns. I could see large citywide hubs of synchronized practitioner research activity that would continue to grow and really build citywide capacity to raise the professional voice. I expected some negotiations in an effort to supplement the misguided neoliberal infatuation with existent crude quantitative analyses with research-informed and evidence-based teaching and teacher education (BERA-RSA, 2014a, 2014b; Furlong, 2013; Whitty, 2014; Carter, 2015). Talk about 'naïve possibilitarianism'!

My experience proved otherwise. At the national level, England stands out across the four jurisdictions of the UK in its embrace of vernacular neoliberal policies (see BERA-RSA, 2014b; Menter, 2013), a peculiar rendition of GERM

(Sahlberg, 2011). In the north of England where I work, politicians, policymakers and powerbrokers seemingly oversee an elite political culture (Ball, 1990/2012) to the point where there is no room for professional input much less teachers' voice on the unremitting performativity focus. I have been shocked by the Local Authority's follow-through on forceful threats of sanctions and 'structural' solutions, urban school closures and takeovers by corporate sponsors. In local urban schools I have witnessed highly dubious 'technicist' directions for teaching from SLT insistent on inspection criteria that mimics Ofsted inspection criteria for quality teaching and the like. These are mostly atheoretical, without any regard to professional debates. I have seen the most extraordinary policy and time demands put on teachers and unrealistic performance targets for disadvantaged students. I have seen teachers crushed by extremely harsh terms of survival in local urban schools with some ultimately forced out of their chosen profession. I am consistently taken aback by both compliant and overly cautious school Heads and teachers, but not surprised by those who harbour professional disquiet and anger yet remain fearful and reluctant to speak out. This is not to forget some brutal experiences of my own on Boards of Governors, with forced resignations to be replaced by Interim Executive Boards with oversight of managed staff reductions.

None of this is to dwell on the negatives because it has not stifled practitioners' deep-felt sense of professional misgivings and resistance; rather it has focused attention on the professional and political challenge. This is not only among unionactive teachers and academics, or indeed the teacher and academic unions who have called on successive neoliberal governments to reconsider their technocratic control of education policy making. The popular democratic call, even at local urban school level, is to countenance the profession's demands for more research-informed and evidence-based responses to matters of professional concern[1]. The situation brings to mind Touraine's (1977) advice on the anti-technocratic struggle, but where he cites the anti-nuclear protest against an energy policy with no scientific, technological or economic argument to show its superiority to any other policy, the same could be said of professional educationalists' protest. As Ball (1990/2012) noted in *Politics and Policy Making in Education*:

> *Policy making in a modern, complex, plural society like Britain is unwieldy and complex. It is often unscientific and irrational, whatever the claims of policy makers to the contrary.*

My concern is with policy advocacy for contextualized school improvement in urban schools (see Angus, 1993; Thrupp, 1999, 2005; Lupton, 2005, 2006). This is on the strength of teacher inquiry marked by contextual understandings and critical social explanations (see Anyon, 2009) of the ways disadvantaged students' lives, learning and urban schooling experiences are inextricably intertwined. This requires academic partners to co-develop a research-informed yet semi-structured teacher education programs on the pre-service–in-service continuum that is contextually sensitive and locally responsive. In the event, working in this northern city in this neoliberal policy regime, academic partners aligned with the non-accredited component of the 'Leading Learning' CPD have to scaffold professional knowledge work and practitioner research activities to be of use in urban schools. This begins with professional learning to equip teacher partners to engage intellectually and critically with social geography and neighbourhood studies (see Lupton, 2003; Thomson, 2007) and with more sociologically informed critical analyses of the official national-school data released as RAISEonline but also school-generated data. It proceeds with school-based investigations, geared to publication (see Beckett, 2014a).

This chapter features the nub of the professional knowledge work done once the non-accredited component got underway to run over 3 years, 2012–2014, with the first cohort of teacher partners called Trailblazers. It confines itself to the shared professional learning and development work that took shape in the very early stages, supported by a small team of academic partners (see Beckett, 2014a, 2014b). It begins with a rationale of populist hope (Touraine, 1977) and describes some select pedagogical strategies for this form of teacher education. It continues with a depiction of teacher partners' concerns, the ways these were channelled into nascent teacher inquiry projects to tell the stories behind the official data and develop more transformative classroom practices. The records of these professional learning activities are used to build banks of developing practitioner research evidence, which takes the form of insider accounts (Anyon, 2009; Cochran-Smith and Lytle, 2001, 2009; Groundwater-Smith and Kemmis, n.d.) but also ethnographic studies of urban education (Campbell and Whitty, 2007). The chapter finishes by saying what it takes to *hold the professional line* and interrupt the dominant ideological message about urban schools' performative practices, mindful to connect with a wider social movement of practitioners in teaching and teacher education motivated to act on professional discord with GERM.

The populist hope

The design of the non-accredited component of the 'Leading Learning' CPD twin-pack connects with Grace (1994, 2007) on 'complex hope' in urban education as a necessary complement to critical analyses of the present state of urban schooling. It is characterized by an 'optimism of the will' that recognizes the historical and structural difficulties to be overcome. Coincidentally, I had used the Gramscian epithet 'pessimism of the intellect, optimism of the will' in my doctoral studies to mean an acknowledgement of the hegemonic processes that have been operating in and through the public education system but an insistence on the democratic control of schooling and the curriculum (Beckett, 1996). Hope is a motif in a number of progressive studies to do with urban schools (see Wrigley, 2003; Lingard et al., 2003; Thomson et al., 2012; Beckett, 2014a, 2014b). This connects with Touraine's (1977) idea of populist hope, the backbone to populist movements, which are founded on the desire of social groups [read teachers in urban schools] experiencing crisis to avoid splitting up and, by strengthening their collective identity, to succeed in regaining control over their own development [cast here as professional learning and development]. I shared this sense of hope in my presentation on the 'Leading Learning' CPD twin-pack to the local school Heads' fora when I cited Lingard *et al.* (2003):

> [T]here remains great hope and some reasons for optimism about a future of learning that is tied in its vision to an empowering, imaginative and inclusive vision for teaching . . .

The non-accredited component is offered in 12 sessions: six on-campus seminar-workshops and six school-based seminar-workshops, with each held once every half term. The first year was designed to support teacher partners' knowledge building strategically focused on 'raising achievement' and 'closing the gap'. This is not to ignore Menter's (2013) advice about the conceptual difficulties if not flaws with these sorts of phrases cum metaphors, which come to characterize our professional learning activities, but first things first. A twin question in preparing the program was how to broach quality teaching and how practical school-based knowledge about it might be identified, portrayed, applied and shared in developing academic partners' pedagogies (see Loughran, 2006). Further critical consideration of the pilot studies pointed to joint discussion of school-focused and system-wide issues against a backdrop of professional reading about international research and experiences; sequential worksheets; and practitioner research activities to support teachers' budding inquiry projects. While there would be no formal assessment in this component (except where teacher partners embark on the optional accreditation in the allied MA 'Achievement in City Schools') there is an expectation they will complete directed activities designed to develop and deepen teacher learning:

1. developing rich descriptions of the urban school/setting;
2. document analyses of urban school prospectus;
3. examining local demographic data;
4. questioning urban school performance data;
5. identifying other classroom/school data;
6. doing classroom observations and lesson studies;
7. analyzing digital photos of students learning activities;
8. writing vignettes/case stories;
9. interviewing students and parents;
10. collecting stories of schooling experiences;
11. tracking students and teachers;
12. presenting practitioner research data;
13. studying urban school improvement plans;
14. instituting and monitoring changes in practice/s;
15. building an urban school learning portfolio; and
16. engaging evidence-informed policy and practice.

Two points need to be made. It is left to teacher partners to make their own selection of directed activities, guided by a sense of professional discretion notwithstanding Lingard and Renshaw's (2010) advice. They took issue with policy directions that championed teaching as evidence-based because it disrupted teaching as a research-informed profession. They argued for teachers' professional knowledge and values to be central to policy production, and preferred evidence-informed, rather than evidence-based, and research-informed rather than researched-based, to pick up on the need for [teachers'] professional discretion.

The first of the six university campus-based sessions to run over the calendar year with Trailblazers was an introduction to the programme: it was billed in the yearly outline to traverse the schedule of events and expectations; the focus on local knowledge building about students achievement, school performance and factors impacting on different and diverse students' academic and social learning outcomes; introduction of designated academic partners; joint discussion of cluster-based case study work and practitioner research foci. In attendance were more than expected practitioner numbers, including school Heads presumably there to double-check on proceedings, but sadly no Local Authority partners.

My introductory session was focused on the big 'O', using graphic design familiar to practitioners, which was intended to attract attention not only on Ofsted as expected, but on Operational principles, the Outcomes of school improvement, being Open to critical thinking, and the Offer of practitioner research methods. One academic partner added 'Ouse-keeping, a reflection of the local dialect[2]. This focus on Ofsted in the first session was in response to school Heads and teacher partners' evident concerns in professional conversations. I am advised there is an expectation that, given an inspection observation by School Leadership Teams or line managers of usually 20 minutes duration in one lesson, teachers should demonstrate so many criteria. This too is writ large in inspection specifications for judging student learning in the colour-coded sheet, provided to me by an urban high school teacher partner who previewed this book: see Figure 5.1.

Yet again the grid is indicative of atheoretical directions while anecdotal evidence suggests teachers' approach is to display a little bit of everything, no matter how pointless. The students are advised it is an 'Ofsted lesson', so they know what to expect when proceedings are interrupted and they are questioned about what they have learnt. Apparently they would prefer to 'crack on with course work' for the GCSEs (now 'Best 8') while teachers 'play the game' and 'fit in all the tricks much like a performing seal'. This adds another dimension to performativity! More seriously, it shows some of the tensions between teachers' efforts in the urban classroom, the performativity focus, mock and/or Ofsted inspections and considerations of disadvantaged students' learning.

This coincided with the release of Ofsted's (2012b) *The Evaluation Schedule for the Inspection of Maintained Schools and Academies: Guidance and Grade Descriptors for Inspecting Schools in England under Section 5 of the Education Action 2005, from January 2012*[3]. The title captured the moment, and gives pause to consider neoliberal government policies on accountabilities. As Ball (1993, 2006) indicated, an

Areas of focus	Outstanding	Good	Requires improvement	Inadequate
Starter including Meet & Greet 1.1	High expectations from teacher and students engaged all in a relevant learning activity from the outset with a clear link to the intended learning.	A starter activity provides a purposeful start to the lesson which aims to link with the intended learning.	The start of the lesson lacks structure and purpose.	Low expectations from teacher and students result in an unstructured start to the lesson.
LO/SC 2.2 14.1	LO/SC are well structured, communicated expertly and used throughout the lesson to focus learning for all students.	LO/SC are structured, communicated and used to focus learning.	LO/SC are conveyed to the students.	LO/SC are not evident or do not inform learning.
Context 2.2	LO/SC are well structured, communicated expertly and used throughout the lesson to focus learning for all students.	The students are clear of LO's relevance and how the lesson fits into the course.	Some effort is made to put the lesson into context.	The lesson is not put in context and has little relevance to the students.
Questioning techniques 6.2	All students show deep understanding, asking and/or answering a range of probing questions in a variety of situations. Questioning is used to assess understanding.	Most students are involved in asking and/or answering questions. Questioning is used to aid understanding and techniques are used to engage most students.	Questioning and discussion are used to aid understanding, but involve a limited number of students.	Questioning and discussion are not used to aid understanding.
Peer & self assessment 1.2/2.5/6.2	All students assess the success of their own and/or others' learning and set targets.	All students assess the success of their own and/or others' learning.	Some students assess the quality of their own work and/or others' work.	Opportunities to engage students in self or peer assessment are missed.
Verbal feedback 2.3/6.4	Verbal feedback is personalized and suggests ways to improve. Praise is consistent, appropriate and specific in supporting students improve their learning.	Verbal feedback is helpful and detailed suggesting ways to improve. Praise is a key feature in the lesson.	Verbal feedback and/or praise is infrequent and may be inconsistent. Some praise is used.	Verbal feedback is not given or is unhelpful. Praise is not a feature of the lesson.
Marking 2.3/6.4	Marking is regular and of consistently high quality. Feedback is constructive and positive and ensures pupils make rapid gains.	Marking is regular. Pupils know how well they have done and how to improve.	Marking is inconsistent. Some pupils know how well they have done and how to improve.	Pupils are rarely, if at all, informed about their progress through marking. Many do not know how to improve.
Plenary 2.3	Plenary activities throughout the lesson engage all students in effectively reviewing what and how they have learned. A connection is made to future learning and interventions are anticipated.	Plenary activities at points during the lesson effectively review learning for most students. Tasks and explanations are reshaped to improve learning.	A final plenary activity summarizes the learning from the lesson.	A plenary activity does not take place hence there is no formal close to the lesson.
Variety of experience	A wide range and variety of learning	A range of learning experience engages	One learning experience	A 'onesize fits all' approach provides

FIGURE 5.1 What does learning look like?

2.4/4.5	experience inspires all students.	most students.	dominates to engage some students.	little variation for students and does not motivate or engage students.
Planning 1.2/2.2/4.1/ 6.3	A clear awareness of prior attainment, performance targets and relevant assessment criteria has been used to pitch the lesson accurately for all students.	An awareness of prior attainment, performance targets and relevant assessment criteria has been used to pitch the lesson appropriately for most students.	Some awareness of prior attainment, performance targets and relevant assessment criteria is evident.	Awareness of prior attainment, performance targets and relevant assessment criteria is lacking.
Use of time 4.1	The management of time in the lesson is exemplary, the lesson is clearly structured and flows seamlessly from one phase to the next.	Good use is made of time and the lesson has structure and pace.	Insufficient use is made of the time available in the lesson and the lesson lacks pace.	Inadequate use is made of the time available in the lesson and the lesson has no clear structure and lacks pace.
Level of challenge 1.2/2.2/5.4	All learners, at all levels, make exceptional progress, through the highly effective tailoring of activities to the learners' capabilities. The motivational effect of this is evident.	Activities are closely tailored to the different capabilities of different groups of learners so that most students can learn well and make good progress.	Activities are insufficiently challenging to ensure that the majority of students including those with additional needs make expected progress.	Activities contain low levels of challenge. The teacher does not have a clear understanding of learners' needs.
Teacher's subject knowledge 3.1/3.2	The confidence generated by the teacher's excellent subject and curriculum knowledge inspires and challenges all students.	The teacher has strong subject and curriculum knowledge which challenges and enthuses most students.	The teacher's knowledge of the subject and curriculum are insecure.	The teacher's subject and curriculum knowledge is inadequate.
Resources 5.1/5.3	Resources, including new technology where appropriate, are used creatively to impact the quality of learning.	Resources, including new technology where appropriate, are used competently to enhance the quality of learning.	Resources, including new technology where appropriate, are used adequately.	Resources, including new technology where appropriate, are not used to support learning.
Use of support staff 8.3	Support provided through other adults is precisely targeted and makes a marked contribution to the quality of learning.	Support of other adults is well focussed to support and challenge individuals and groups of students.	There is a role implied for other adults who are deployed to support learning.	Inadequate use is made of the time available in the lesson and the lesson has no clear structure and lacks pace.
Level of challenge 1.2/2.2/5.4	All learners, at all levels, make exceptional progress, through the highly effective tailoring of activities to the learners' capabilities. The motivational effect of this is evident.	Activities are closely tailored to the different capabilities of different groups of learners so that most students can learn well and make good progress.	Activities are insufficiently challenging to ensure that the majority of students including those with additional needs make expected progress.	Activities contain low levels of challenge. The teacher does not have a clear understanding of learners' needs.
Teacher's subject knowledge 3.1/3.2	The confidence generated by the teacher's excellent subject and curriculum knowledge inspires and challenges all students.	The teacher has strong subject and curriculum knowledge which challenges and enthuses most students.	The teacher's knowledge of the subject and curriculum are insecure.	The teacher's subject and curriculum knowledge is inadequate.
Resources 5.1/5.3	Resources, including new technology where appropriate,	Resources, including new technology where appropriate,	Resources, including new technology where appropriate,	Resources, including new technology where appropriate,

FIGURE 5.1 continued

	are used creatively to impact the quality of learning.	are used competently to enhance the quality of learning.	are used adequately.	are not used to support learning.
Use of support staff 8.3	Support provided through other adults is precisely targeted and makes a marked contribution to the quality of learning.	Support of other adults is well focussed to support and challenge individuals and groups of students.	Insufficient use is made of the time available in the lesson and the lesson lacks pace.	Inadequate or inappropriate use is made of other adults in the classroom.
Independent learning 2.5/4.1/4.2	Teachers facilitate and empower all students to work independently and collaboratively; learners explore, seek clarity and think critically and imaginatively.	Planned opportunities for all students to work increasingly independently exist in order to share and apply their knowledge.	Little independent learning takes place and learners are overly dependent on the teacher.	No independent learning takes place and learners are excessively passive.
Homework 4.3	Appropriate homework is set which meets the needs of individuals accurately so they can consolidate and extend their knowledge understanding and skills. The vast majority of pupils regularly compete their homework.	Appropriate homework is set. It matches nearly all pupils' needs allowing them to consolidate and extend their knowledge understanding and skills. The majority of pupils complete their homework.	Appropriate homework is set. It matches most pupils needs.	Homework is not set regularly or it does not contribute to learning.
Attitude to learning 1.1/5.2/701/7.3	All students show excellent attitudes to their learning and clearly enjoy what they do. Students are inspired and enthused. The lesson proceeds without interruption.	Students show good attitudes to their learning and enjoy what they do. Students are motivated and engaged. Low level disruption to the lesson is uncommon.	Too few students show positive attitudes to their learning. A lack of motivation is evident. There is occasional low level disruption.	Attitudes to learning are poor. Teaching fails to promote students' learning, progress or enjoyment. Low level disruption reduces learning and/or leads to a disorderly classroom.
Behaviour management 7.1/7.2/7.3/7.4	Behaviour management is exemplary. Bahveious is managed skilfully and consistently and as a result behaviour in the lesson improves or is outstanding.	Behaviour management is normally good and most inappropriate behaviour is dealt with effectively.	Some inappropriate behaviour managed adequately. Major disruption is rare.	Behaviour is often inappropriate and is not adequately managed.
Literacy & Numeracy 3.3/3.4/3.5	Teachers respond expertly to exploit all opportunities for students to develop their skills in literacy and/or numeracy. This is well planned and results in highly effective development.	A range of planned strategies are employed for students to develop their skills in literacy and/or numeracy.	The lesson provides some opportunity for students to develop their skills in literacy and/or numeracy.	Opportunities to develop literacy and numeracy are missed.
Spiritual, Moral, Social & Cultural opportunities 1.1/1/3/5/3	Teachers respond expertly to exploit all opportunities for students to develop their skills in literacy and/or numeracy. This is well planned and results in highly effective development.	A range of strategies are employed for students to develop SMSC.	The lesson provides some opportunity for students to develop SMSC.	Opportunities to develop SMSC are missed.

FIGURE 5.1 continued

Health & Safety	The health and safety of learners is not endangered.		The health and safety of learners is endangered.	
Observer to reflect upon areas above and cross-reference overleaf before formulating a final judgement.					
Teaching over time 2.1/2.3/4.3/ 6.1/6.4	All students have played an active part in the lesson and therefore made very good progress by the end; the impact of learning is evident in what they do and say. Students demonstrate that they will be able to use and apply the knowledge and skills they have gained in future learning with confidence. Students understand in detail how to improve their work and are consistently supported in doing so through written and verbal feedback. Understanding is checked throughout the lesson with tasks and explanations reshaped in order to improve learning. Frequent and varied homework is set which consolidates and extends the knowledge and understanding students have acquired. Student work is assessed consistently in accordance with the whole school marking policy. Summative and formative feedback is used to secure student progress.	Most students have played an active part in lesson and therefore demonstrate good progress by the end. Student outcomes are secure and will be helpful for future learning. Students know how well they are performing and can articulate how to sustain this good progress. Teachers listen to and observe in order to improve learning. Homework is set which consolidates and extends the knowledge and understanding students have acquired. Some student work is assessed generally in accordance with the whole school marking policy. Evidence of both summative and formative feedback exists.	Some students have not engaged in the lesson or there is evidence of passivity. As a result progress is hindered. Student outcomes are insecure given their starting points. Students are unclear about progress and/or how to improve. Teachers monitor students' work during lessons. Arbitrary homework tasks are set that do not consolidate or extend knowledge and understanding acquired by students in lessons. Student work is not assessed in accordance with the whole school marking policy. Evidence is lacking of summative and/or formative assessment.	Too few students are engaged by the lesson or the majority of learning is passive. Progress is not sufficiently evident. Student outcomes are superficial or unclear to students. Students are not informed with sufficient regularity about progress and/or how to improve. Teachers take too little account of students' understanding and do not help students improve. Homework is not set in line with whole school policy. Student work is not assessed.

FIGURE 5.1 continued

important aside is the question 'what is policy?' and his advice is not to be misled into unexamined assumptions about policy as 'things', which requires an awareness of policies as processes and outcomes. The mock classroom inspections are highstakes for teachers and also the urban school, but they have potential negative effects on pedagogies and the continuity in students' preparation for equally high stakes examinations. It is as if the complexities around socioeconomic context, notably the effects of poverty and cumulative multiple deprivation are not enough. One urban primary school Head put it this way:

> [some of] the complexities are the family circumstances [from] the emotional well-being of parents and their mental health to their economic status [with attendant] stresses within the family around money, around housing, around resources, around food. So some of those really basic things can have a massive impact on children. . . . There are other indicators around deprivation. It might be mobility, for example, has the child got a bed to sleep in? It might be language used/spoken at home, in the community, and there could be lots of other factors involved.

This data is supplemented by further anecdotal evidence, this time an urban high school teacher's concern about a student given the pseudonym David, who has undiagnosed dyslexia at least in written form by way of medical report. He does not cope with mainstream class work, which requires the teacher's time to not only personalize learning activities but to build a relationship in order to coax him along. Another student given the pseudonym George often comes into class all worked up and has emotional outbursts, which requires the teacher's inordinate patience and encouragement to settle into class work. This is often only accomplished if the lad is sitting in close proximity to the teacher. Neither of these professional demands can be located on the observation grid titled 'What does learning look like' in Figure 5.1. For example, here is what another urban high school Head had to say on Ofsted inspections:

> An Ofsted inspection team coming in might have 5 hours to look at the background information. The lead inspector will have a bit longer time to have a look but [in actual fact it remains] very, very little time. So what they see is what they see when they get to the door. We no longer get the pre-inspection briefing document so you've got to be absolutely ready all the time.

This data dovetails with the ongoing public disquiet about Ofsted in the print media, for example. *The Guardian* journalist Zoe Williams[4] in a recent article, 'The entire schools inspection culture is the problem', questions the inspection system at both theoretical and methodological levels: measuring schools according to Ofsted grades but also specious process. As she put it, 'Our problem is the fact that the entire culture – targets and terror, name and shame, compete and count – discourages what education thrives upon: trust, cooperation, participation'. The same urban high school Head more or less agreed:

> *[An alternative]* is a professional conversation in a peer-led system whereby you've got people coming in and saying: right, this is what it looks like, this is what your data's saying, let's go and see what's going on in the classroom; it's a far better way of doing it because it doesn't feel like it's being done to you, it feels like it's been done with you.

Teachers' nascent criticality

This stated concern to be working in collaboration provoked me to return to first principles. Groundwater-Smith and Kemmis (n.d.) provided advice on capacity building, aimed to find and develop the sense of capacity and agency of schools, teachers, students, families and communities that went past blame and victim roles. More pointedly, Kemmis and Robottom's (1989) published guidelines or 'principles of procedure' for the evaluation of projects was for the purposes of protecting different interests in the procedures of an evaluation: commissioned evaluators, sponsors, participants in projects and programmes. It has not been updated since.

The first worksheet for teacher partners was intended to provide draft 'thinking' material for an agreed set of Operational Principles. It was laid out in a table and provided a template for others to follow. The point was made that our joint work is not designed for the evaluation as such of teachers' work in urban schools, though it will be useful to practitioners and participants in different projects and programmes being evaluated and to those concerned to contribute to evidence-informed practice and policy. Trailblazers were provided with Kemmis and Robottom's article and invited to comment, which was a way to encourage professional reading, engage ideas, concepts, theories, and trigger critical reflections and reviews of literature. Their worksheets were photocopied for the academic partner to collect and become a store of research data. Here is a sample, with one urban primary school teacher partner's response (in italicized print):

Kemmis and Robottom noted the contexts of evaluation are complex; and they can change over time. A multitude of variables interact at any one time, and independent participants' perspectives are important. They put a premium on negotiation, deliberation & diplomacy.	*A school's context is complex + important and changes frequently over time and all these elements impact on efforts to raise achievement within clusters and individual schools. The opportunity to work together in a safe professional circle will help practitioners support each other.*
Kemmis and Robottom counselled against determining effectiveness using pre-specified standards or criteria for evaluation, which can be insensitive to participants.	*Criteria for evaluation must be relevant and support participants in a constructive way.*

Kemmis and Robottom underlined the intent of their 'principles of procedure' was to be fair to everyone concerned.	*This fairness not only needs to include the professionals involved but also the students.*

It is possible to read a concern with ethicality and a sense of equity and academic partners learned much from what these practitioners had to say. For example, this teacher partner drew attention to student voice, which to date had only ever featured in the pilot studies and first attempts at teacher inquiry projects. To be honest I was totally preoccupied with generating the teachers' voice, under the most onerous set of circumstances. It had been broached in the pilot studies with trial student interviews and latterly emphasized by working with Trailblazers on research methods. This included focus group interviews with students, as the non-accredited CPD came into the 'practice' practitioner research activities.

It happened the six university campus-based sessions to run over the calendar year were interspersed with local urban school-based cluster meetings, where academic partners visited teacher partners in context: the first one was billed in the yearly schedule as joint discussion of urban school cluster priorities and expectations, teachers' knowledge and ideas about students' achievement and urban school performance, and critical challenges in different urban schools; deciding on the focus of cluster-based case study work, e.g. white British students' underachievement; developing skills of practitioner research; sample directed activities. These too had been tabulated in a worksheet to provide teacher partners with some ideas and tools for practitioner research with academic partners to furnish some guidelines to support select activities. Again here is an extract, with one urban primary school teacher partner's response (in italicized print):

Choose 3/4 select activities in addition to the one highlighted in yellow (a universal expectation)	What are you investigating? In what ways would these methods be useful?	What questions would the information generated allow you to answer?
Examining local demographic data	*How the community/ parents can support the school and vice versa; it would help gain an understanding of what the community provides.*	What can the community provide to support achievement? What issues do the children face in the community?
Interviewing students & parents	*In what ways can we support and engage parents/gain parents' opinions*	How can we get parents more involved in their child's learning? How can we support parents in their education?

Tracking students & teachers	How we could achieve a normal distribution in all [primary] years of schooling/looking at tracking results	How can parent/community involvement support children's achievement?
Building a learning portfolio	How parent/community support has an effect on 'raising achievement'.	How do we understand what the community provides?

Two points are noteworthy in this data. It shows teacher partner's ongoing concerns with 'raising achievement' but also a cognisance of the social determinants of students' learning. This is identified as a concern with community, family and parents, intimates another use of ACORN[5] data. As noted earlier, this is used to make comparisons with 'like' schools to inform decisions about student targets and rates of progress, but it could become a different source of data in the teacher partner's preliminary planning for a teacher inquiry project. This was a focus in the follow-up campus-based session[6], billed in the yearly schedule as discussion of the extant policy frameworks, fault lines of achievement, which includes identifying inequalities; feedback on joint discussion of cluster-based case study work; developing practitioner research questions. What follows are the notes from the first slide:

Build on foundations laid 27 Jan to bring teachers together with academic partners and Local Authority School Improvement partners, tapping school improvement across the world, and keeping abreast of international literature to inform practitioner research into classroom practices in local [city] schools; The international literature, reminds us that the challenges and pressures are global and, alongside more UK-centred literature, help us reflect on our practice experiences here.

Reviewing teachers' responses, given academic partners de-briefed with everyone, collected completed worksheets to date and began the task of building loops of feedback learning given our critical reflections & analyses (syntheses and theorisations);

'Making sense' of statutory targets, one focus for today's seminar, which are derived from Secretary of State for Education (SoS) Michael Gove's blueprint *The 2010 Schools White Paper* and new Ofsted (2012) guidelines and Her Majesty's Chief Inspector (HMCI) Sir Michael Wilshaw's amendments;

Ofsted under scrutiny, a second focus, which is to begin the task of a critical engagement with the new system of regulation and inspection and furnish you with ideas and vocabulary in your dealings with inspectors *et al.*;

Connecting and mapping backwards to research, a third focus, which takes a cue from Lingard and Renshaw (2010).

It is apparent academic partners had not given up on Local Authority partners, and the focus was on developing teacher partners' criticality (see Burbules and Berk, 1999). Coincidentally an invitation to attend this second campus-based session was extended to Lingard, who was at the university to present the 2012 Winifred Mercier public lecture[7] titled 'Confronting Schools and Social Inequality: Policy, Practices and Pedagogies'. He sat with a cluster of teacher partners in the interactive workshop session, and one element of his contribution to a digitally recorded discussion would have struck home:

> *Do you know what's always struck me about great teachers? They're teaching. [For example] I don't know photosynthesis, but what you do is take this concept and actually break it up, have hooks in and link to what the kids know. You actually turn it into [an activity] which is teaching . . . it's what's core. It's why I like the word pedagogy . . . you know how to actually take the knowledge and engage young people for learning by turning it into something else.*

Conversely it would have been interesting for Lingard to read teacher partners' reviews of professional readings, his own included. A worksheet titled 'Teachers' responses to key messages/ideas' was laid out in a table with a précis of Lingard et al.'s (2003) work, among others, to trigger theorizing about ideas that inform their school practices. Again here is a sample of two out of nine readings, with one urban high school teacher partner's response (in italicized print):

Key messages/useful ideas	What other ideas in these readings are useful to you and why?
Lingard et al.'s (2003) work on 'leading learning' provided a shining example of principled work for school leaders as they consider outcomes from schooling, classroom practices and leadership practices.	*Provided 'food for thought' on giving students space to negotiate their own approaches to work and teachers 'letting go' of the direction of the lesson. This involves taking risks but some colleagues are reluctant to do so in a culture of judgement. This way of working can also be constrained by a content-heavy and assessment-heavy curriculum.*
Lupton's (2006) chapter on disadvantaged schools was concerned to map the effects of poverty, the importance of school context, and the need for contextualised policy response.	*Interesting to note that school improvement is unlikely to come about by implementing practices that have been successful elsewhere and that establishing the school context is fundamental in effecting change. The four case study schools [in Lupton's chapter] highlighting the importance of understanding the challenges faced by [our school].*

This data exemplifies teacher partners continuing to engage with critical thinking to inform professional conversations. The next worksheet, on statutory targets, does the same: what it takes to achieve excellence, meet new floor standards, raise achievement, increase attainment/results, improve students' progress, and secure 'outstanding' judgement. In an effort to equip Trailblazers to undertake a critical reading of extant school data, they were provided with Johnson's (2002) chapter 'Talking about data'. Here is an extract from the accompanying worksheet, noting the first row and first column with directions and then cells with one urban high school teacher partner's response (in italicized print):

Case story from Johnson (2002)	Comment on students' progress	What more can be said?
The chapter is a case story from the USA that suggests reading beyond what data describes, to construct an interpretation in practice terms. Use the following questions to focus your discussions.	Summarise here the key points of your discussion in answer to the questions.	In thinking about students' progress and the sorts of information that could be used to indicate progression, are there any important factors/points that need to be considered?
• In your school what, if any, are the multiple types of indicators used to find out how different groups perform?	• FSM • Gender • EAL • Ethnic groups • SEN • G&T • Attendance *Teacher assessment levels; controlled assessment; FFT data[8]; KS5: AZPS & PANDA*	*High exclusion rate among FSM & SEN students; also high for white + black Caribbean, any other black and mixed background; also poor attendance rate among students eligible for FSM*
In your school are there any gaps among different groups of students in the same class/grade/year level, and why?	*Gap btw FSM (22 per cent) and all students (47 per cent) for GCSE grades 5A*-C English and Maths (5ACEM); EAL 5ACEM (36 per cent); SEN 5ACEM (12 per cent): underperforming ethnic groups, [notably] white & black Caribbean and Pakistani.*	*Groups performing significantly below average for value added: white British; white and black Caribbean; Pakistani; any other mixed background; boys & girls (particularly mid-high ability) . . . Where to start?*

This sample begins to bring to light the complexities of teachers' work in local urban schools in this neoliberal regime. In reply to the teacher partner's question 'where to start?' the answer has to be firmly on the classroom and a 'local' solution. However, as Connell (2009) put it,

> [t]he divisiveness of the neoliberal agenda for education is clear, and many experienced educators are deeply unhappy with it. But there is not yet a substantial alternative to offer. In the complex task of defining educational futures, an important focus is to develop a better conception of good teachers.

This sort of critical thinking all fed into the following local urban school-based cluster meeting, which was billed in the yearly schedule as a joint discussion of getting the cluster-based case study work started, priorities, planning details, logistics, problems (if any); building teachers' knowledge and ideas; developing practitioner research foci; sample directed activities. I am advised by an urban primary school teacher partner, the visits by academic partners were invaluable because they provide the necessary support to come to grips with the idea of a 'local' solution, key issues, directions for 'practice' practitioner research, and developing criticality. As a direct result of these visits, the school Head and school staff, led by the teacher partner, started to look at their urban school data differently and ask more questions.

An indicative commitment

The next citywide session had in attendance invited Local Authority partners, including the Deputy Chief Executive of Children's Services and School Improvement Advisors, along with academic colleagues in leadership and management positions[9]. I planned to reiterate school–university partnership ways of working with long-term sustained CPD focus on students' learning; classroom practices; teachers' needs; school priorities[10]; and cluster concerns. I led a critical discussion about government expectations but drew attention to school control of improvement; set improvement priorities; inspection to drive and support school improvement; school actions; and early teacher inquiry findings with an acknowledgement of risk.

I also reiterated the big 'O' theme and led another critical discussion of Ofsted, which followed some fieldwork where I became aware of another teacher partner's concern about mock inspection observations by the school Head, himself an Ofsted inspector. This involved one class per teacher and a report to the Board of Governors that 48 per cent of teachers were inadequate. I then constructed teacher learning activities around sample Ofsted lesson observations and a sample Local Authority observation form, which includes questions for the mock inspector:

Strengths:

- *How well have the students responded, learned, or attained?*
- *How has the teaching impacted on this learning?*

Two areas of development:

- *In what areas might the students have under-achieved or under-performed?*
- *How might the teaching have improved this?*

Learning prompts [focussed on whether or not students are, for example]:

- *Engaged, focussed?*
- *Challenged/stretched?*
- *Communicating ideas?*

Teaching prompts [focussed on whether or not teachers, for example]:

- *Establishes purpose, stimulates interest and inspires curiosity*
- *Links to students' previous learning: KUIS*
- *Provides additional challenge stretching highest performing students*

I naïvely hoped with the Local Authority in attendance, there would be an interactive professional conversation if not some negotiations with Trailblazers and academic partners, who could provide critical feedback on these sorts of classroom observation schedule. I expected this might be in the light of the literature reviewed so far (Groundwater-Smith, 2007a; Hayes et al., 2006; Lingard et al., 2001). This also prompted me to construct a different template for a first attempt at lesson study and work with colleagues to participate in observations of each other's lessons for their professional learning and development, not for teacher inspection and judgement (see Figure 5.2). This proved popular among Trailblazers. As an urban primary school one put it:

> *The QSRLS coding sheet is really useful for lesson observation. It helped steer us away from the narrow Ofsted focus on technical aspects of teaching, and addressed lots of issues we were beginning to question.*

It came as no surprise after the third citywide session to field criticisms via my Head of School, who reported a phone call from the Deputy Chief Executive agitated about the workload in the non-accredited component. I was perplexed that teacher partners had not come to me with constructive feedback, and I was mindful of local power plays, given my past experiences in the pilot studies. I put faith in the way I engage in critical theorizing: always professional, research-informed and evidence-based while the effort to showcase alternatives and SPEAK TRUTH TO POWER is always respectful.

The Local Authority officials may have been anxious. After all they had lent their support to the 'Leading Learning' CPD twin-pack at least in principle and

Teacher inquiry project: lesson observation template

Project name:_____
School/Class:_____
Teacher:_____

No of Boys:		No of Girls:		Target group focus:	FSM	ethnicity	Other detail	Other detail	Other detail

Describe the lesson/its place in sequence/content/rationale:
_____
_____
_____

State the teacher's concerns/questions:
_____
_____

Describe the agreed focus for classroom observation/lesson study:
_____
_____
_____

Comment on the lesson plan e.g. teachers' considerations, strategies, hopes	Suggestions for de-briefing
Comment on class as a whole e.g. quick to settle; distracted at times; aware of observer's presence	Suggestions for de-briefing
Comment on lesson progression e.g. retained class attention, or not	Suggestions for de-briefing
Comment on the pedagogies e.g. engaging, or not	Suggestions for de-briefing
Comment on pupil responses to classroom activities	Suggestions for de-briefing
Name the evident barriers to pupil learning	Suggestions for de-briefing
Comment on observer's overall impression of the lesson	Suggestions for de-briefing

Provide notes on tentative suggestions for further investigations into the teacher inquiry project:
_____
_____
_____
_____
_____

FIGURE 5.2 Leeds Met 'Leading Learning' CPD Programme 2012–2014

they gave approval to use their logo on the marketing flier. Their endorsement had provided some weight if not respectability to our work, which was promoted in Local Authority correspondence to all primary schools, again at the citywide school Heads' fora, the citywide Governors' fora, and the Advanced Skills Teachers' meetings. The Local Authority may have simply been concerned by the role of academic partner, acting as critical friend (Groundwater-Smith and Kemmis, n.d.; Beveridge et al., 2005) but also secretary (Apple, 2009) to support and mentor teacher partners to find their voice. That said, I fully acknowledge my stand against compliance and conformity, especially when it goes against my better professional judgement, which invariably leaves me open to criticism. Indeed I wondered if our more formalized school–university partnership work, already subjected to QA, was to be disrupted, influenced to change direction, or become the butt of interference.

These were recurring thoughts as our Head of School long reminded me of the Deputy Chief Executive's report of dissatisfactions with the volume of work in the non-accredited component. Perhaps it was more his anxiety about upsetting Local Authority officials, compounded by the silence in reply to the Local Authority's promotion of our work. One incident makes the point. I often saw reference to the 'Leading Learning' CPD twin-pack in the Local Authority's material, but there was no evident follow-up by way of enquiries. I was not alert to further action taken so that in the end nothing eventuated from these promotional activities, at least from my perspective. A penultimate chance to continue the work with the Local Authority came with an invitation to a meeting with the Deputy Chief Executive, the new manager of the School Improvement team and seconded school Heads. It was on the proviso academic partners agreed to tailor the non-accredited component to students' achievement in maths, one of the target areas in the neoliberal performative agenda. This was obviously a blatant attempt at co-option.

The invitation was declined and after more than 7 years academic partners stopped attending these meetings with local officials although I continued to issue invitations to attend citywide sessions and to public events[11]. Once again naïvely, it was many years before I came to see these meetings with few exceptions were less a case of commitment to partnership (see Sirotnik and Goodlad, 1988; Kruger et al., 2009; Bevins and Price, 2014) and more likely a case of academic partners' usefulness. We were possibly a ready supply of research intelligence to the Local Authority's managerialist oversight of their local area plans for urban schools, in line with authoritarian politicians' decrees. Then one of our colleagues, long established in this northern city of England, suggested that our ongoing meetings could have provided the Local Authority with an indication of partnership useful to its own tick-a-box inspection data for Ofsted[12].

A confirmation of my inclination not to dwell on the negatives can be derived from two sources. The historian E.P. Thompson's (in Winslow, 2014) counsel is that suggestive forces cannot be resisted by fostering a negative current of critical resistance alone. They must be met by other positive forces which can only come from a vigorous movement in which the political minority [read research-active teachers] and intellectuals [read academic partners] *make common cause*. This is matched by Touraine's (1977) guidance that anti-technocratic battles are waged by two categories of actors: a fraction of professionals [read academic partners] who speak in the name of knowledge against an apparatus that seeks to subject knowledge to its own interests . . . they ally themselves with those [read teachers in so-called 'failing' schools] who are forced to the sidelines by a central apparatus and submitted to its power. In the ongoing non-accredited component of the 'Leading Learning' CPD twin-pack, there was almost a union of these protesting categories but as Touraine (1977) noted, it does not occur easily.

It must be said the Local Authority's criticisms via our Head of School were not lost. I certainly recognized a need to recalibrate, not least the pace and direction to engage teacher partners in this out-of-the-ordinary in-service teacher education programme. Without meaning to sound defensive, the pace was a conscious decision: one school Head from the pilot studies had emphasized the need to provide value for money, given each urban school was funding the teacher partners' participation and CPD budgets were tight. I figured that in the light of these expectations, teacher partners would devote some part of each work week to so-called 'homework' activities. In the first four sessions, which spanned a school term of approximately 12 weeks, 13 readings with accompanying worksheets were provided. On a practical level, this had to be reconsidered. Under extreme policy and time pressures in a performative culture there is little or no time for professional learning activities much less practitioner research.

At a more substantive level academic partners needed to be sure they were *making common cause* with teacher partners to co-investigate matters of professional concern in regards 'raising achievement' and 'closing the gap'. Some self-consciously reflective questions needed to be asked if academic partners had Trailblazers' trust to guide the non-accredited component so it meets urban schools' needs. In effect this required further critical theorizing of our self-proclaimed research-informed teacher education practice, both theoretical and methodological. So much of this had been conceptualized in bids for research funding, the design of the 'Leading Learning' CPD twin-pack, the formal application for Operational Approval and the validation of the allied MA 'Achievement in City Schools'. Another question related to how the co-developed professional knowledge work was being rolled out in practice.

Teacher partners' identified concerns

The next local urban school-based cluster session was a 'make-or-break' point in that teacher partners really had to indicate a commitment to continue on the programme. In the yearly schedule it was billed to be a joint discussion of progress with the cluster-based case study work and necessary collaborations; building teachers' knowledge and ideas; developing skills for practitioner research/inquiries;

sample directed activities. It happened I digitally recorded the session with the permission of a team of urban high school teacher partners and their senior colleague who had assumed the role of Coordinator of the teacher inquiry projects. Once we had passed the introductory discussion, the pace and direction soon came to light:

> Coordinator: *There's a lot to think about so I'd quite like a breakdown, almost like a step-by-step paint-by-numbers guide. How to go from step one: have you done this? Step two, now do that. Otherwise it might all get jumbled up inside my mind about what to do when. So almost a bit of a guide: first identify the class that you want to [research] and write a rationale of why you have chosen that class. Step two, then step three and four and so on.*
>
> Teacher partner: *Personally I would like a set task by a set day, with some kind of structure, not necessarily a form, but even just an email, that's broken down, almost step-by-step, to say do this first, do that and then write something about what you have done. Then in a couple of weeks [the Coordinator] could say 'you should have done x, y and z'.*
>
> Lori: *In reply, it's us trying to hit our stride and find a way of working together because the last time I came the focus was on RAISEonline. Then I sent an email follow-up [to confirm agreed directions]. I came today expecting all of you to contribute with critical questions [of the national-school data], thinking to myself from those critical questions we're going to develop an interview [schedule for a focus group of students].*

Crucially, this data shows that teacher partners and their Coordinator made a commitment to continue the work. In charting a way forward, I indicated a willingness to be flexible and patient, alert to the huge policy and time pressures they had to endure and to 'just roll with it'. At the same time I indicated I needed to know where this cluster of teacher partners was in planning their teacher inquiry project/s and how I could support them as an academic partner. The discussion continued with a focus on the extant school data, including Year data, which evolved into a professional conversation about the student census and community demographics related to student groups at risk of underachieving, 'attitudes to learning'[13], attendance and exclusions. The concern for teacher partners was to find where and how they could contribute what is known as 'value added' (see Ray, 2006). A tentative decision was made to collectively focus on Year 9, and as two teacher partners put it:

> First: *[In this year group] there's massive free school meals, massive EAL (English as an Additional Language), though not so massive G and T (gifted and talented) but literacy is huge and 'thinking skills' is a huge issue for them.*
>
> Second: *[yes] this is a massive research-rich year group!*

This data shows this cluster of Trailblazers had registered Cochran-Smith and Lytle's (2001) recommendation to treat their own classrooms and schools as sites for intentional investigation, which augured well for planning their teacher inquiry project/s. They continued to explicate the complexities although this began with the compensatory programs then in place: behaviour management, setting, and 'on access'. I learned this was a nurture group that carried over from primary school, where students stay in the same class with the same teacher with responsibility for multiple subjects in the early years of high school. This included a programme called SEAL focused on the social and emotional aspects of learning. A significant breakthrough came with teacher partners organizing themselves to prepare the brackets of questions for student interviews though they would need support and mentoring on practitioner research[14] (see Menter et al., 2011). This included methods and data gathering but also critical analyses and triangulation with national-school RAISEonline data and local area data. As one of the teacher partners was wont to highlight:

> The interesting bit in the RAISEonline [is] where it put which [local area electoral] ward they come from, and [noted] the high density housing and the percentage of those [who live there] . . . how do we find that about the students in front of us? Whether we've got that information in school or whether we ask them?

This data suggests teacher partners are prepared to engage intellectually and critically with social geography and neighbourhood studies but also with ethnographic case studies to tell the stories behind the official data. Moreover, this data in the form of transcripts is stored along with the RAISEonline report, School Development Plan and 'other' data generated in the course of teacher inquiry in each teacher partner's learning portfolio. This provides a record of our co-developed professional knowledge work but also useful material as the basis of conference presentations (see Nuttall, 2014; Nuttall et al., 2015) and publications[15]. This data also provides academic partners with material for their research-informed deliberations about subsequent interactive workshop sessions in the non-accredited component of the 'Leading Learning' CPD twin-pack.

It happened the next citywide session, delivered by Lupton (2014), was billed in the yearly schedule to canvass disadvantaged schools, poverty and deprivation; social markers like class, race, gender; effects of context; and building school databases. Lupton also provided two readings (see Lupton, 2004a, 2011) and I prepared the associated worksheets. Here are sample extracts with input in italics from one of the urban primary school teacher partners:

| What is your explanation for the discrepancy in school results? | *Different starting points – children in poor schools start at lower levels. Some make limited progress due to factors such as life experience, parental support, attendance, etc. . . .* |

Do you agree with the dominant view? Why/why not?	*No! Not all children have the same starting points so some are at an advantage compared to others from early childhood. Schools can't make up for everything!*
Lupton puts her case that there is a problem of school quality in disadvantaged areas, and suggests that in general the most disadvantaged students are served by the least good schools. Do you agree? Why/why not?	*No!! Measure of 'good' schools is by results and Ofsted inspections – schools in disadvantaged areas have more factors which can prevent them from achieving, e.g. children starting school with below average speech/knowledge/skills, behaviour problems, etc. . . . Schools in disadvantaged areas have to work harder to get the same results/behaviours as schools in middle class areas.*
Lupton continues to argue that the problem largely rests on the assumption that it is to be tackled on terms internal to the school, rather than a product of the local context. In your experience, does this assumption hold for work in our current school?	*No!!! Local context impacts on all areas of learning and education – not to take it into account will inhibit children's progress as their full need will never be met.*
Lupton's chapter contained an argument in favour of a social analysis (structural account) of schools' work. Please name three points in that argument:	• *Teachers in the inner-city school who perceived white children had no rules at home dealt with more behaviour problems than at the school where ethnic minority children were taught by parents to respect authority.* • *Primary school in middle class area had PTA, parent donations and therefore a better learning environment/more enrichment activities.* • *Disadvantaged had a wider range of abilities and more extreme learning needs.*

    This data exemplifies Trailblazers coming to grips with debatable ideas about urban school contexts, in the larger sense but also the minutiae via their own illustrations: engaging alternative viewpoints and touching on established and long-standing debates about interventions, say about compensation strategies, in the academic literature but also the public media[16] (see Bernstein, 1970; Power, 2008). This exposure to research insights continued in the remaining three campus-based and three school-based sessions in that first year of the non-accredited component geared towards drafting teacher inquiry questions, looking for data, building descriptive and critical analyses. The latter part of the year's programme continued to scaffold shared professional learning activities.

The penultimate campus-based session turned out to be one of my watershed moments, when a teacher partner provided an article 'Don't call me a chav' by the rapper, actor and film-maker called Plan B, featured in the Radio Times[17]. This served to underline the point that this professional knowledge work is indeed co-produced! I was instantly reminded of Jones' (2011) book and Toynbee's (2011) article, *Chav: the vile word at the heart of fractured Britain*[18]. I got the impression these teacher partners found an archetypally local term to describe their 'school mix' or social class composition (Thrupp, 1999). I sensed they took umbrage not only at government and Ofsted criticisms of their teaching and the derisory discourses about their urban schools but also at the demonization of the working classes that included their students. The academic partners' ongoing task was to help unpack these professional concerns and then assist Trailblazers to channel them into their teacher inquiry projects.

The last task of the year was for teacher partners to complete a template provided for their 2012 Annual Report, a pedagogical strategy trailed in the final pilot study, now revised to consolidate Trailblazers' professional learning and share with school Heads, among others. It began with a narrative description of the non-accredited component, followed by a series of bullet points that invited input, as per the following examples:

- *Some preliminary analysis of school data to inform thinking about our definition of student's progress and the terms of our analyses. We used a case story from Johnson (2002) to probe an instant of student's progress, for example* [insert sample detail from #8 worksheet];
- *An exercise to examine a sample of new Ofsted inspection advice in order to backward map to research and identify what might need investigation. For example the advice to focus on* [insert example from #9 worksheet] *suggested a further look into* [ditto];
- *A second review of literature to encourage teachers' thinking about key messages in the literature and theorising about ideas that inform their school practices. For example, one key message was* [insert sample from #10 worksheet];

The completed reports were also returned to me as university Course Leader of the 'Leading Learning' CPD twin-pack, and I was keen to receive teacher partners' evaluation, given they were invited to comment. Here is a sample from a team in an urban primary school:

> Overall [teacher partners in this urban primary school] would rate this 'Leading Learning' CPD program experience as [indicate as appropriate – very good/ good/satisfactory/poor/very poor] *for the following reasons:*

> The development of a shared vocabulary to discuss the impact of context in group sessions has been followed up and strengthened in the readings then utilised in school-based meetings. Looking closely at a small group of children in a series of lessons has allowed us to home in on [student] learning and pedagogies from a new angle, not just achievement data.
>
> The critical commentary activities using proformas and Ofsted statements has given us a voice within the group but also a platform to continue the conversations with other stakeholders like the Board of Governors and other colleagues in staff meetings.

Conclusion

This is useful feedback and the non-accredited component is mostly graded 'good' year-on-year with unanimous support from teacher partners to continue the program into subsequent years, which is some testament of its worth. As the following evaluative comment from a high school teacher partner shows, practitioners see value in this sort of out-of-the-ordinary professional learning and development at an institutional level but also at a personal level:

> This 'Leading Learning' CPD was a real opportunity to re-connect with the reasons teachers came into teaching. It reminds professionals to question what we do and why? What's best for our students? It supports real research in our settings to really 'make a difference'. . . . It allows me to take ownership of my thoughts and ideas and move forward with pedagogies in a research-informed way. It is the only CPD that challenged me to push myself intellectually.

This data confirms my intuition that teacher partners would want to deflect criticisms of academic partners, who received no systemic support, only veiled criticisms in the form of concerns raised by the Local Authority about workload coupled with ongoing reminders from Head of School about such dissatisfaction. In the end, teacher partners are the best judges and the ones to lend support to the 'university project' in teacher education (Furlong, 2013; Whitty, 2014) but also to 'make common cause' (Thompson in Winslow, 2014) with academic partners. This is best explained by Furlong (2013), who argues the discipline of education is not only a coherent field of study; it has a political life, argued for, supported, challenged and debated. This can be gleaned from the Trailblazers' publications, developed in the non-accredited component of the 'Leading Learning' CPD twin-pack and showcased in the next chapter.

110 Making common cause

"Mr. Wickers called me 'gifted' in front of the whole class. I'm ruined."

© Andrew Toos. Reproduced by permission of Cartoon Stock. www.CartoonStock.com (image ID: aton853).

Notes

1 See, for example, the NUT successive annual conference agenda and proceedings: www.nut.org.uk
2 Again I must acknowledge academic partner Dr Jon Tan, who in his own way provided backup and assistance, including his contributions to teaching and research that informs the 'Leading Learning' CPD twin-pack. I learned much from him about teachers' identity.
3 See www.gov.uk/government/uploads/system/uploads/attachment_data/file/391531/School_inspection_handbook.pdf
4 See www.theguardian.com/commentisfree/2014/oct/19/schools-inspection-ofsted-rachel-de-souza
5 This is a commercial package purchased by local urban schools to provide detailed demographic data about the local area: http://acorn.caci.co.uk/
6 In order to clarify respective roles, it should be said this second and sixth session was developed by Dr Jon Tan who presented to teacher partners while I furnished all readings and all worksheets throughout the non-accredited CPD component and developed the template for the 2012 Annual Report, noted later in this chapter. We did much the same for the following years, and I developed the template for the teachers' journal articles.
7 I (usually) invite a prominent woman to speak on matters of concern, though to date Bob Lingard has been the exception.
8 See www.fft.org.uk/about-us/Fischer-Family-Trust.aspx

9 Invitations were consistently issued to this wider group, always in the hope that they would accept and hopefully come onto a proposed Reference Group, as suggested by Lieberman and cited earlier in this book.
10 I should here again acknowledge the contribution of Dr Jon Tan, who brought to the fore school priorities, which took a cue from Ofsted inspections, School Evaluation, etc.
11 This includes the Winifred Mercier public lecture, a major event in the calendar year.
12 I am told that the Local Authority, apparently renowned over many years for its conservatism, is constantly resistant to different ways of thinking and innovation. I can only imagine what sort of challenge an outsider, even an English-speaking white Australian with some English heritage, might present: see Beveridge *et al.*, 2005 p. 705 on outsiders.
13 The 'Attitude to Learning' survey is an instrument devised by other school staff and used school-wide, which signals an attempt at practitioner research however blunt. The ongoing conversation with teacher partners yielded no evident indication of how school staff might view such inquiry and how it might affect student learning in and outside the classroom (see Campbell and Groundwater-Smith, 2010).
14 One of the readings and accompanying worksheets to follow was by Menter *et al.* (2011).
15 This cohort of Trailblazers, who like to be known as RaTs (research-active teachers), are all published authors given the special collection of journal articles published in *Urban Review*, 46, 5, December, 2014. The details about developing this publication are discussed in the next chapter.
16 See www.newstatesman.com/node/139246 also www.theguardian.com/education/2010/jan/05/schools-cbi-social-changes-standards
17 See www.radiotimes.com/news/2012–06–17/plan-b-dont-call-me-a-chav
18 See www.theguardian.com/commentisfree/2011/may/31/chav-vile-word-fractured-britain

6
TEACHERS' VOICES

Introduction

At the foreground of each year's work in the non-accredited component of the 'Leading Learning' CPD twin-pack programme is critical discussion of participants' professed values and sense of ethical practice in urban schools in this northern city of England. This includes a recap of the 'principles of procedure' that cement teachers' and academic partners' joint commitments to disadvantaged students, families and communities with deep needs in Austerity Britain. This logic of ethicality and appeal to moral purpose is part of a tactical professional reply to successive neoliberal governments' insistence on 'structural' solutions for so-called 'failing' schools to be replaced by semi-privatized academies.

Again, political wit to the fore. The case for this Conservative-led academies programme is often made on the same grounds by right-wing politicians. For instance, former Secretary of State for Education Michael Gove instituted a more 'radical-conservative experiment' to boost quasi-market relations, opportunities for edu-business (Hatcher, 2010) and 'the retail model of schooling' (Ball, 2012). This has more or less come to be regarded as an insidious 'common-sense approach' (Apple, 2001) to urban schooling. Gove[1] put it this way:

> *Introducing the next generation to the best that has been thought and written is a moral enterprise of which we can all be proud. Giving every child an equal share in the inheritance of achievement which great minds have passed on to us is a great progressive cause.*

This data shows Gove's hubris and arrogance. His presumptuous appeal to ethicality and moral purpose has harnessed the language and discourse of an assemblage that characterizes fairer, equitable and socially just approaches to urban schooling (see Connell, 1993; Sturman, 1997; Smyth *et al.*, 1998; Gale and Densmore, 2000; Thrupp and Lupton, 2006). It is then linked to a Conservative neoliberal restructuring of the public schooling system, which is shored up by a new managerial construction of an audit culture that goes past the limits of older versions (Apple, 2009). The upshot is that politicians, policymakers and power-brokers are bound to uphold the derisory and demonizing notion of 'failing' schools to extend marketization and privatization in the school system. This is driven by material class interests that are conceptualized and operationalized in ideological terms (Hatcher, 2010).

The cohort of Trailblazers eventually came to build practitioner research evidence that went past crude national-school data distributed in RAISEonline but also school-generated performance data about student attainment and progress, co-opted to the dominant ideological message. The 'case for the defence' (Gorton *et al.*, 2014) relies on developing critical contextual understandings of urban schooling and professional conversations about, say, student cohorts and individuals like Plan B colloquially known as 'chavs'. Teacher partners know to align the derisory and demonizing 'failing' schools misnomer with wider practical-politicized debates about social theories like neoliberalism (see Ball, 2008/2013, 2012; Anyon, 2009; Apple, 2001, 2009; Lingard, 2009, 2011; Beckett, 2013a, 2013b). At a more practical level, they also see the need to provide disadvantaged students with responsive and meaningful curricula with access to powerful knowledge synchronized with equally expressive forms of pedagogies and assessment (see Lingard, 2009).

This chapter comes to the crux of Trailblazers' co-developed professional knowledge work, which foregrounds the processes of practitioner research and teases open the interconnections of disadvantaged students' lives, learning needs and urban schooling experiences. It throws a spotlight on professional concerns about the social determinants of students' learning but also the social and political realities in urban schools. There is a special emphasis on the ways these research-active teachers and their academic partners have to negotiate practice-focused investigations, given huge policy and time pressures. This includes what can and cannot be said not only to maintain professional respectability but to stave off fears about 'putting one's head above the parapet' and drawing attention to their local urban school. Significantly, this chapter shows the steps taken towards this cohort's first published work with only one exception[2] since everyone agreed to publicize the research-informed professional voice. It concludes with a précis of their journal articles to showcase their classroom action and policy advocacy for contextualized school improvement plans. This is no small feat in the current conjuncture.

Channelling teachers' concerns

Teacher partners in this local network of urban schools are concentrated on 'raising achievement' and 'closing the gap' in line with government policy and practice dictates. Strategically they pool their collective intelligence and co-develop knowledge of poverty and cumulative multiple deprivation with academic partners whom they trust. They also glean insights from guest lecturers whom we call 'consultant academic partners': Lupton (2004a, 2006, 2011), Lingard (2009), Park (2013) and Cahill (2012). There is also the virtual team of academic partners who came together in response to my call to demonstrate practitioners' necessary intellectual activity to wrest back professional control from non-educationalists who dictate the terms of teaching and teacher education (see Beckett, 2013a, 2013b). Two teacher partners made their own contribution to this edited collection (Arthurs, 2013; Ghale and Beckett, 2013), and in many respects acted as an advance party on 'going public', and spearheaded an alternative to the norms of privacy and secrecy (see Lieberman and Miller, 2001, 2008). As well, public commentator Melissa Benn (2013) took what they had to say to demonstrate policy advocacy in the run-up to the 2015 UK election.

The same cohort of Trailblazers continued into the second year with some withdrawals and one addition. One teacher partner took a school Headship, one was preoccupied with a Deputy Headship, and one transferred to a new school and deemed the workload enough! At the same time, a union-active teacher partner from one of the urban high schools engaged in a school-closure campaign after the TDA-funded pilot study joined the cohort. The replacement Acting school Head finally relented and agreed to fund her participation, which was a cause for celebration given our previous ongoing work had been majorly interrupted. The proviso this time round was for a directed teacher inquiry project to be focused on a Year 7 group overseen by the School Improvement Advisor (see Gallagher and Beckett, 2014). Coincidentally he had told me on a previous occasion that practitioner research was not a really useful strategy to improving student learning outcomes because it takes too long and it is too long-term[3].

I was taken aback but I could see the influence of the Local Authority's directions for standardized school improvement, evident in the following extract from a report to the then-citywide Governors' Forum:

> *In [this city] Local Authority we have taken the intentional strategic decision to respond proactively to national and local changes [in national policy and funding arrangements]. Recent developments, particularly the academies program, provide the opportunity for schools to act with great autonomy, but we also know that to improve outcomes for children and young people in [this city] we need to continue to build on the strong culture of partnership across the city. To do this we have looked at the existing 'landscape' and refreshed our approach to provide a framework in which strong partnerships between schools and other services can grow.*

Two points need to be made about this data. First, it signifies buy-in to the prevailing neoliberal agenda, which again reflects the Local Authority's imprimatur for local officials to operate as civil servants in support of the incumbent national government and to tailor their work accordingly. Again this focuses attention on vested or positional power, given their role in 'failing' school closures. It also mirrors the machinations of education politics at the local government level, where elected city councillors, some political party-affiliated and others independent, run the Local Authority. There is a haunting spectre of failed Ofsted inspections: first, of the education department that brought into being a not-for-profit company allied to a business entity to run it, then a second, on safeguarding children, that led to its demise. Most recently the Children's Services Directorate, marked by its redeveloped corporate plan, is rated 'highly satisfactory' by Ofsted.

Second, the Local Authority's point on partnerships between schools and other agencies, no doubt a reflection of the new integrated Children's Services Directorate model worked up for the city, suggests scope for the sort of partnership ways of working put forward by this book. The political reality is that the Local Authority's School Improvement Plan 2011–2015 is a reply to Gove's letter 'Improving Underperforming Schools' and chimes for the duration of the previous Coalition Government. It makes very clear it takes direction from the 2010 *Schools White Paper* and interestingly "other international publications". These are not named, but a scan of the research literature shows professional debate of dominant constructions of School Effectiveness and School Improvement (see Slee and Weiner with Tomlinson, 1998; Thrupp, 1999, 2005). The Local Authority (LA) named four elements that sit with these dominant constructions:

Monitoring	Statutory functions of the LA including analysis of data
Challenge	Supported self-review to schools, clusters and professionals
Support	Signposting good practice in schools and partners
Intervention	Direct work to strengthen leadership and governance

At the same time, we followed much the same format as the first-year non-accredited component: 6 on-campus and 6 in-school sessions (one each per half term) over the school year. There are interactive workshop activities, readings and specially devised worksheets for teacher partners to engage in professional learning including practitioner research activities to build their portfolios in-between sessions. It must be said this paperwork was much reduced, in the light of Local Authority criticisms of the CPD workload in first-year and academic partners' ongoing recalibrations. However, it takes nothing away from teacher partners' preparedness to engage intellectually with the international research literature and tease out socially critical positions. Under the circumstances, we need to take a measured approach to identify and name the vernacular forms of GERM (Sahlberg, 2011) that influence their work in local urban schools.

Sahlberg (2011, 2014), who coincidentally delivered the inaugural BERA Annual lecture, provides good direction. In the campus-based session[4] devoted to 'Strategies for practitioner research and data generation', teacher partners' reading about research-active teachers in the Finnish system could see a working alternative to GERM. Lieberman's Series Foreword to Sahlberg's (2011) book consolidates the argument:

116 Teachers' voices

- We learn what it means to have a teacher-preparation program that is 'research-based' and its effects on students' learning;
- [we need] time to study pedagogy as well as practice and to learn how to do research;
- [we learn] inquiry into teaching is part of what it means to teach;
- teaching is an intellectual enterprise enhanced by the teacher's own research questions and subsequent findings;
- we have much to learn from the examples written about in this book: ... research as an important focus for learning to teach; and leadership emanating from the teachers themselves.

A question for teacher partners: How do Lieberman's observations play out in a justification (rationale) for practitioner research? Prompts for their deliberations in the purposefully devised accompanying worksheet include:

- its effects on students' learning;
- inquiry into teaching is part of what it means to teach;
- teaching is an intellectual enterprise;
- research is an important focus for (continuously) learning to teach; and
- it equips teachers for leadership (and leading learning).

As noted throughout this book, the effects of poverty and cumulative multiple deprivation are by now upheld as 'mitigating circumstances' (Arthurs, 2012, 2013) to be named as such in marshalling the evidence and building the 'case for the defence' of urban schools (Gorton et al., 2014). However, this does not confine professional concerns to what disadvantage means to teacher partners in terms of the social determinants of disadvantaged students' learning. This requires academic partners to engage them in more practical-politicized dialogue about ongoing investigations into disadvantaged students' lives and urban schooling experiences. This teases open professional concerns named earlier: disadvantaged students' health and welfare; lack of sleep/tiredness; hunger; and bringing personal/family problems into school, all of which can result in lateness, emotional tensions and being ill-prepared for the day's school work. Then there is lack of interest, disaffection, disengagement, alienation and absenteeism, which all say something about students' views about the school system.

Teacher partners will talk openly about students whose priorities lie elsewhere, towards immediate caring responsibilities for siblings, parents who are sick/dependent, to showing a mindset for survival without adequate coping strategies or any sense of future security much less improving their school performance and attainment. To reiterate the point, it is important to revisit academic partners' pedagogical efforts to support teacher partners' draft teacher inquiry questions, as this example from a worksheet shows with one of the urban primary school teacher partner's answers (in italics):

> Restate your 4 sample questions that were derived from your student vignette, now that you have had a chance to consider the annotations with your academic partner:
>
> - *What pedagogies seemingly engage students with low attendance?*
> - *How can productive pedagogies be best developed to engage FSM children in the process of their learning?*
> - *How do we secure level 2 for high functioning EAL students?*
> - *How do we raise standards for white British students across KS1?*

As expected, these draft teacher inquiry questions reflect a major concern with Ofsted preoccupations such as low attendance, the category of students eligible for free school meals, levels of learning and raising standards, which are also indicative of a standardized school-improvement agenda. In many ways it is to acknowledge Lieberman and Miller's (2008) advice that:

> [t]eachers are always working from tacit knowledge and implicit theories that they often don't recognise as such. . . . Teachers develop the capacity to become self-conscious knowledge workers. . . . They begin with experience and work their way toward theory.

This takes some time and ongoing structured professional learning opportunities to engage with school-generated 'other' data (see Johnson and La Salle, 2010) like student work samples and teaching episodes to make the connection between practice and its theorizations[5]. This is to provoke critical discussion about 'local' solutions and the sort of practitioner research Trailblazers might be doing with their academic partners. It connects with Whitty's early advice about naïve possibilitarianism and democratic professionalism (Whitty, 2008) with a sense of 'complex hope' (Grace, 1994, 2007), which brings to mind historical and structural difficulties.

It happened Trailblazers needed more guidance on the minutiae of practitioner-research processes in the form of readings about qualitative methods with some expansion on feminist perspectives to provide a better understanding of how social class and race interacts with gender (Menter *et al.*, 2011; Punch, 2009; Burns and Walker, 2007). Table 6.1 shows a specially tailored worksheet that uses a sample set of teacher inquiry questions with details of possible responses to prompts (in the LHS column). This worksheet is paired with another one that has blank cells for teacher partners to register their own responses. The two tabulated worksheets are purposefully constructed to connect with Trailblazers' current preoccupations but also to help them structure their teacher inquiry projects.

A turning point

The co-developed teacher inquiry projects require ethical approval from each urban school as well as the university, which in many ways became the lynchpin to the school–university partnership way of working with teacher partners. The process

TABLE 6.1 Sample teacher inquiry worksheet

Draft your 3 questions in the adjacent boxes	1st draft question	2nd draft question	3rd draft question
	Why are achievement scores so low for some students in my class?	How and what are students learning?	How do my colleagues understand learning?
What data is at hand?	RAISEonline data (disaggregated); subject-specific achievement data/patterns; grades & test scores & comparisons; performance assessments; HLTA's advice	National curriculum specs; schemes of work/content/knowledge & skills; lesson plans & plan books; FFT data & targets for students; outcome data & test information	Lesson plans; suggested activities; assignments & assessment tasks; student grades and work samples; standards/information on what needs to be taught, e.g. vocabulary/reading
What ideas/themes are useful from your readings/review of literature?	The 'pedagogies of poverty'	There are ritualistic acts in the classroom that do not necessarily foster students' learning.	'Old hands' at teaching have some set ways to handle disengaged students to maintain control, but this may not ensure students' learning.
What thoughts can you add?	There are poverty and deprivation effects on students (see Lupton, 2004a; 2006), but also on teachers (see Haberman, 1991)	Lesson observations are revealing because they sketch the 'do's and don'ts'; map the expectations of teachers and students; delineate what is considered the way to operate	If the staff/faculty want to experiment (say with productive pedagogies★) then we need to do it all together to effect a change/reform that all students will accept.
What are your lines of inquiry?	The sorts of pedagogies in operation★; the classroom atmosphere; the teachers' role/function in class; the students' experiences of teaching/learning	The students' responses to what's on offer; the way they adapt/react to different pedagogies; teachers' resources/strategies; intervention strategies	Student compliance/resistance/engagement; Teachers' efforts at control/engagement; The indicators of good/exemplary teaching★; types of assessment
How do these connect with the Faculty/School Development Plan?	Improving performance, achievement, progress	Implementing intervention strategies but also improving classroom practice	Embedding quality teaching
What 'other data' do you need?	Photos; student vignettes; interviews with parents/students; self-assessment of my strengths/needs; ditto for the teaching team; information on teachers' grading (how/why)	Teaching and learning policies/procedures; extra data on expectations of students; students' and teachers' schedules/diary entries	A survey/questionnaire with closed/open questions; ★coding sheets; classroom observations; recording de-briefing sessions with teachers/students

of drafting the application for Ethics Approval to the university served a few purposes: it alerted teacher partners not used to research formalities to the necessity to name the ethics of our work together, which added to their sense of ethicality and moral purpose; it became the basis for ongoing campus- and school-based workshop sessions, given it required ongoing support and mentoring of practitioners; and it brought into sharp relief a contrast between the university's Ethics Policy and Procedures, which demands precision in regards to research practice to secure Ethical Approval, and other ways of overseeing policy-practice implementation. This points to neoliberal governments and corporate sponsors seemingly not bothered with the profession and its debates about research evidence, never mind ethical hinterlands.

This work with Trailblazers on an Ethics Application connected back to the year's opening work on 'Ethics: a question of quality' and the professional learning activity geared to Groundwater-Smith and Mockler's (2007) argument that ethics is an orientation to research practice that is deeply embedded in those working in the field in a substantive and engaged way. Trailblazers are alert to their ethical guidelines where Quality Assurance is named as quality of evidence, purpose and outcome. This needs to be read in conjunction with the Ethics guidelines issued by the university Faculty's Ethics Committee (also see Campbell and Groundwater-Smith, 2007).

Strategically, this professional learning activity came to be a consolidation of what the non-accredited component is geared towards: professional learning communities of teachers and academic partners to focus on poverty and cumulative multiple deprivation in a local network of urban schools in a former industrial northern city of England. The task is to co-develop the profession's preferred practitioner research-informed 'local' solutions, stated clearly in the formal requirements for an Ethics Application then done in two lengthy parts[6]: Stage 1 is on risk assessment and application/project details, and here is an extract submitted to the Faculty Ethics Committee:

> ***A practitioner research investigation of 'raising achievement' and 'closing the gap' in a city-wide network of schools in [this city]***
>
> *This city-wide collaborative practitioner research project, coordinated by Beckett, will be undertaken by a team of designated academic partners (Beckett, Tan, Ford) and [19] teacher partners located in [10] urban primary and high schools to address two major issues of concern: 'raising achievement' and 'closing the gap', acknowledged locally and nationally as problems for challenging schools serving students and communities marked by poverty and cumulative multiple deprivation. Having secured school Heads' approval to proceed, teachers and academic partners will together identify and address the effects of social disadvantage on students' learning and urban schooling experiences, and develop action plans for classroom and school improvement.*

Stage 2 also required templates for the information sheets and consent forms and templates for data collection; for example, surveys and interviews. This was all shared with teacher partners, who learned about consent forms for school Heads, students, parents/caregivers, and teachers (including their own consent forms). The task of securing approval was not necessarily straightforward given school-level jurisdictions over teachers' practitioner research activities and the university's jurisdiction over academic partners' teaching and research activities[7], but an articulation of the purpose and aims was a particularly helpful shared professional learning activity:

> *Done under the auspices of the 'Leading Learning' CPD programme co-sponsored by [our] Faculty and participating schools, the practitioner research aims to examine extant data and generate new data on the learning outcomes of students whose academic performance is below national targets, and on teachers' classroom practices including their use of National curriculum aligned with different pedagogies and assessment strategies. The practitioner research also aims to facilitate collaborative professional learning about the meanings and effects of urban schools' local context (demographics, area factors, socio-economic factors, institutional factors), especially its impact on those cohorts of students designated free school meals (FSM), the officially recognised marker of poverty and multiple cumulative deprivation. The intention is that the collaborative team of practitioner researchers will critically reflect on the speculation, in light of the evidence, that poverty and cumulative multiple deprivation are distinctive features of challenging schools' work in local disadvantaged areas and therefore require responsive tailored action plans for classroom and school improvement.*

It should be noted that midway during the non-accredited component, the allied accredited part of the 'Leading Learning' CPD twin-pack got underway. The MA 'Achievement in City Schools' (MAACS) had been through validation and a marketing exercise. Visiting Professor Terry Wrigley[8] took a lead role to develop the Course Handbook and module handbooks along with teaching materials and distance learning materials. Seventeen teacher partners took up the two-for-one opportunity, which certainly added to their CPD workload but they made the commitment[9]. Significantly the non-accredited and accredited component parts aligned not only in conceptualization but very often in delivery. For example, Trailblazers' focus on teacher inquiry data on different disadvantaged student cohorts timed with the MAACS Module 1 'Diversity and achievement: geographies of opportunity' focus on disaggregated achievement data. This sort of theoretical work gave depth and breadth to teacher partners' practitioner research.

By this stage in the non-accredited component, the interactive workshop sessions on-campus and in-schools are planned to lay out the extant data on disadvantaged students, all anonymized, so teacher partners can share it with each other and academic partners. The suggested maximum number of students is ten, but the advice is to keep the cohort at a small manageable number because the exercise generates a good deal of data. It should trigger ongoing professional conversations about the student census, bearing in mind the 'chavs' epithet, so that practitioners come to theorize 'school mix' related to the social class intake (see Thrupp, 1999). The exercise is also supposed to support practitioners' decisions about the further collection of qualitative data, past their 'practice' practitioner research activities. It is painstaking work under the circumstances, but eventually, the teams of Trailblazers guided by their academic partners' advice selected the following cohorts of students in the different urban schools:

- a group of preschool-to-Reception students across a cluster of urban primary schools
- a group of vulnerable urban primary school students targeted through 'Pupil Progress'
- a mixed-age cohort of disaffected boys in another urban primary school
- an urban high school bottom set English high school class of minority ethnic students
- a group of students targeted as persistently absent in another urban high school
- a group of students labeled 'Pupil Premium' in yet another urban high school

This selection, in many cases arbitrary, shows a number of things: an indication of teacher partners' professional concerns, the social realities of teachers' work but also the shortcomings of the simple categories of students that are used in extant data banks like RAISEonline and school-based performance data summaries. For example, the official category of FSM, the proxy indicator of poverty and deprivation, tends to miss the complexities and nuances of social class and other social markers, disadvantaged students' lived experiences, and what this means for their schooling and life chances. This comes to light in another professional learning activity that calls for more detailed 'other' data on student cohorts. The prompts alert teacher partners to list students with a code/pseudonym and age; name the class/group; provide student census data, including family/social background; expand details, e.g. IMD data; provide any further in-school data; and include a commentary on reasons for selection of student cohort. The following reply was constructed by an urban primary school teacher partner, who gathered qualitative data for a mixed-age cohort of ten disaffected boys, though only a sample of three is shown in Table 6.2.

This sort of 'other' data homes in on the students' lived experiences of poverty and cumulative multiple deprivation and speaks to the importance of professional learning about teacher inquiry in CPD that is locally sensitive and contextually specific. It brings to light the intense intake-related pressures that accrue to school Heads and teachers (see Thrupp, 1999) but also students' and families' economic hardship: whether or not there is impoverishment, brutality, ignorance and numbing emptiness, limited horizons, few options, and restraints or distractions in regards love, caring and warmth (Boomer, 1999). It also illustrates a sensitivity to gender and its intersection with other social markers, hopefully in the light of feminist methodologies canvassed earlier. This all demands interrogation and interruption, past the neoliberal penchant for a 'politics of blame' and colonization of ethics and

TABLE 6.2 Sample of student 'other' data spreadsheet

Name	D.O.B.	Address	Parents	Siblings	Support	Significant events
Student 1	19.12.02	7 previous addresses including temporary accommodation in homeless shelter	Live together but unstable	4 younger siblings at home One younger half-sibling	No family network. Social care Children's centre Family outreach worker Signpost (via police) CAF Previous CP plan	Police involvement (anti-social behaviour) Lack of supervision Arson (set fire to own bedroom) Possible drug dealing Family bereavement (Grandma)
Student 2	27.6.03		Live together	2 older siblings and 1 younger. 1 much older half-sibling with own child (sometimes lives at home address depending on circumstances)	PCSO	Police involvement (anti-social behaviour of children) Speech and language difficulties (all siblings affected) Lack of supervision in and out of home (parents go to bed and leave unsupervised)
Student 3	2.4.03		Lives with father, mother deceased	2 older and 1 younger, plus 2 much older with own children	No family network Older brother had much multi-agency support but none so far	Older brother – drugs and prison Dad – alcohol misuse Brought up by older sister Lack of supervision

moral purpose to win consent for marketization and privatization. In contrast, practitioner research in support of 'local' solutions is informed by an orientation towards equity and social justice, which translates into a fairer distribution of educational opportunities, outcomes and rewards (see Boomer, 1999; Perry and Francis, 2010).

Towards critical social explanations

Another watershed moment came in the non-accredited component with the critical reviews of literature focused on the achievement gap, which shed light on neoliberal orientations to human capital as well as the negative or dangerous effects of the ways the school system in England is currently structured (see Lingard, 2009; Carter, 2015; BERA-RSA, 2014a, 2014b; Furlong, 2013; Whitty, 2014). Here are a few edited extracts from the 2013 Annual Report template, which again proved to be a worthwhile pedagogical strategy to not only fuse Trailblazers' professional learning and their intention to 'go public' but also to remind colleagues in urban schools of alternatives to GERM (Sahlberg, 2011).

- Ladson-Billings (2006) *From the Achievement Gap to the Education Debt: Understanding Achievement in U.S. Schools*. This provokes teacher partners' thinking and theorizing about the focus of practitioner research activities in their urban school. It helps hone practioners' critical perspectives, notably on the intersection of social class, race and gender, and the ways this intersection informs social and educational inequities;
- Milner (2013a) *Rethinking Achievement Gap Talk in Urban Education*. It directly follows on from Ladson-Billings 2006 Presidential Address to AERA to map out a set of questions to help teacher partners rethink the talk about achievement. An accompanying exercise requires teacher partners to re-conceptualize and move beyond achievement discourse (or gap talk);
- Anyon, J. (1981) *Social Class and School Knowledge*. This is read at two levels: (1) for its structure, to guide teacher partners' thinking about the focus of practitioner research activities but also how to frame it and write it up; and (2) for its substance, to glean some ideas about curriculum and school knowledge and their role in what teacher partners might want to find out (then say) about achievement;
- Moll et al. (1992) *Funds of Knowledge for Teaching: Using a Qualitative Approach to Connect Homes and Classrooms*. Like Anyon's article, it forms part of the lineage of arguments about curriculum. Again it is read (1) for its structure, and (2) for its substance, to follow aspects of the curriculum debate, noting how the authors describe the knowledge students bring to school (and how that knowledge relates to achievement). It prompts teacher partners to name their own main idea and why it is important;
- Dinkins, D. (2009) *Teachers Talk about Race, Class and Achievement*. This chapter is one of the practitioner's contributions to Cochran-Smith and Lytle

(eds) *Inquiry as Stance, Practitioner Research for the Next Generation*. It is an exemplary model for teacher partners thinking about a co-developed teacher inquiry project, and provokes a consideration of how findings might be presented to colleagues in school.

These readings and accompanying worksheets proved to be extremely valuable professional learning activities, not only as a strategic consolidation of what the non-accredited component is all about. They continue to trigger contextual understandings and critical social explanations (see Anyon, 2009), this time round focused on the impediments to teachers' core business in urban schools, including disadvantaged students' disillusionment, disengagement and the like. For example, Milner's (2013a) efforts to problematize achievement discourse or 'gap talk' in North America stuck a chord with teacher partners in the north of England. As this extract from the accompanying worksheet notes:

- *He drew attention to the focus on standardized tests but also the standardization of policies and practices (in our parlance, the 'one size fits all' model);*
- *He claimed these standardized reform efforts advance a sameness agenda for different and diverse groups of students;*
- *He posited results on outcomes (e.g. SATS tests) provide information about a particular socially constructed way of thinking about students;*
- *He drew attention to other research (Milner, 2013b; Apple, 2006) to articulate an argument about students' knowledge;*
- *He concluded that certain areas of achievement are privileged and valued over others, and there appears to be a socially constructed hierarchy of which and what achievements and knowledge matter more than others.*

In another effort to encourage teacher partners' critical reflections on the arguments, a set of purposefully constructed questions provides an opportunity to register professional concerns about the performative culture. The following extract from the worksheet accompanying Milner's (2013a) article shows an urban primary school teacher partner's responses (in italics):

What can you say about the problem with 'gap talk'?	*Does not allow for discussion of multiple gaps. Produces a deficit model where white middle class students are considered academically superior.*
What can you say about the 'one size fits all' model in your school?	*Standardised assessments do not recognise the challenges children face in their education, or the wide range of starting points. SATs favour white middle class children with a range of life experiences many of our children will not have.*

What can you say about the sameness agenda in your school?	*Socio-familial factors are very diverse, as is the culture and ethnicity of children. Cannot expect all children with such diverse experiences to respond in the same way to the same curriculum.*
What can you say about different and diverse students' knowledge (NB. productive pedagogies)?	*Need connectedness to the curriculum and socially supportive pedagogies. Need to value children's experiences rather than have a deficit view.*
What can you say about hierarchies of achievement and knowledge?	*What children need to know and how they show their knowledge is defined by policymakers. Irrelevant for many children and serves to widen the 'gap'.*

This data typifies teacher partners' increasing capacity to do professional knowledge work, a far cry from the view of most teachers that theory and research are considered irrelevant if not useless (see Lieberman and Miller, 2008). We saw this in the very first pilot study, echoed in Chapter one, a reflection of Hargreaves' (1984, cited by Lieberman and Miller, 2008) view that 'Experience counts, theory doesn't'. The Trailblazers' engagement with Milner (2013a) and others is a promising indication of what is to come, which is the main message of this book: that professional teams of teachers and academic partners – all educationalists – come together in school–university partnership ways of working, reclaim professional responsibility to co-develop research-informed teaching and teacher education and school action plans. These are more in line with contextualized school improvement that connects with outside agencies. This of course includes other stakeholders like students but it requires a scaffolding of ongoing professional learning and development that is tailored to practitioners' needs and shared more widely.

'Going public'

The Trailblazers and their academic partners responded well to my suggestion that we collectively embark on a publication project and prepare our co-developed responses to critical scholars like Milner (2013a) to be included in a special collection of journal articles. We are all agreed on the need to showcase the teachers' voice, honed by the practical-pedagogical work done against the odds to advocate more realistic policies and practices. I made contact with Pink (see Pink and Noblit, 2007; also Pink, 2012), who had not only invited my contribution to his edited book, *Schools for Marginalized Youth*, with a chapter on one of the campaigns against school closure (see Beckett, 2012a), but he also invited a sequel for the international journal, *Urban Review*, which became an outlet for Trailblazers' critical perspectives on 'raising achievement' and 'closing the gap'. As I described them in my editorial (Beckett, 2014a):

The teachers, school Heads, assistant Heads and academic partners assembled in this special edition are the first to collectively tell a story about achievement in urban schools in England, or more specifically in a citywide network of urban schools in the north of England, in the hope that better school policies will be put in place to quell the professional disquiet if not anger about extant school policy.

It was a pedagogical strategy par excellence to focus attention on reporting the teacher inquiry projects, intended to develop formalized action plans for the classroom and plug into their urban School Development Plan. Again it required much of academic partners to support and mentor teacher partners to hone the focus on sample cohorts of disadvantaged students' levels of achievement and any gaps; continue to review more select literature on their practitioner research activities; further develop capacity for critical social explanations; and finalize their teacher inquiry projects. This was something of a daunting task, with incredible policy and time pressures in urban schools and looming publication deadlines, but we made a joint commitment. The rationale is summarized in my PowerPoint presentation to the cohort in a campus-based session on the matter:

> *Publication has two functions. It opens work to*
>
> *criticism and consequently to refinement; and it*
>
> *also disseminates the fruits of research and*
>
> *hence makes possible the cumulation of*
>
> knowledge.
>
> (Stenhouse, in Rudduck and Hopkins, 1985)

Yet again, a template proved to be a worthwhile tool to support the transfer of fieldwork notes, school-generated data from worksheets and teacher partners' learning portfolios into narrative form for a journal article. The task is to fill in the detail, share critical thinking, and report on practitioner research processes. As noted in the 2013 Annual Report:

> #14 worksheet was the template that required paragraph-long statements in the Introduction about the achievement gap in our school/class; then under sub-headings about (1) the tasks of 'raising achievement' and/or 'closing the gap'; (2) a critical discussion of Milner (2013a) and Ladson-Billings (2006) and British-based authors; (3) a description of our school/cluster and our teacher inquiry project; (4) a description of the substance of our project; (5) an elaboration on our findings and our critical analysis; and (6) our conclusions to wrap up the argument, re-visit Milner (2013a) and Ladson-Billings (2006), and provide advice.

This helps encourage teacher partners to share their critical perspectives on extant school policy and its links to classroom practice: their teacher inquiry questions; the circumstances, constraints and barriers they confront in their efforts to improve the academic and social learning outcomes of students disadvantaged by poverty and cumulative multiple deprivation; the externally imposed directions to urban schools, framed by political agendas; their findings that could provide evidence and be triangulated; and their data analyses feeding into conclusions and recommendations on school improvement (see Beckett, 2014a).

The last task of the second year of the non-accredited component of the 'Leading Learning' CPD twin-pack was for teacher partners to complete a template provided for their 2013 Annual Report to share with School Leadership Teams. It began with a narrative description of the professional learning and development programme, followed by a series of bullet points that invited input as for last year, but it also reiterated intentions:

> *The aims of the 'Leading Learning' CPD programme remained constant as academic partners were mindful of local/national policy agendas to improve school performance as well as the social realities of schools serving disadvantaged students, families and communities. The academic partners wanted it to be responsive to these urban schools' needs, but also to demonstrate a commitment to equity and social justice. They stand by their views of a central role for practitioners in school improvement, and 'knowledge-practice relations' that leans towards knowledge-of-practice, not simply knowledge for and about practice. To this end they see a crucial role for practitioner research with academic partners mentoring and supporting teachers and school Heads develop local knowledge and collective intelligence.*
>
> *This year the team of academic partners continued to promote useful habits of mind, emphasising practitioners' critical thinking so they can develop critical social explanations of students' achievement and any gaps, but also using/making school data and 'other' multiple data sets. As for last year, the intentions are for the 'Leading Learning' CPD programme to result in evidence-based policy and practice at the local school, but also the national level so that the English system of education is marked with practitioners' 'change-power'.*

The *final third year* of the non-accredited component was given over to co-develop more detailed knowledge of the fields of School Effectiveness and School Improvement (SEI). This included a book chapter by Thrupp (1999) who issues sound advice on governments and the way they use the SEI arguments to construct school failure as the responsibility of schools alone with any reference to the broader socio-political context, such as the impact of poverty, ruled out as an excuse for poor performance. This helps teachers and academic partners make sense of politicians, policymakers and powerbrokers' pronouncements[10] about Ofsted, school inspections, entrance exams, standards, and discipline plus links between state- and fee-paying schools and claims of the politicization of schooling policies. As for previous years, the third year featured guest lectures from consultant academic partners mentioned earlier, ongoing professional readings and associated worksheets with a particular focus on the following:

- ethical practices[11];
- debates[12] re school improvement plans;
- teachers' inquiry projects;
- school priorities and school development;
- local knowledge and larger concerns;
- policy advocacy and dissemination.

This simply underlines the agreed strategy for professional learning geared to 'going public' via the production and dissemination of a special collection of journal articles. For all intents and purposes, it harks back to my efforts to construct the non-accredited component of the 'Leading Learning' CPD twin-pack as a sociology of action twinned with practitioner research methods to help develop democratic 'local' solutions as practical actions. Again this sits well with advice gleaned from Touraine (1977) that a conception of society [read one that is concerned for disadvantaged students, families and communities with deep needs in Austerity Britain] is of no use unless it produces a sociological practice. This is a rationale devoted to sociological intervention, a method devised to meet the demands of a sociology of action. The cue is for a method based on three principles: the self-analysis which teachers perform on their social-educational actions; interaction with social partners or stakeholders such as disadvantaged students, urban School Leadership Teams and multi-agency workers; while the academic partner is an intermediary.

Teachers' budding sociological practice

One teacher partner, with support of an academic partner (Nuttall and Doherty, 2014), did her teacher inquiry project in an urban primary school situated on the outskirts of this de-industrialized city in the north of England. Her focus is on a small group of white British boys in receipt of free school meals (FSMs), who are identified by the school as disaffected and as a consequence vulnerable in terms of their educational achievement (see also Nuttall, 2014). The task is to identify the contributory factors that prompted these boys' disaffection, described in patterns of disruption and disengagement. The published article argues for teacher partners to problematize and take into account the social context of schooling and considers the complexities of these boys' lived experiences and the ways these impact on their learning and achievement. In developing this argument, the article draws on the work of Johnson (2002) and Johnson and La Salle (2010) in regards to the 'other' data that needs to be generated to show factors which perpetuate poor student performance and which hide real issues of inequity: 'the wallpaper effect'.

A team of three teacher partners, with support of an academic partner (Darbyshire *et al.*, 2014), report on their interconnected teacher inquiry projects considered to be works in progress in a neighbourhood cluster of three urban primary schools. Their published article registers concerns with the ways the so-called 'achievement gap' is portrayed in policy announcements in England. It charts a challenge to the current view that it is the task of urban nursery and primary schools to train young children at ever younger ages to be school-ready. It portrays a collective professional judgement that some young children from less affluent backgrounds face a range of barriers to their learning on entry, which hampers their success in these urban primary schools. Further, it argues these barriers arise from children's multiple vulnerabilities which cannot be encapsulated by a single category of need such as eligibility for free school meals or a special educational need represented in official categorizations used by Ofsted, RAISEonline and the Local Authority. This article proceeds to report on the three research-active teachers' efforts to define and identify the range of vulnerabilities faced by some young children and consider intervention measures that will address their academic and social learning needs. The intention is to show that a more refined view of identifiying these needs based on a research-informed reading of young children's multiple vulnerabilities, framed by their social context, will lead to more equitable provision of urban primary schooling experiences.

Another teacher partner, this time writing a sole-authored article (Wilson, 2014) but with support from her academic partner, reports on efforts to embed quality teaching in a local urban primary school in the north of England, under pressure from the Local Authority to raise standards because it is well below national expectations on SATs tests. This initially means embracing Ofsted's 'first wave quality teaching' notably through this urban primary school's Teaching and Learning Strategy and professional learning opportunities, including joining the 'Leading Learning' CPD. She began with identifying and naming professional concerns about student achievement and what this meant for classroom practices, including pedagogies or instruction, as it is called in the USA. The teacher set out to investigate student learning needs and develop responsive schemes of work. The social realities of the Year 3 classroom, and the research evidence, all point to recognition that official versions of 'quality teaching' are not enough to improve student learning outcomes. This published article shows how she developed an 'inquiry stance' (Cochran-Smith and Lytle, 2009) on quality teaching drawing on two Australian initiatives (Hayes *et al.*, 2006; Munns *et al.*, 2013) to develop responsive teaching episodes and subject them to critical scrutiny. It also shows some of the impediments that surface in her urban primary school context, from student disengagement to student ill-health, which calls into question the inequitable opportunities that exist together with the need for a contextualized understanding of school improvement.

The union-active teacher partner, an English teacher in one of the urban high schools targeted for closure who came late into the LLCPD, shares a joint investigation with her academic partner (Gallagher and Beckett, 2014). They recount the circumstances of forging a partnership way of working in the face of externally imposed directions, framed by political agendas, which are major barriers to practitioner research activities beyond crude quantitative national-school data analyses. Their published article shows how this is connected to performance and achievement against Ofsted inspection criteria and school data benchmarked against national data. The article proceeds with a recollection of this teacher's battle for professional recognition when it comes to the intellectual and practical arguments for curriculum and classroom practices that are tailored to the learning needs of different minority ethnic students, who have to negotiate language barriers to schooling. This more professional view of what is to be done draws on evidence built up in the course of a determined teacher inquiry project, which needed the sanction of the Local Authority's School Improvement officer, who recommended a focus on achievement in the teacher's bottom set Year 7 English class. This setting, in part a result of reduced student numbers and corresponding financial resources, along with being compelled to 'teach to the test' are identified as obstructions to addressing these disadvantaged students' complex learning needs. This joint work illustrates the NUT argument that teachers' professional responsibilities are linked to a struggle to reclaim the right to make professional decisions, as noted earlier in this book.

Another team of three teacher partners (Arthurs et al., 2014), located in the other urban high school forced to close and reopen as a sponsored academy, began their teacher inquiry project long before their transfers and wrote their published article with support from academic partners with whom they worked in the two component parts of the LLCPD twin-pack. Together they homed in on the attendance-achievement link in the then-most recent government quantitative data for secondary schools in England: persistent absentees stands at 6.6 per cent for all children, but it raises to 9 per cent for students who are classed as 'Pupil Premium', which is an official measure of poverty. In the urban high school and site of this case study, this data indicates it is 15 per cent for all students and 20 per cent for 'Pupil Premium' students, and that these students are predominantly white British at 22.9 per cent while another category of 'any other white background' is 26.9 per cent. This totals 50 per cent of the school census and the research-active teachers argue that if half of the student population are persistent absentees, with Gypsy Romany traveller students more persistently absent, there is a problem that needs investigation. They constructed a teacher inquiry project to ascertain the extent of student absences at the school level, to probe the reasons, scrutinize achievement, and develop a responsive urban school action plan. They furnished sound evidence for a more enlightened alternative to the standardized punitive quick-fix solution of enforced attendance with financial penalties for families who experience significant levels of poverty and deprivation, which does not work.

A team of four teacher partners (Firth et al., 2014), all senior leaders in a large comprehensive urban high school on the outskirts of this northern city, work with their senior colleague who acts as Coordinator of their teacher inquiry project and their academic partner. In their published article, they show this work has school-wide significance, given recent history going from being graded as a 'failing' school by the Office for Standards in Education (Ofsted) in 2009, to being judged a 'good' school in 2013. The team's work developed in response to Ofsted's recommendation to identify features of 'effective' pedagogies so cognisant of 'pedagogies of poverty' (Haberman, 1991), they trialled productive pedagogies (Hayes *et al.*, 2006) in their own subject-department lessons, with a view to disseminating these through school in an attempt to progress further. These research-active teacher partners argue that, despite the pedagogical improvements made to date, the data used to measure the success of the school still reads unfavourably when compared to similar schools nationally. They challenge what 'counts' as knowledge, achievement and success, and further argue that constraints placed on the school by budget, the standardized reform agenda, and high stakes accountability restrict attempts by this urban high school to work in a more creative way as it strives to raise achievement and aims for an 'outstanding' judgement from Ofsted.

Conclusion

A significant addition to the special collection, indicative of sociological interventions, is from two urban school Heads who each respectively sponsor urban primary school and high school staff to sign up for the CPD twin-pack, learn the processes of teacher inquiry, and report back to School Leadership Teams. Here they co-author with the support of an academic partner (Gorton *et al.*, 2014). Their published article begins with the phenomenon of 'official' Ofsted judgements of urban schools that question work in 'raising achievement' particularly in areas of deprivation. It points to deep flaws in the operation of 'policy-as-numbers' and high stakes accountability, contrasting the punitive style and consequences with collaborative principles of leadership and school change. The article looks at how summative judgements gloss over the complexities of students' lives and teachers' work, and ignore school-generated evidence of what is actually being done to meet policy expectations. The conclusion is that more intelligent forms of school accountability are needed which do not constantly undermine the improvement processes of urban schools' efforts and damage reputations with labels such as 'requires improvement', 'special measures' or more colloquially 'failing' school. The argument is 'intelligent accountability' might begin to support a more community-orientated 'moral purpose' in leadership and pedagogy. This takes us full circle to where Trailblazers began their professional learning journey with academic partners.

132 Teachers' voices

TOLES © *The Washington Post*. Reprinted with permission of UNIVERSAL UCLICK. All rights reserved.

Notes

1. www.gov.uk/government/speeches/michael-gove-on-the-moral-purpose-of-school-reform
2. This teacher partner had just accepted a school Headship and so withdrew from the task of writing for publication but kept up with the LLCPD citywide workshop sessions and allied MAACS studies.
3. I will be curious to see a longitudinal study of standardized school improvement efforts in regards urban schools' performance within the Local Authority's jurisdiction. Perhaps my next research focus should be on the results over the decade since my arrival to work in this city in the north of England, where I have battled to institute 'local' solutions. The evidence on 'structural' solutions might be telling!
4. As noted in the previous chapter, there was some job-sharing with the teaching. In this second year I delivered the first campus-based session, which was followed by Dr Jon Tan's session on practitioner research in two parts, purposefully designed to introduce further strategies for data generation. This included my selection of readings and worksheets though it was Tan's idea for a 'homework' exercise on practice-generated data. I then followed teaching the remaining sessions and into the third year, interspersed with visitors' sessions.
5. Here I must again acknowledge Dr Jon Tan's contribution as these were his ideas.
6. This process is much streamlined now with university applications done online while schools retain oversight of their own ethical research approvals.

7 In the end it was decided that the university had jurisdiction over academic partners' collection of secondary data developed in the course of the 'Leading Learning' CPD twin-pack project.
8 Wrigley left at the end of 2014 and took up a Visiting Professor position at Northumbria but continued to take an active role in teaching the Trailblazers on the MAACS and accepted supervisory responsibilities for some dissertations, which got underway just as this book went into print production.
9 Of the seventeen Trailblazers, fourteen proceeded onto the MAACS: of the three who declined the offer, one had already done an MSc; one was seconded to the local NUT office and one was pregnant expecting a first child. Midway through another two withdrew, given one's promotion to school Head and another's school transfer. This leaves twelve of the original cohort.
10 See www.gov.uk/government/speeches/michael-gove-speaks-about-securing-our-childrens-future
11 We spent some time engaging the invited seminar organized by Martin Thrupp in New Zealand: see Barbara Comber's presentation on ethical accountability: www.education2014.org.nz/?page_id=274
12 See www.theguardian.com/politics/2014/mar/21/education-secretary-michael-gove-backs-school-inspection-overhaul

7
PROFESSIONAL CONTROL OVER SCHOOLING

Introduction

Throughout this book, which spans my first decade's work in the north of England, I have foregrounded a sense of educational politics in a local effort to establish school–university partnership ways of working in a local network of urban schools. What focuses my attention is the writ of democracy and the whole way of struggle to co-plan, trial, then bring to fruition an *appropriate professional response* to the charge of 'failing' schools. As the preceding chapters show, the quest ended in a showcase of the teachers' collective voice in a special collection of journal articles from the first cohort of teacher partners affectionately called Trailblazers and RaTs (research-active teachers) and their academic partners. They have shown a way to challenge the derision and demonization of disadvantaged students and their families with a will to SPEAK TRUTH TO POWER, anchored in their collective intelligence and practitioner research evidence. This supports their right to make professional decisions intertwined with the right to expect professional and political attention. The task is to negotiate contextualized school improvement to meet the deep needs of these local school communities in Austerity Britain.

It is poignant that Lupton (2004a, 2006, 2011), who does so much as a consultant academic partner to guide and support the co-development of the teacher inquiry projects, made a contribution to the special collection with an Afterword (Lupton, 2014). In many ways it is a recognition of the distinctive work being done in the 'Leading Learning' CPD twin-pack by the different teams of teachers and academic partners:

> *In this edition of* Urban Review, *we have a whole collection of rich narratives and formidable insights: an unusual, perhaps unique, set of papers. Lori Beckett has pulled together a collection which brings out teachers' voices, as well as academic ones. Speaking from the front-line, or chalk-face, they paint a detailed picture of the realities of school*

improvement in areas of deep poverty and social deprivation. The collection speaks loud and clear about the inadequacies of current policy prescriptions. It should be widely read in this country and I have no doubt that it will also resonate in others where high stakes testing and marketised school systems are transforming the meaning of learning and the nature of teachers' work.

One might expect some professional engagement with these ideas, mostly published by teachers with the support of their academic partners, who have all raised their voices thoughtfully and respectfully. One might even hope for some negotiation if not a battle of ideas, given the burden of decisions made by authoritarian politicians, policymakers and powerbrokers when it comes to dictatorial directions to teachers with some worrying consequences. I find that any sort of practical-politicized dialogue about *what is to be done* in contextualized school improvement to be somewhat subdued by a palpable fear that permeates urban schools and universities, at least in the north of England where I work. This is not surprising in light of the force and threats of sanctions that often results in school (and university faculty) closures, managed staff reductions, job losses and the like. This is not to forget the fearful voices of disadvantaged students, families and communities with deep needs, who are the leitmotif of the teacher partners' published work.

This struggle, being made public, is guided by twin questions: Who reads this professional literature and what comes of it? I have certainly witnessed intense policy and time pressures that preclude such professional activity among teachers and academic partners working in urban schools, which is to acknowledge their social and political realities. Such a problem is identified by Menter (2013) in his BERA Presidential Address, who posits two significant but related arguments. The first is to interrogate the political rhetoric about the achievement gap between rich and poor and look to the educational research from the 1960s onwards, which consistently demonstrated that educational achievement is closely associated with socioeconomic patterns. The second is to acknowledge the important contribution that educational research should be making, say to reconstituting 'closing the gap' as 'preventing the gap', although it is not having that kind of influence. As Menter put it, either it is not happening or it is being ignored[1].

This is certainly my experience, which brings me full circle back to Lingard's (2009) advice in an article for the Queensland Teachers' Union's Professional Magazine:

> *For a whole range of reasons – including policy borrowing, the flows of individual policy advisors between the countries, and political alignments – the English situation has had real policy salience in Australia. But we should see the English situation as a warning, not as a system from which to learn.*

This chapter elaborates on the warning, not just for Australia but for other countries who are battling the GERM (Sahlberg, 20111), and it documents the lessons I learned in the process of developing school–university partnerships in this northern city. From the outset, I canvassed advice on professional concerns about vernacular neoliberal reforms troubling teaching and teacher education. It always came back to focus on professional knowledge work and the ways to build the practitioner research evidence to put the case. There is a clear need to question the dominant policy logic, if that is the right word given some illogical neoliberal policy directions like excessive performativity then hounding so-called 'failing' or 'coasting' schools[2]. Then it is always a question of ways to publicize the professional voice, modestly at first, with each other and with School Leadership Teams, then policy advocacy in wider arenas. I always had the sense I was continuing a tradition of 'holding the line'. It is a good metaphor that speaks to what practitioners might do in the face of threats to professional practice, which is what is at stake. These are no doubt driven by global edu-businesses[3] and although the English vernacular neoliberal policy agenda latterly named 'disadvantage'[4], there is seeming refusal to recognize the effects of poverty and cumulative multiple deprivation on urban school teachers' work. This gives rise to professional disquiet and anger (see Beckett, 2013b, 2013c), and it may well come down to the academic and teacher unions to organize and represent the professional concerns of practitioners and orchestrate a *choreography of urban schools policy conflict*.

Standing on the shoulders of giants

Ten years ago I came to the north of England with fresh experience in Sydney as an academic partner to a few urban schools in the NSW Priority Action Schools Program (PASP) and an inner-city predominantly Aboriginal urban high school, as noted in previous chapters. I saw the task to initially build a shared vocabulary about how to engage disadvantaged students, families and communities in learning, and I took a cue from the Priority Action Schools Program, jointly devised by NSW Teachers' Federation and the Department of Education and Training to develop 'local' solutions. I was struck by Groundwater-Smith and Kemmis' (n.d.) meta-evaluation of the knowledge-building work being done in a network of self-identified disadvantaged schools. I was also struck by their use of Stenhouse's (1975) ideas about 'systematic inquiry made public', reiterated by Rudduck and Hopkins (1985) in their co-edited book on Stenhouse's inspiration for research as a basis for teaching, and again by Rudduck (1995) on Stenhouse's notion of teachers' empowering education.

There is a fine tradition of this teacher-research work in England (see Menter, 2013; Menter and Murray, 2011; Menter *et al*., 2011; Campbell and Groundwater-Smith, 2010). Not long after my arrival I turned to distinguished academics whose work on disadvantaged schools is renown: Lupton (2004a, 2004b, 2006) and Whitty (1985, 2014), who presciently advised me to embark on a critical analysis of the possibilities *and* problems of teacher-initiated change to improve student learning outcomes and simultaneously be cognizant of 'naïve possibilitarianism'. They certainly reminded me to reflect ideas about democratic professionalism (Whitty, 2008) with a sense of 'complex hope' (Grace, 1994, 2007).

I was then fortunate in the extreme to host at my university so many visiting academics, all critical scholars who generously gave invaluable professional guidance: Lingard and Rizvi (2009), Mills (2014), Groundwater-Smith (2007a, 2007b), Brennan (see Furlong et al., 2011), Gale (see Gale and Densmore, 2000; Gale, 2010), Lieberman (see Lieberman and Miller, 2001, 2008), Wrigley (see Thomson et al., 2012; Smyth and Wrigley, 2013; Gorton et al., 2014), Cahill (2012) and Maguire (see Maguire et al., 2006; also Hoskins and Maguire, 2013). I also met others who were onshore like Cochran-Smith (see Cochran-Smith, 2006; Cochran-Smith and Lytle, 2001, 2009; also Cochran-Smith et al., 2013) and those active in education-political circles like Benn (2013) and Park (2013). So many pieces of their collective research-informed advice stuck, which are worked into the 'Leading Learning' CPD twin-pack and elaborated on in preceding chapters. Perhaps the most striking piece of advice, pertinent to this book, is to be mindful of how our work with research-active teachers might articulate with other interventions and wider social movements.

I take this to mean urban schools, battling policy ideas about strategic change, are ripe for teachers' collective action. My first foray into publicizing an instance was around school closures and I framed the story in terms of a case for democratic schools (see Beckett, 2012a). I drew on Mouffe (2005), who pointed the way when she said the task of democratic politics is not to overcome this 'we/they' discrimination through consensus, but to construct it in a way that energizes the democratic confrontation. In so many ways this advice to play out any potential antagonisms in agonistic ways still stands as teachers and academic partners in this northern city are bothered by the 'them against us' attitude and try to negotiate the dominant ideological policy and practice dictates imposed. At the time I flagged the public spaces for the expression of dissensus in the 'Leading Learning' project, marked by a need to attend to contextualized school improvement, anchor the action plans in theoretical argument, and keep up written and verbal communications with the Local Authority.

My second attempt was to rouse teachers' collective action in an invited article titled 'Giving teachers voice – getting school democracy' for the NUT's journal, *Education Review* (Beckett, 2013b). There I declared that teaching in urban schools requires more than incessant policy demands and hounding of teachers and students because it is more than training to deliver predetermined content to be tested and graded. I argued for recognition of the complexities in teachers' work with disadvantaged students, which should call into play some nuanced thinking about social markers like poverty, deprivation and social class. At the same time, there needs to be a detailed interrogation of the meanings of 'closing the gap' and the ways this is inextricably intertwined with social and educational inequalities.

The third and most significant attempt to showcase the teachers' voice, as noted earlier, was the work done in the non-accredited component of the 'Leading learning' CPD twin-pack to hone teacher partners' professional concerns and engage in the processes of practitioner research. It was always geared to raising the professional voice, and two teacher partners showed the way with publications. Arthurs (2013) documents the reality of working life as a teacher in an urban high school and questions the multi-faceted policy pressures on teachers. She turns to the construction of the 'futuristic teacher' who is seemingly required to acquiesce to demands and directions and, after Menter (2009), what is required to be a teacher for the future who engages intellectually with teaching and teacher education. Ghale and Beckett (2013) discuss teachers' politicization. They exemplify the role of a teacher working with an academic partner, in school and in the university but also in wider political arenas. They reflect back on what it is that might encourage colleagues, especially practitioners, to engage with ideas and with their mutual issues of professional concern, and what it is that gives their concerns such political significance.

Teachers' voice as research-informed

The silence to so many of these efforts to encourage teachers' collective actions and raise the professional voice has been deafening. I come to realize, as Crossley (2005) rightly points out, there are a wide-ranging number of operational definitions with some blurring of boundaries between social, religious and political movements but also terms like 'collective' and 'protest' that are fuzzy and ambiguous. However, I find solace in Touraine (1977) on social movements and the aim of social (read the teaching profession's) struggles, especially where these movements are not yet able to act as general political and ideological mouthpieces; the few attempts that have been made in this direction have met with failure. I take his advice to heart:

> *What might potentially become a social movement can still emerge in no other way than as a pressure group, taking advantage of the elections to make itself known. On the whole, new movements either fall back on past experiences, sentiments, and a sense of spontaneity in their challenge to political institutions, or else they become paralyzed by the political and ideological categories . . .*

This is not to give up on the quest to find a new connection between a social movement in and among urban schools and institutional democracy in the north of England and beyond, across the four jurisdictions of the UK, in Australia and globally. Of salience is a recent British Educational Research Association (BERA) initiative by six of its special interest groups to develop the *Fair and Equal Education* manifesto detailing how research should serve as the basis for future education policies[5], which sits well with the NUT *Stand Up for Education* manifesto[6]. Coincidentally these follow calls for more nuanced structural accounts of working class educational achievement (see Perry and Francis, 2010) and concerns about the 'politics of blame' (see Power, 2006), both attuned to critical gender analyses of teachers' work in urban schools. That said, I appreciate the situation for teachers and academic partners. One local urban high school Head indicated the dilemmas for colleagues:

> *The language coming out from the Minister's office is a real issue. I read something this morning that teaching morale is at a particular low ebb. Any wonder. It's a long time since I read anything that was coming out nationally that was positive about urban schools. The calls and claims just keep coming, whether it is 'right now look at white working class boys' or 'it's Muslim radicalization' . . . [all this] is hitting very hard at the moment, and people are really concerned to see if we can track things through, if we can prove that we are challenging these students. Then next week there'll be something else.*

If nothing else this demands some collective action for teachers' professionalism, but this is not to deny the policy and social context of teaching and the barriers to the enhancement of professional practice (see Gewirtz et al., 2009). I take advice from Lieberman and Miller (2008) on developing capacities. There is an identified need for academic partners to work with teachers in semi-structured ways to help co-develop the ability and disposition to do knowledge work and engage with theory and research as well as practice. As Apple (2009) indicated, it is clear that one of the most important steps in continuing the process of rebuilding and extending what it means to be a respected, responsive and critical professional is creating compelling analyses of what is going on now. This is what I set out to do in this book, and my main aim here is to recap my reflexive account of working with teachers and academic partners in a local network of urban schools in the north of England.

The lessons learned

I certainly learned much from a study of the history of ideas on poverty and schooling in England, which no doubt influenced policy initiatives in Australia. I can see the NSW Priority Action Schools Program (PASP) in England's Educational Priority Area programmes of the 1960s and 1970s (see Halsey, 1972; Smith, 1987 cited by Mortimore and Whitty, 1997/2000). The question of course is what happened to these programs, no doubt seriously interrupted by the 'Baker revolution' in Thatcher's Britain, which provided directions to Australian politicians who wanted to follow the neoliberal dictates of the 'new right' (see Beckett, 1996; also Ball, 2008/2013; Lupton and Obolenskaya, 2013; Lupton and Thomson, 2015).

I readily admit my work as academic partner in this local network of urban schools began in unchartered territory (see Beckett, 2009) and I had to forge a critical understanding of school–university partnership work (see Beckett, 2011). At the time, as I was grappling with these conceptualizations, I came up face-to-face with the politics of 'failing' schools compounded by Ofsted inspection judgements and all the negative publicity around threats of sanctions real and otherwise. I soon learned this has such a significant impact on teachers in urban schools and disadvantaged students while their parents/caregivers struggle to survive in Austerity Britain [7]. As one urban primary school Head exemplified it:

> *Church schools tend to get outstanding judgments. Schools with better data tend to get outstanding judgments and schools within urban environments tend to be the schools that get the 'require improvement' or get put in 'special measures'. I don't believe that there's any greater concentration of poor teaching in an urban environment any more than it is in any other school.*

I also came to learn that practitioners – school Heads, teachers and teacher educators – over a long period of time have had to cede more and more professional control to politicians in successive neoliberal governments that rolled out performative school policies. It did not take long to recognize the politicians, policymakers and powerbrokers enjoy 'a privileging of the policymakers' reality' (Ball, 1993, 2006). This is described as the adjustment of teachers and context to policy, not of policy to context. Of note is Ball's (1993, 2006) advice that 'resistance' is a crude and over-used term that is a poor substitute which allows for rampant over-claims and dismissive under-claims, to bring about the way policy problems are solved in context. There are other lessons to be learned here (see Ball et al., 2012), but for now I take heed of a local urban high school Head:

> *The political push behind all of it is something that worries everybody. We have two urban high schools either side of us; one is in 'special measures' and the other one 'requires improvement'. One has had its senior leadership team removed and has become a 'forced academy'. It has therefore been taken over; it's what's called a 'structural' solution.*

This frightening set of circumstances is shored up by never-ending announcements of popular media sound bites. An example was the Ofsted scheme to deploy outstanding teachers into urban schools to redress the situation for white British students[8], as if other teachers need to be told yet again they have it wrong. This is consistent with my argument in Chapter 1 about the Ofsted Regional Report. More than that, the deployment suggests one white British community is the same across the country, irrespective of regional and local differences and dialects from north to south, east to west. One urban primary school Head reacted this way:

> *[Urban schools] should be challenged and there should be a mechanism by which we consider and vet our practice. Part of that is an inspectorate and another part maybe the politician's voice but that is not everything. There is teachers' professional voice and there's the academic voice as well and at the moment, certainly, we know politicians' voices are dominant in that conversation.*

This data speaks to another lesson learned in that the effort to encourage the professional voice via the sort of school–university partnership work documented by this book is extremely difficult in such hostile neoliberal policy regimes. Tantamount is the stranglehold of the performativity agenda, which brings enormous time and policy pressures, but there is a compounding problem in urban schools. The policy directions or 'goal posts' are forever shifting, as noted in previous chapters in regards changes to GCSE (now 'Best 8') specifications for course work and/or examinations. I am reminded by an urban high school teacher partner who previewed this book that it seems as soon as targets are met, then a charge is made that 'ah, the examinations are too easy', benchmarks are raised, achievement targets are conflated, and controlled tests are introduced.

This might be a moot point to develop practitioner research on assessment for accountability at the expense of assessment for learning (see Doherty, 2013), but teacher partners all say they are up against 'crisis politics' (Harvey, 2005) or constant firefighting that is not sustainable. Anecdotal evidence, which will have to do in the absence of centrally held figures about staff resignations forced or otherwise in a school-led system, is quite disturbing. I already mentioned teachers on 'capability procedures', stress and high pressure, but I recently learned about 'disciplinaries' where teachers are targeted for infringements like having their personal mobile phones at hand. This suggests obsessive micromanagement of staff, who are continuously observed, monitored and scrutinized not only on levels and targets for performance-related pay but to the point where it is said 'they are never off our backs' or 'there is no let-up'. This comes back to the 'we/they' discrimination, but far from energizing a democratic confrontation, the constant surveillance means teachers have no sense of professionalism and no voice. Instead they resort to grievance procedures, although I am told these are rarely upheld and eventually lead to resignations[9].

Ironically the 'structural' solution of school closure and forced academization with corporate sponsors does not ease the pressures on urban schools. The forced academy discussed in earlier chapters was recently judged by Ofsted as 'requires improvement' and the school Head appointed by the corporate sponsor retired to be replaced with a celebrity school Head renowned for TV appearances. This is not before more than 80 per cent of experienced staff, including the heads of departments in English, Maths and Science, were on stress leave then left the school. These were teachers with 5, 10, 20 years' experience, which means some loss of continuity and institutional memory, which is crucial when it comes to providing stability for disadvantaged students and dealing with siblings, parents/caregivers and families in communities with deep needs. Apparently this forced academy now runs with a staff of approximately 60 per cent unqualified teachers on temporary contracts while the rest are newly qualified teachers (NQTs), Teach First and SCITT teachers. One wonders how excessive performativity is to play out, given this extract from an urban primary school teacher's diary:

> In amongst all the above, assessments were made, planning was written, resources were created, routines were set, parents were counselled, work was marked, new staff were inducted, staff meetings were held, assemblies were attended, trips were risk assessed, special visitors invited, budgets negotiated, Ofsted statements chewed over, lessons were taught, children were welcomed and learning took place.

This data speaks to the pressures of performativity on teachers' workload. Yet another lesson for me took some time to reveal itself but only after school Heads and teachers indicated time and again they wanted to work with us and often said they were 'on the edge', a metaphor for teacher stress, burnout, and being on the brink of (forced) resignation. I often ponder if it is enough to say in reply they need to 'stay strong' and find the courage to voice their concerns about the situation in which they find themselves in these neoliberal regimes. This requires some interrogation of teachers' feelings and the ways they are impressed in this neoliberal regime to steer particular courses of action (see Beckett, 2015). This harks back to my concern to find the *most appropriate professional response*, not dwelling on the negatives but keeping a focus on the positives and the future.

The ongoing need for practical-politicized dialogue

So many of these teachers and school Heads in urban schools take to heart the interests of disadvantaged students, particularly those who experience poverty and cumulative multiple deprivation, which coincidentally intersects with the BERA *Fair and Equal Education* manifesto and NUT *Stand Up for Education* manifesto. Yet practitioners including union-active teachers are nearly always confronted by politicians with hubris. Prime Minster David Cameron's insistence was telling in a roll-out of the Conservative's strategy for the 2015 UK election, heralded on the front page of a major newspaper:

> *PM to send rescue teams into failing schools*[10]

Apparently Cameron was anxious to move away from the main news stories of Europe and immigration that had dominated populist political debate and so made an announcement about the establishment of a National Teaching Service (NTS). This effectively tried to sideline mainstream political debate about Britain's membership of the European Union and immigration, which requires critical scrutiny, but also distract the media and public policy debates away from the major news concerns of the day in the run-up to an election. In all likelihood it was contrived as part of a propaganda war given the populist minor United Kingdom Independence Party's (UKIP) then-first victory in its concerted efforts to win parliamentary seats in by-elections.

The Prime Minister's concerns to spotlight 'failing' schools might, at first glance, be seen as a calculated move, but it suggests a fake concern with teachers' work and teacher quality, which cuts to the heart of teaching and teacher education. It was a curious electoral strategy on Cameron's part to home in on urban schools given he bought straight into educational politics, in itself fraught with controversy. Witness Gove's term of office, whose vernacular versions of global neoliberal education reforms were replete with news reporting until he was ultimately deemed a political liability and replaced[11]. What is the political mileage to be gained? Urban schools are, for the most part, situated in local areas that score high on the

Index of Multiple Deprivation given families and communities disadvantaged in Austerity Britain. This sort of political attention is so misplaced, but it comes back to an argument of this book about derision and demonization to deflect criticism from government social policies, including welfare and education. Cameron would do well to hear this urban primary school Head's retort in response to a question about the work that is actually being done to meet government policy expectations, including 'raising achievement' and 'closing the gap':

> *I could put 30 [student] files in front of you or we could sit on the computer for the rest of the day, going through every piece of evidence. At the end of the day what it says is that all our conversations, all our work in school is around trying to bring about some purposeful improvement in a child's development. Whether it's National curriculum; whether it's key skills around literacy and numeracy; whether it's social, emotional resilience; whether it's understanding themselves and others. All of our work [from] half past 7 in the morning 'til half past 6 at night, what is taking place in [these] schools is this, all of the time, constantly, nothing else, other than this.*

This data speaks to practitioners who are cognizant of research evidence as well as the ways to serve the deep needs of disadvantaged students, which provokes me to think more about their commitments. My quest for some theorizations actually brought me back to Lieberman and Miller's (2008) advice on 'Forging commitments' in that there is no such thing as an instant community nor a single template for its form and content. This is still another lesson for the 'Leading Learning' CPD twin-pack even in view of the semi-structured nature of the non-accredited component and all the recalibrations. Taking heed, I recognize it takes time for a community of teachers working with their academic partner to take hold in an urban school and for the school Head to consider a way to share professional learning and school-generated practitioner research evidence. Certainly my work on Boards of Governors is witness to the time it takes to develop effective ways to talk, think and learn together.

This need to acknowledge different paths for professional learning communities is best exemplified in the urban primary school that hosted our first pilot study. As noted in an earlier chapter, they were resistant to the label 'disadvantaged' school but also in many ways to so-called academic vocabulary, professional readings, research and theory (see Lieberman and Miller, 2008; Hargreaves, 1984). For all intents and purposes the teacher partners were seemingly resistant to follow through with their teacher inquiry projects and generate school-based 'other' data, contrary to initial negotiations about working in partnership. Yet they signed up with other Trailblazers, and a senior leader and a classroom teacher published the results of their joint work in our special collection with support from their academic partner (see Harridge et al., 2014). They portray an idiosyncratic approach to teacher inquiry, reporting their joint work constructed as a conversation piece intended to be a representation of their developmental learning journey and professional dialogue. Their narrative is said to be indicative of a continuous analysis of different national and school data sets that contribute to an understanding of practitioner research in challenging urban schools under huge policy and time pressures.

My search for theorizations of commitment also brought me to the historian E.P. Thompson (in Winslow, 2014), featured throughout this book. His work titled 'Commitment in Politics' sheds some light on the plight of staff in urban schools, including research-active teachers and their academic partners who 'go 'public':

> [T]he record of our working class can appear as an instinctual, almost vegetable, evolution in which the active role of the minority, as the agent of social change, is belittled, as well as the moral and intellectual resources which have been called forth in a whole way of struggle. Our society today – our democratic liberties and our social services – is in great part the product of this struggle, and of the adjustments to it on the part of capitalist interests.

This sense of history helps with a recognition of the forces at work that corrupt efforts to build urban schools on the strength of research-informed teaching and teacher education. In view of practitioners' evident commitment in the local network of urban schools, I was incensed by the Prime Minister's announcement of 'hit squads' so I replied with a letter to the editor[12] that is worth quoting in full:

> *The idea of a hit squad dispatched into so-called 'failing schools' (Wintour, The Guardian, 13 October) should sound an alarm on a few counts. It signals the continuation of the use of force that engenders fear in urban schools, labelled not as challenging schools or more pertinently disadvantaged schools in local areas that usually rank high on the Index of Multiple Deprivation. It wages a propaganda war against teaching staff and multi-agency workers who are working extremely hard to try and combat exceptional social and educational inequalities in school-communities who have suffered much from austerity policies. The charge of failure, code-named 'inadequate' by Ofsted, is a political ploy to mask the effects in teachers' classrooms of poverty and deprivation, which should be seen as mitigating circumstances when it comes to exam results, national benchmarks and floor targets.*
>
> *This is a dangerous social experiment with these disadvantaged schools, overseen by the Prime Minister and led by authoritarian politicians like Gove and now Morgan, who is seemingly content to carry on with a deliberate misrepresentation of the social realities of these front-line workers and subject them to intense policy pressures and sanctions including job losses. More worrying, in the absence of adequate research-informed system support to meet pupils' academic and social learning needs, is the power allocated to these politicians to shut down these schools, which are then cut adrift from the local authority and re-opened as academies with corporate sponsors intent on profit-making and wealth creation. This then paves the way for global edu-businesses to come in and take over the nation's state school system, which in turn raises serious questions about knowledge control and the control of teachers' work not to forget the*

fate of pupils from poor and deprived family and social backgrounds. The fall-out from these vernacular forms of global neoliberal policies will echo down the twenty-first century, and as history has shown, there are dangerous precedents.

This letter shows my exasperation with political assaults on urban schools and speaks more to my concern about protest veering towards direct political struggle. However, the most pronounced lesson from my work with teacher partners is not to underestimate their steely determination to posit an *appropriate professional response*. They want to learn from academic partners how to co-develop '*local*' solutions to *local* problems, and then how to 'go public' with alternatives to dominant ideological practices. These are well represented in Trailblazers' published articles for *Urban Review*, which all flag the historical and structural difficulties of 'raising achievement' and 'closing the gap' for disadvantaged students marked by poverty and cumulative multiple deprivation.

Professional-political arenas

In an effort to strengthen tactical professional relations between academic partners and union-active teachers locally but also with a view to the future, I invited NUT General Secretary Christine Blower to deliver the 2015 Winifred Mercier public lecture. This is an annual event to celebrate the life and legacy of the first Vice Principal of the City of Leeds Training College, and in many ways it is a tribute as well as an acknowledgement of the long history of teacher education in the institution that stretches back more than a century. These public lectures provide an opportunity to hear the work of distinguished scholars and researchers who are working on schools policy. Blower did not disappoint. Her title 'Standing up for Education' was a call to practitioners to engage with the NUT *Stand Up for Education* manifesto.

These were Blower's opening words to her public lecture:

> *Education is a Human and Civil Right and a public good. This assertion is central to the philosophy and politics of the Global Union Federation for Education unions, Education International, an organisation bringing together 30 million teachers, through their unions, worldwide.*
>
> *It is also central to the philosophy and policies and politics of the National Union of Teachers. Finally it is even enshrined in the constitution of a country to which I shall refer several times this evening, namely Finland.*

There is no need to recount Blower's public lecture now published with a post-event story[13], but attention is drawn to three matters. First, Education as a Human and Civil Right and a public good in contradistinction to GERM (Sahlberg, 2011) given schooling and education is being mined for its potential for profit. Second, the Global Federation called Education International in Brussels coordinates with an international conglomerate of teachers' unions to campaign against global edu-businesses. Third, she declared, 'Social Movement Trade Unionism means making the union into a vehicle through which its members can not only address their bargaining demands but actively lead the fight for everything that affects working people in their communities and the country' (see Gindin, 1995, cited by Blower, 2015). Blower's public lecture was evidently research-informed, given her list of key characteristics of social movement trade unionism:

- Concern with issues that affect life in the workplace but not limited to sectional interests
- Concern with equality, democracy and justice in wider society
- Seeks to address underlying causes not just symptoms
- Seeks allies and coalition partners (community organizations, etc.) with shared issues and concerns
- Notion of solidarity (international) is central
- Non-instrumental: based upon a vision rather than 'pragmatic' response, although sometimes a healthy dose of pragmatism is required
- Based upon maximizing participation and democracy within unions at various levels: local, regional, national, international

This shows Blower's conceptualization of the NUT's *appropriate professional response* to the predicament for schooling and education in the current neoliberal regime. In my vote of thanks, I reiterated two points: Blower's endorsement of social movement trade unionism dovetails with my concerns to encourage teachers' collective actions and raise the professional voice. The NUT *Stand Up for Education* campaign puts it on an industrial footing as well as a professional, social and political footing of concern to everyone in England, the UK, Australia, globally! I also highlighted potential in a local interest group of teachers and academic partners who come together in support of the NUT campaign and tentatively explore likely possibilities for examining the manifesto, homing in on the policies/ideas/evidence that underscore schooling, and combining a local/global analysis. I posed the following questions, ripe for practitioner research and 'local' solutions:

Q. What does achievement and student learning look like in local schools?

Q. What is the fallout from teaching to the test in local schools?

Q. What is the situation on qualified teachers/retention/recruitment locally?

Q. What does child poverty look like locally?

Q. What are the effects of poverty and deprivation in local classrooms?

Q. What does the shortage of places look like locally?

Q. Who stands up for the children and young people?

Afterwards I spoke to Blower about the work of the NSW Priority Action Schools Program, jointly devised by NSW Teachers' Federation and the Department of Education and Training. I gave her copy of Groundwater-Smith and Kemmis (n.d.) and drew attention to our local knowledge-building work in a local network of urban schools. I still harbour hopes that the NUT might work with a government in England to consider a systematic evaluation of the work done in self-identified urban schools, with each assisted by an academic partner experienced in school-based research. This would go further than the work proposed by the previous Cameron-Clegg Coalition Government, spearheaded by enquiries from the then-Minister for Schools, Liberal Democrat The Rt Hon. Mr David Laws, MP. His letter to the University Council for the Education of Teachers (UCET) was a request of the national Initial Teacher Training community to feed into policy deliberations on 'closing the gap'[14].

It is this that requires rigorous analyses by each and every one concerned about disadvantaged students marked by poverty and cumulative multiple deprivation, exemplified by allies of the NUT *Stand Up for Education* campaign[15]. It happened I issued numerous personal invitations to the citywide network of politicians, policymakers and powerbrokers for Blower's public lecture, and the only one to attend was the local Deputy Director of Children's Services. My follow-up email afterwards presented a final opportunity to suggest yet again we might work in a productive partnership in respectful and trustworthy ways and broach some of the questions ripe for practitioner research. Perhaps naïvely I continue to be puzzled by the silences because I always expect the professional courtesy of a reply if only to decline the invitation! Then there is the matter of the right to expect professional and political attention!

Once again it is important to revisit the terms of my analyses, and Ball's (1993/2006) theorization of policy as text and discourse is helpful. Power, he says, is multiplicitous, overlain, interactive and complex; policy texts *enter* rather than simply change power relations. This shows the complexity of the relationship, as he says, between policy intentions, texts, interpretations and reactions. When it comes to the local struggle to establish professional learning communities focused on poverty and cumulative multiple deprivation, I am certainly open to advice. As Ball indicated, we cannot rule out certain forms and conceptions of social action simply because they seem awkward or theoretically challenging or difficult. Others in local positions of authority evidently think differently!

Teachers' policy advocacy

This raises questions about to what extent practitioners are confident in making their voices heard on what happens or should happen in the classroom, which is the domain of their professional practice. That academics and teacher partners might be encouraged to collectively join in the BERA *Fair and Equal Education* and NUT *Stand Up for Education* campaigns requires diligence, however, professional-political motivated work at local level ideally grows organically in the networks of urban schools. This is dependent on whether or not they have capacity, given enormous policy and time pressures to engage with each other and School Leadership Teams, notwithstanding the school Head's power bases and the problems with micro-management mentioned earlier. Any expectation of a remonstration against GERM and its vernacular forms in England, including toxic forms of accountability, needs to be mindful of the ambiguities around these sorts of terms and the fear circulating among practitioners. It is also crucial to remember there is a politics around the unionized workforce, as one of the local urban high school Heads said:

> *The teacher unions will do what they can, but the problem is they are not particularly heard as our professional associations. That no one is listening is one of the big issues.*

After the 2015 Winifred Mercier public lecture, the General Secretary Christine Blower invited me to attend the 2015 NUT annual conference. Once again there is no need to recount proceedings published in a précis form[16] but serious consideration should be given to a series of motions. What follows were items in the final agenda, moved and seconded with supporting arguments, subject to debate, amendments, and rights of reply before being put to the vote. Whatever, these extracts serve to illustrate professional concerns that are both research-informed and evidence-based:

> *Social movement trade unionism:* Conference notes that neoliberal politicians the world over claim for their 'reforms' that they are intended to improve the quality of working class children. Conference believes, however, that standardized tests, league tables, a climate of fear generated by Ofsted, performance-related pay, academisation and privatization are of no real benefit to working class children. These neoliberal reforms are a smokescreen designed to shift the blame for failings in the system onto teachers; they are based on a free-market ideology that is diametrically opposed to the real interests of working class children.
>
> *Resisting the GERM:* Conference believes that the domination of the ideas of the Global Education Reform Movement means that none of the three main parties are offering policy that will properly address the problems (the permanent state of crisis; shortage of school places and impending shortage of teachers; the government's austerity and privatization programs; and the central issue of inequality in education).
>
> *Reclaiming our professional development:* Conference believes that new appraisal systems are invariably being used to find ways of punishing teachers. Conference believes that it is in everyone's interests for teachers to improve their practice but that harsh and punitive appraisal is not achieving this, particularly given that many schools now link teachers' pay to appraisal.
>
> *Ofsted:* Conference instructs the Executive to work with other teachers' unions and academics to campaign for the abolition of Ofsted and promote evidence-based models of effective and supportive school improvement systems which are trusted by teachers, fair, developmental, and which offer structured and properly funded CPD.

I certainly lend my support as academic partner not only to union-active teachers at the local level but also to the teachers' trade union movement more generally. I trust this book has shown the necessity of what it takes to co-develop a knowledge-building programme in networks of urban schools, not only to draw invaluable lessons apropos school–university partnerships but to reclaim professional control of teaching and teacher education. This is fertile ground for a social movement of practitioners to develop *an appropriate professional response* to some of the urgent problems for English society. It is in the grip of damaging consequences from globalization not least for students and families already disadvantaged by changes in national social and economic policies. I wholeheartedly agree with the NUT conference delegates' call for urgent and collective action across the profession and in conjunction with parents, Local Authorities and other stakeholder organizations. One question that bothers me is why teachers' right to make professional decisions intertwined with the right to expect professional and political attention, which sits well with the writ of democracy, has become a trade dispute. In searching for an answer, I came across E.P. Thompson's (Winslow, 2014) advice:

> *It is the old debate continued. The same aspirations, fears and tensions are there: but they arise in a new context, with new language and arguments, and a changed balance of forces. We have to try and understand both things – the continuing traditions and the context that has changed.*

The point is that it may well come down to teacher and academic unions if not BERA and UCET to organize and represent the professional concerns of practitioners about teaching and teacher education, and emphasize the need for *policy conflict*. As Sennett indicated in his Foreword to Touraine's (1977) book, *The Voice and the Eye*, the emphasis is on the relation between theory and action. This is best exemplified in the NUT's work in the run-up to the 2015 UK elections, notably in a local event called 'Education Question Time', held in a local urban school in a marginal constituency[17]. The press release advertised it to draw attention to education politics, critical in a key battleground given the Conservatives' then-hold on the electorate with 1,650 votes:

> *Education is one of the most controversial and contentious issues in this election with political parties and educational experts offering contrasting visions for our children's education. Local Authorities are no longer able to build new schools to meet local demand for places and record numbers of teachers are leaving the profession.*
>
> *There have been considerable changes made to our school system with the introduction of Free Schools, the expansion of Academies and considerable changes to the curriculum, examinations and testing. Have these changes improved education or have they been a dangerous experiment on our children?*

The NUT Regional office and local branch office arranged it so the public, teachers, parents, governors and students could hear from the main parties' parliamentary candidates and a special panel of education experts, who put advertised questions to them in a 'Question Time' format:

- Is Ofsted fit for purpose?
- Are free schools the solution or part of the problem?
- Are standards of education falling?
- Should students be tested at 4 years of age?
- Do we need a Royal College of Teachers?
- Why do teachers strike?
- Should schools be run for profit?
- What's next for education after the election?
- Why do teachers need to be qualified?

The Conservatives unexpectedly won this seat and the election with an outright majority given a net gain of 24 seats, a 0.8 per cent increase share, though it is crucial to study analyses of results especially given non-compulsory voting and 66.1 per cent of voter turnout compared with 65.1 per cent in 2010[18]. Prime Minister David Cameron remained leader and confirmed Nicky Morgan as Secretary of State for Education. She very quickly announced policy intentions to target schools that 'require improvement' and retain the nomenclature of 'failing' and 'coasting' schools. With a bill confirmed in the Queen's Speech[19] this consolidates the academies and free schools programme, only to continue with authoritarianism and frightening scenarios for school Heads and teacher partners including replacement of urban school leaders and job losses. This is not without controversy, going by the public commentary[20] including a statement from NUT Deputy Secretary Kevin Courtney who told the BBC there was 'no convincing evidence' that academies improve standards: 'This is serious error that the government is making. They are following something which has no evidence base'[21].

Cameron also appointed the former Secretary of State for Education Michael Gove, who had been demoted to Chief Whip in the Cameron-Clegg Coalition Government, as the new Justice Secretary in the new Cameron Conservative Government. Gove's apparent brief, widely published, is to dismantle the Human Rights Act though this too is not without controversy but interestingly opposition is from the Conservative party in the first instance[22]. Taken together, these twin policy initiatives herald a dark future for urban schools and the idea of education as a Human and Civil Right as well as a public good. Consequently it is all the more pressing to contemplate what a *choreography of urban schools policy conflict* might look like post-election and over the possible 5-year course of this government, if the idea of research-informed teaching and teacher education is to take root. Of significance is the need to look ahead and think strategically about the run-up to the 2020 election.

Yet again I am inspired by Touraine's (1977) book *The Voice and the Eye* to encourage practitioners – school Heads, teachers and teacher educators along with student teachers – to breathe life into a social movement in an 'effort to say what

Professional control over schooling **151**

it is [threats to professional practice], to see its contours [holding the line] in order to speak its name [of democratic control]' (see Sennett's Foreword). This is a struggle in urban schools to combine action and analyses, while history shows there are alternatives to government models of intervention that rely on derisory and demonizing discourses about disadvantaged students' progress and performance. Like Sennett intimates, it might be best to think of this sociology as radical rather than ideological dominance of the profession: radical in its conceptual scheme of professional learning and progressive teacher inquiry projects; radical in its refusal to accord with the vernacular neoliberal destiny of forced urban school closures and corporate takeover; radical in the professional responsibility it therefore places on practitioners for the pains and freedoms in their lives but also for the disadvantaged students in their remit.

If we balk at the term 'radical', it needs unpacking as we situate ourselves in real work settings dealing with the real politics of urban schooling, globalization and university-based teacher education, teaching and research. Indeed I prefer to go with Thrupp (2005) on his point about contesting official school improvement, which takes time and energy working with whole school staff engaging ideas/concepts/theories and which must not be discouraged with promises of radicalism. That said, in the face of brute force from authoritarian politicians, policymakers and powerbrokers, I also lean towards Boomer's (1999) idea about being a pragmatic radical:

> *The radical teacher must be a hard-nosed pragmatist keeping alive principles and long-term goals, but having a canny sense of what is achievable, what is not worth the energy and what, however slight, might constitute strategic gain. The radical teacher must also seek out networks of support.*

Wizard of Id © Parker & Hart. Reproduced by permission of Creators Syndicate International.

Notes

1 Menter (2013) quite rightly points to some significant developments: the BERA-UCET (2012) report on major threats to research capacity across the UK, and the BERA-RSA (2014a, 2014b) *Inquiry*.
2 See the report on the Conservative manifesto 'How five more years of Cameron would look' in *The Guardian*, Wednesday 15 April, 2015. A point on education key policies read: Turn 'failing and coasting' state secondary schools into academies.
3 See Beckett (2013c) on Gove's links to Murdoch, a major powerbroker.
4 See the latest pronouncements from Ofsted on disadvantage: http://dashboard.ofsted.gov.uk/sdd_guidance.pdf
5 See www.bera.ac.uk/project/respecting-children-learning-from-the-past-redesigning-the-future
6 See www.teachers.org.uk/manifesto
7 Curiously there is so much said about parental choice of schools, yet this hardly ranks among parents/caregivers in urban school communities, where mobility is by far one of the biggest issues for the poorest families forced to move around and relocate because of welfare policies (see Menter, 2013).
8 See www.theguardian.com/teacher-network/teacher-blog/2013/jun/20/failing-schools-michael-wilshaw-ofsted-teacher
9 It is difficult to cite the frequency of incidents because in England's school-led system marked by fragmentation what's missing are central banks of exit data that shows teachers' reasons for resignations such as pressures, stress, ill-health. The NUT's central office conducts surveys of members and compiles national data while local branches are invariably taken up with member teachers' caseloads so there are local logs of data. Other unions no doubt have their own data, along with the DfE, but there is no ready reference.
10 See www.theguardian.com/politics/2014/oct/12/failing-schools-rescue-teams-squad-teachers-assist
11 It is interesting to see reports that Gove, although demoted to Chief Whip, was said to be still driving the then-Conservative-led education portfolio: see www.independent.co.uk/news/education/education-news/sacked-education-secretary-michael-gove-still-sees-papers-via-allies-allowing-him-to-backseat-drive-department-10016118.html
12 See www.theguardian.com/politics/2014/oct/14/teaching-oaths-hit-squads-and-reality-of-life-at-chalkface
13 See www.leedsbeckett.ac.uk/news/0315-nut-general-secretary-delivers-leeds-beckett-guest-lecture/
14 I should here mention I was asked to draft our university Faculty contribution to the UCET (2013) discussion paper on 'closing the gap': see www.ucet.ac.uk/4954
15 See www.teachers.org.uk/files/reclaimingschools-essays-9963.pdf
16 See www.teachers.org.uk/node/21275 also http://schoolsweek.co.uk/teacher-union-conference-round-up-what-happened-at-nut-2015/
17 See www.eventbrite.co.uk/e/pudsey-education-question-time-tickets-16352917015
18 See www.bbc.co.uk/news/election-2015-32624405. It is worthwhile following the public debates around electoral reform, given an apparent gerrymander of electoral boundaries for parliamentary seats: see www.electoral-reform.org.uk/ and an allied editorial in *The Guardian* that describes the problems without proportional representation at www.theguardian.com/commentisfree/2015/jun/01/guardian-view-lessons-2015-general-election
19 See www.gov.uk/government/topical-events/queens-speech-2015
20 See http://schoolsweek.co.uk/why-morgans-plan-to-fire-heads-probably-wont-solve-coasting-school-problems/
21 See www.bbc.co.uk/news/education-32763097
22 See www.theguardian.com/law/2015/may/22/falconer-scrap-human-rights-act-thrown-out-house-of-lords-gove

© Mike Konopacki. Reproduced by permission of Huck/Konopacki Labor Cartoons.

BIBLIOGRAPHY

Angus, L. (1993). The sociology of school effectiveness. *British Journal of Sociology of Education, 14*(3).
Anti-academies Alliance. Accessed 22 May, 2013. Retrieved from http://antiacademies.org. uk/2013/03/school-improvement-held-back-by-the-academy-solution/
Anyon, J. (1981, Spring). Social class and school knowledge. *Curriculum Inquiry, 11*(1), 3–42.
Anyon, J. (1997). *Ghetto schooling: A political economy of urban educational reform.* New York: Teachers College Press.
Anyon, J. (2009). *Theory and educational research: Toward critical social explanation.* London and New York: Routledge.
Apple, M. (2001). *Educating the 'right' way: Markets, standards, God and inequality.* London and New York: RoutledgeFalmer.
Apple, M. W. (2006). Understanding and interrupting neoliberalism and neoconservatism in education. *Pedagogies: An International Journal, 1*(1), 21–26.
Apple, M. (2009). Foreword. In S. Gewirtz, P. Mahony, I. Hextall and A. Cribb (Eds), *Changing teacher professionalism: International trends, challenges and ways forward.* London and New York: Routledge.
Apple, M. W. and Beane, J. A. (1999). *Democratic schools: Lessons from the chalk face.* Buckingham, England: Open University Press.
Arshad, R., Wrigley, T. and Pratt, L. (2012). *Social justice re-examined: Dilemmas and solutions for the classroom teacher.* Stoke-on-Trent, England: Trentham.
Arthurs, N. (2012). *Raising white British students' achievement* (Unpublished Master's thesis). Leeds, England: Metropolitan University.
Arthurs, N. (2013). Stop! Cloning teachers as Stepford wives. In L. Beckett (Ed.), *Teacher education through active engagement: Raising the professional voice.* London and New York: Routledge.
Arthurs, N., Patterson, J. and Bentley, A. (2014). Achievement for students who are persistently absent: Missing school, missing out? *Urban Review, 46*(5), 860–876.
Ball, S. J. (1990/2012). *Politics and policy making in education.* London and New York: Routledge.
Ball, S. J. (1993). What is policy? Texts, trajectories and toolboxes. In S. J. Ball (2006), *Education policy and social class: The selected works of Stephen J. Ball.* London and New York: Routledge.

Ball, S. J. (2003). The teacher's soul and the terrors of performativity. *Journal of Education Policy, 18* (2), 215–228.

Ball, S. J. (2006). *Education policy and social class: The selected works of Stephen J. Ball.* London and New York: Routledge.

Ball, S. J. (2008/2013). *The education debate.* Bristol, England: The Policy Press.

Ball, S. J. (2012). *Global education inc: New policy networks and the neo-liberal imaginary.* London and New York: Routledge.

Ball, S. J. (2013). *Education, justice and democracy: The struggle over ignorance and opportunity* (Policy paper). London: Centre for Labour and Social Studies. Retrieved from: http://class online.org.uk/docs/2013_Policy_Paper_-Education,_justice_and_democracy_(Stephen_Ball).pdf

Ball, S. J., Maguire, M. and Braun, A. (2012). *How schools do policy: Policy enactments in secondary schools.* London and New York: Routledge.

Baumfield, V. M., Beckett, L. and McLaughlin, C. (2011). *A different way of thinking about work: The challenges and opportunities of school-university research partnerships.* Paper presented at the annual meeting of the American Association for Research in Education (AERA), New Orleans, 8–12 April.

Beckett, L. (1996). *The radical-conservative experiment in NSW education: 1988–1996* (Unpublished PhD dissertation). Geelong, Australia: Deakin University.

Beckett, L. (2009). School-university partnerships in disadvantaged communities in the UK. International keynote address for the 'Social Inclusion in Education' conference, Sydney, 22–23 October.

Beckett, L. (2011). Professional learning in community: Teachers and academic partners focussed on disadvantaged students in schooling and higher education. *Australian Educational Researcher, 38*(1), 109–124.

Beckett, L. (2012a). Engaging democratic politics against school closure. In W. Pink (Ed.), *Schools for marginalized youth.* New York: Hampton Press.

Beckett, L. (2012b). Trust the teachers, mother!: The leading learning project in Leeds. *Improving Schools, 15*(1), 10–22.

Beckett, L. (Ed.). (2013a). *Teacher education through active engagement: Raising the professional voice.* London and New York: Routledge.

Beckett, L. (2013b). Giving teachers voice – getting school democracy! National Union of Teachers' *Education Review,* Summer, *25*(1), 51–58.

Beckett, L. (2013c). Power struggles over teacher qualifications. In L. Beckett (Ed.), *Teacher education through active engagement: Raising the professional voice.* London and New York: Routledge.

Beckett, L. (2014a). Raising teachers' voice on achievement in urban schools in England. *Urban Review, 46*(5).

Beckett, L. (2014b). Research-active teachers. Second keynote address presented at the British Educational Research Association – National College of Teaching and Learning (NCTL) *Supporting Teachers as Researchers* conference, Manchester, 30 June.

Beckett, L. (2015). *Leaving an impression: The indelible marks of toxic forms of school accountability on teachers in urban schools.* Paper presented at the Gender and Education Association conference, Roehampton University, June.

Beckett, L. and Wood, J. (2012). Talking honestly in a challenging primary school: England. In T. Wrigley, P. Thomson and B. Lingard (Eds), *Changing schools: Alternative ways to make a difference* (pp. 140–151). London and New York: Routledge.

Beckett, L. and Gallagher, K. (2014). *Practitioner research to improve students' learning outcomes in the north of England: Possible or impossible?* Paper for BERA Annual Conference, London, 23–25 September.

Bibliography

Benn, M. (2013). Afterword. In L. Beckett (Ed.), *Teacher education through active engagement: Raising the professional voice*. London and New York: Routledge.

BERA-UCET Working Group on Education. (2012). *Research prospects for education research in education departments in higher education institutions in the UK*. Retrieved from www.ucet.ac.uk/4371

Bernstein, B. (1970). Education cannot compensate for society. *New Society* (London), *15*, 387.

Beveridge, S., Groundwater-Smith, S., Kemmis, S. and Wasson, D. (2005). Professional learning that makes a difference: Successful strategies implemented by priority action schools in New South Wales. *Journal of In-service Education*, *31*(4), 697–710.

Bevins, S. C. and Price, G. (2014). Collaboration between academics and teachers: A complex relationship. *Educational Action Research*, *22*(2), 270–284.

Blacker. (2013). *The falling rate of learning and the neoliberal endgame*. Alresford, England: Zero Books.

Boomer, G. (1999). Pragmatic radical teaching and the disadvantaged schools program. In B. Green (Ed.), *Designs on learning: Essays on curriculum and teaching by Garth Boomer*. Canberra: Australia Curriculum Studies Association.

British Educational Research Association (BERA) – Royal Society Action and Research Centre (RSA). (2014a). *The role of research in teacher education: Reviewing the evidence interim report*. Retrieved from www.bera.ac.uk/wp-content/uploads/2014/02/BERA-RSA-Interim-Report.pdf

British Educational Research Association (BERA) – Royal Society Action and Research Centre (RSA). (2014b). *Research and the teaching profession. Building the capacity for a self-improving education system. Final report of the BERA-RSA inquiry*. Retrieved from www.bera.ac.uk/wp-content/uploads/2013/12/BERA-RSA-Research-Teaching-Profession-FULL-REPORT-for-web.pdf

Burbules, N. C. and Berk, R. (1999). Critical thinking and critical pedagogy: Relations, differences, and limits. In T. S. Popkewitz and L. Fendler (Eds), *Critical theories in education*. New York: Routledge. Retrieved from http://faculty.education.illinois.edu/burbules/papers/critical.html

Burgess, T. (2007). *Lifting the lid on the creative curriculum: How leaders have released creativity in their schools through curriculum ownership*. Report for the National College for School Leadership. Retrieved from http://dera.ioe.ac.uk/7340/1/download%3Fid%3D17281%26filename%3Dlifting-the-lid-on-the-creative-curriculum-full-report.pdf

Burns, D. and Walker, M. (2007). Feminist methodologies. In B. Somekh and C. Lewin (Eds), *Research methods in the social sciences*. London: Sage.

Cahill, K. (2012). *What class are you in? A critical ethnography of school choice, social class and student identity in an urban post-primary school; ethnographic research on social class* (Unpublished doctoral dissertation). Ireland: University College Cork.

Campbell, A. and Groundwater-Smith, S. (2007). *An ethical approach to practitioner research: Dealing with issues and dilemmas in action research*. London and New York: Routledge.

Campbell, A. and Groundwater-Smith, S. (2010). Introduction. In A. Campbell and S. Groundwater-Smith (Eds), *Connecting inquiry and professional learning in education: International perspectives and practical solutions*. London and New York: Routledge.

Campbell, A. and McNamara, O. (2010). Mapping the field of practitioner research, inquiry and professional learning in educational contexts: A review. In A. Campbell and S. Groundwater-Smith (Eds), *Connecting inquiry and professional learning in education: International perspectives and practical solutions*. London and New York: Routledge.

Campbell, C. and Whitty, G. (2007). Urban education dystopia, 2050: A response from the United Kingdom. In W. Pink and G. W. Noblit (Eds), *International handbook of urban education*. New York and Philadelphia: Springer.

Bibliography

Carr, W. (Ed.) (1989). *Quality in teaching*. Lewes, England: The Falmer Press.
Carter, A. (2015). *Independent report: Carter review of initial teacher training*. Retrieved from www.gov.uk/government/publications/carter-review-of-initial-teacher-training
Cochran-Smith, M. (2006). Policy, practice and politics in teacher education. *Journal of Teacher Education*. Thousand Oaks, CA: Corwin Press.
Cochran-Smith, M. and Lytle, S. (2001). Beyond certainty: Taking an inquiry stance on practice. In A. Lieberman and L. Miller (Eds), *Teachers caught in the action: Professional development that matters*. New York: Teachers College Press.
Cochran-Smith, M. and Lytle, S. (2009). *Inquiry as stance: Practitioner research in the next generation*. New York: Teachers College Press.
Cochran-Smith, M., Piazza, P. and Power, C. (2013). The politics of accountability: Assessing teacher education in the United States. *The Educational Forum*, 77(1), 6–27.
Compton, M. and Weiner, L. (2008). *The global assault on teaching, teachers and their unions*. New York: Palgrave Macmillan.
Connell, R. W. (1993). *Schools and social justice*. Leichhardt, Australia: Pluto Press.
Connell, R. W. (2009). Good teachers on dangerous ground: Towards a new view of teacher quality and professionalism. *Critical Studies in Education*, 50(3), 213–229.
Connell, R. W., Ashenden, D. J., Kessler, S. and Dowsett, G. W. (1982). *Making the difference: Schools, families and social division*. Sydney: George Allen and Unwin.
Connell, R. W., White, V. and Johnston, K. M. (1991). *'Running twice as hard': The disadvantaged schools program in Australia*. Geelong, Australia: Deakin University Press.
Crossley, N. (2005). *Key concepts in critical social theory*. London: Sage.
Darbyshire, N., Finn, B., Griggs, S. and Ford, C. (2014). An unsure start for young children in English urban primary schools. *Urban Review*, 46(4), 816–830.
Darling-Hammond, L. and Lieberman, A. (Eds). (2012). *Teacher education around the world: Changing policies and practices*. London and New York: Routledge.
Department for Communities, Schools and Families. (2009). *Deprivation and education: The evidence of pupils in England, foundation stage to key stage 4*. Retrieved from http://dera.ioe.ac.uk/9431/1/DCSF-RTP-09-01.pdf
Department for Education. (2010). *The importance of teaching: Schools white paper*. Retrieved from www.education.gov.uk/schools/toolsandinitiatives/schoolswhitepaper/b0068570/the-importance-of-teaching
Department for Education. (2011). *Training our next generation of outstanding teachers*. Retrieved from www.gov.uk/government/publications/training-our-next-generation-of-outstanding-teachers-implementation-plan
Department for Education and Employment. (1997). *Excellence in schools*. London: HMSO.
Department for Education and Skills. (2003). *Aiming high: Raising the achievement of minority ethnic pupils*. Retrieved from www.education.gov.uk/consultations/downloadableDocs/213_1.pdf
Dinkins, D. (2009). Teachers talk about race, class and achievement. In M. Cochran-Smith and S. Lytle (Eds), *Inquiry as stance: Practitioner research for the next generation*. New York: Teachers College Press.
Doherty, J. (2013). The thorny matter of assessment. In L. Beckett (Ed.), *Teacher education through active engagement: Raising the professional voice*. London and New York: Routledge.
Dorling, D. (2011). *Injustice: Why social inequality persists*. Bristol, England: The Policy Press.
Dorling, D. (2014). *Inequality and the 1%*. London: Verso.
Firth, B., Melia, V., Bergan, D. and Whitby, L. (2014). 'No ceiling on achievement': Breaking the glass ceiling or hitting a steel plate in urban schools? *Urban Review*, 46(5), 877–890.

Frankenburg, E., Taylor, A. and Merseth, K. (2009). Walking the walk: Teacher candidates' professed commitment to urban teaching and their subsequent career decisions. *Urban Education*, 45(3), 312–346.

Furlong, J. (2013). *Education – an anatomy of the discipline: Rescuing the university project?* London and New York: Routledge.

Furlong, J., Cochran-Smith, M. and Brennan, M. (2011). *Policy and politics in teacher education: International perspectives.* London and New York: Routledge.

Gale, T. (2010). Social inquiry and social action: Priorities for preparing school leaders. *Scholar-practitioner Quarterly*, 4(4), 316–318. Retrieved from http://dro.deakin.edu.au/eserv/DU: 30040192/gale-socialinquiry-2010.pdf

Gale, T. and Densmore, K. (2000). *Just schooling: Explorations in the cultural politics of teaching.* Buckingham, England and Philadelphia: Open University Press.

Gallagher, K. and Beckett, L. (2014). Addressing barriers to minority ethnic students' learning in a performative culture: Possible or Aan u SuuraGelin? Niemożliwe? Nemoguće? ناممکن ? *Urban Review*, 46(5), 846–859.

Gewirtz, S., Mahony, P., Hextall, I. and Cribb, A. (Eds). (2009). *Changing teacher professionalism: International trends, challenges and ways forward.* London and New York: Routledge.

Ghale, B. and Beckett, L. (2013). Teachers' politicisation. In L. Beckett (Ed.), *Teacher education through active engagement: Raising the professional voice.* London and New York: Routledge.

Gindin, S. (1995). *The Canadian auto workers: The birth and transformation of a union.* Toronto, Canada: James Lorimer.

Glenny, G., Menter, I. and Todd, L. (2013). How should teacher education take account of poverty? Paper presented at annual conference of British Educational Research Association, Brighton, 3–5 September.

Gorton, J., Williams, M. and Wrigley, T. (2014). Inspection judgements on urban schools: A case for the defence. *Urban Review*, 46(5), 891–903.

Grace, G. (1984). *Education in the city.* London: Routledge and Kegan Paul.

Grace, G. (1994). Urban education and the culture of contentment: The politics, culture and economics of inner-city schooling. In N. Stromquist (Ed.), *Education in urban areas: Cross-national dimensions.* Westport, CT: Praeger.

Grace, G. (2007). Urban education theory revisited: From the urban question to end of millennium. In W. Pink and G. W. Noblit (Eds), *International handbook of urban education.* New York and Philadelphia: Springer.

Grace, G., Menter, I. and Maguire, M. (2006). Series editors' preface. In M. Maguire, T. Woolridge and S. Pratt-Adams (Eds), *The urban primary school.* Maidenhead, England: Open University Press.

Groundwater-Smith, S. (2007a). Lesson study as formative assessment in secondary schools. In T. Loughland (Ed.), Proceedings of the authentic assessment practices for student learning conference (pp 5–18). Sydney: The University of Sydney.

Groundwater-Smith, S. (2007b). *Practitioner researchers: Today's children of mother courage. What can we learn from them?* Keynote address presented at annual conference of British Educational Research Association, London, 5–8 September.

Groundwater-Smith, S. and Kemmis, S. (n.d.). *Knowing makes the difference: Learnings from the NSW Priority Action Schools Program.* Sydney: NSW Department of Education and Training.

Groundwater-Smith, S. and Mockler, N. (2007). Ethics in practitioner research: An issue of quality. *Research Papers in Education*, 22(2), 199–211. Retrieved from www.tandfonline.com/doi/abs/10.1080/02671520701296171#.U7v4yZRdWSo

Haberman, M. (1991). The pedagogy of poverty versus good teaching. *Phi Delta Kappan*, December, 73(4), 290–294.

Halsey, A. (1972). *Educational priority. EPA problems and policies. Volume 1.* Report of a research project sponsored by the Department of Education and Science and the Social Science Research Council. London: HMSO.

Hammersley, M. and Atkinson, P. (2007). *Ethnography: Principles in practice*. London and New York: Routledge.

Hargreaves, A. (1984). Experience counts, theory doesn't: How teachers talk about their work. *Sociology of Education*, October, 57(4), 244–254.

Hargreaves, A. (2006). Four ages of professionalism and professional learning. In H. Lauder, P. Brown, J-A. Dillabough, and A. H. Halsey (Eds), *Education, globalization and social change* (pp. 673–691). Oxford: Oxford University Press.

Harridge, S., Stokoe, S. and Tan, J. E. C. (2014). That's another story: An alternative to the 'official' way the urban school story is told. *Urban Review*, 46(5), 244–254.

Harvey, D. (2005). *A brief history of neoliberalism*. Oxford: Oxford University Press.

Harvey, D. and Reed, M. H. (1996). The culture of poverty: An ideological analysis. *Sociological Perspectives*, Winter, 39(4), 465–495.

Hatcher, R. (2010). Marketisation, privatisation, autonomy and democracy. *The Journal for Drama in Education*, 26(2), 50–61.

Hayes, D., Mills, M., Christie, P. and Lingard, B. (2006). *Teachers and schools making a difference*. Sydney: Allen and Unwin.

Hoskins, K. and Maguire, M. (2013). Teaching the teachers: Contesting the curriculum. In L. Beckett, (Ed.), *Teacher education through active engagement: Raising the professional voice*. London and New York: Routledge.

House of Commons Education Committee. (2014). *Underachievement in education by white working class children*. Retrieved from www.publications.parliament.uk/pa/cm201415/cmselect/cmeduc/142/142.pdf

Hulme, M. and Livingstone, K. (2013). Curriculum for the future. In D. Wyse, V. M. Baumfield, D. Egan, C. Gallagher, L. Hayward, M. Hulme, R. Leitch, K. Livingston and I. Menter with B. Lingard (Eds), *Creating the curriculum*. London and New York: Routledge.

Husbands, C. (2013). *Education research and education practice in a diversifying school system*. Keynote annual conference of the British Educational Research Association, Brighton, 3–5 September.

Johnson, L., Finn, M. E. and Lewis, R. (2005). *Urban education with attitude*. New York: SUNY Press.

Johnson, R. S. (2002). *Using data to close the achievement gap: How to measure equity in our schools*. Thousand Oaks, CA: Corwin Press.

Johnson, R. S. and La Salle, R. A. (2010). *Data strategies to uncover and eliminate hidden inequities: The wallpaper effect*. Thousand Oaks, CA: Corwin Press.

Jones, O. (2011). *CHAVS: The demonization of the working class*. London: Verso.

Jones, O. (2014). *The establishment and how they get away with it*. London: Allen Lane.

Karmel, P. (1973). *Schools in Australia. Report of the interim committee for the Australian Schools Commission*. Canberra: Australian Government Publishing Service.

Kemmis, S. and Robottom, I. (1989). Principals of procedure in curriculum evaluation. In ECS801 Curriculum Evaluation monograph. Geelong, Australia: Deakin University.

Kruger, T., Eckersley, B., Davies, A., Newell, F. and Cherendnichenko, B. (2009). *A Study of effective and sustainable university school partnerships: Beyond determined efforts by inspired individuals*. Retrieved from www.aitsl.edu.au/docs/default-source/default-document-library/effective_and_sustainable_university-school_partnerships

Ladson-Billings, G. (2006). From the achievement gap to the education debt: Understanding achievement in U.S. schools. *Educational Researcher*, 35(7), 3–12.

Leitch, R. (2013). Critical analysis of personal and social education in UK primary curricular. In D. Wyse, V. M. Baumfield, D. Egan, C. Gallagher, L. Hayward, M. Hulme, R. Leitch, K. Livingston and I. Menter with B. Lingard (Eds), *Creating the curriculum*. London and New York: Routledge.
Lieberman, A. and Darling-Hammond, L. (2012). *Teacher education around the world: Changing policies and practices*. New York: Routledge.
Lieberman, A. and Miller, L. (Eds). (2001). *Teachers caught in the action: Professional development that matters*. New York: Teachers College Press.
Lieberman, A. and Miller, L. (Eds). (2008). *Teachers in professional communities: Improving teaching and learning*. New York: Teachers College Press.
Lingard, B. (2009). *Testing times: The need for new intelligent accountabilities for schooling*. Brisbane, Australia: Queensland Teachers' Union. Retrieved from www.qtu.asn.au/files/9113/2780/3358/29–01–2012_1315_170.pdf
Lingard, B. (2010). Policy borrowing, policy learning: Testing times in Australian schooling. *Critical Studies in Education*, *51*(2), 129–147.
Lingard, B. (2011). Policy as numbers: Accounting for educational research. *Australian Educational Researcher*, *38*(4), 355–382.
Lingard, B. and Rizvi, F. (2009). *Globalizing education policy*. London and New York: Routledge.
Lingard, B. and Renshaw, P. (2010). Teaching as a research-informed profession. In A. Campbell and S. Groundwater-Smith (Eds), *Connecting inquiry and professional learning in education: International perspectives and practical solutions*. London and New York: Routledge.
Lingard, B. and Sellar, S. (2012). A policy sociology reflection on school reform in England: From the third way to the big society? *Journal of Educational Administration and History*, *44*(1), 43–63.
Lingard, B., Mills, M. and Hayes, D. (2000). Teachers, school reform and social justice: Challenging research and practice. *Australian Educational Researcher, 27*(3), 93–109.
Lingard, R., Hayes, D., Mills, M. and Christie, P. (2003). *Leading learning*. Maidenhead, England: Open University Press.
Lingard, R. L., Ladwig, J., Mills, M. D., Bahr, M. P., Chant, D. C. and Warry, M. (2001). *The Queensland school reform longitudinal study*. Brisbane, Australia: State of Queensland (Department of Education). Retrieved from http://espace.library.uq.edu.au/view/UQ:40247
Little, G. (Ed.) (2015). *Global education 'reform': Building resistance and solidarity*. London: Manifesto Press.
Loughran, J. (2006). *Developing a pedagogy of teacher education: Understanding teaching and learning about teaching*. London and New York: Routledge.
Lupton, R. (2003). *Poverty street: The dynamics of neighbourhood decline and renewal*. Bristol, England: The Policy Press.
Lupton, R. (2004a). Understanding local contexts for schooling and their implications for school processes and quality. *Research Intelligence*, November, *89*, 21–26. Retrieved from www.bera.ac.uk/publications/Research%20Intelligence?page=15
Lupton, R. (2004b). *Schools in disadvantaged areas: Recognising context and raising performance* (Case paper 76). London: Centre for Analysis of Social Exclusion, London School of Economics and Political Science.
Lupton, R. (2005). Social justice and school improvement: Improving the quality of schooling in the poorest neighbourhoods. *British Educational Research Journal*, *31*(5), 589–604.

Lupton, R. (2006). Schools in disadvantaged areas: Low achievement and a contextualised policy response. In H. Lauder, P. Brown, J-A. Dillabough and A. H. Halsey (Eds), *Education, globalization and social change* (pp. 654–672). Oxford: Oxford University Press.

Lupton, R. (2011). Local context, social relations and school organisation. In C. Day (Ed.), *International handbook on school and teacher development*. London and New York: Routledge.

Lupton, R. (2014). Raising teachers' voice on achievement in urban schools in England: An afterword. *Urban Review, 46*(5): 919–923.

Lupton, R. and Obolenskaya, P. (2013). *Labour's record on education: Policy, spending and outcomes 1997–2010*. Retrieved from http://sticerd.lse.ac.uk/dps/case/spcc/wp03.pdf

Lupton, R. and Thomson, S. (2015). *The coalition's record on schools: Policy, spending and outcomes 2010–2015* (chart). Retrieved from http://sticerd.lse.ac.uk/dps/case/spcc/wp13.pdf

MacBeath, J. (2012). *Future of teaching profession*. Retrieved from http://download.ei-ie.org/Docs/WebDepot/EI%20Study%20on%20the%20Future%20of%20Teaching%20Profession.pdf

MacBeath, J., Gray, J., Cullen, J., Frost, D., Steward, S. and Swaffield, S. (2007). *Schools on the edge responding to challenging circumstances*. London: Paul Chapman.

Maguire, M., Woolridge, T. and Pratt-Adams, S. (2006). *The urban primary school*. Maidenhead, England: Open University Press.

Mahony, P. and Hextall, I. (2000). *Reconstructing teaching: Standards, performance and accountability*. London and New York: Routledge.

Menter, I. (2009). Teachers for the future: What have we got and what do we need? In S. Gewirtz, P. Mahony, I. Hextall and A. Cribb (Eds), *Changing teacher professionalism: International trends, challenges and ways forward*. London and New York: Routledge.

Menter, I. (2013). *Educational research – What's to be done?* Presidential address, annual conference of British Educational Research Association, Brighton, 3–5 September.

Menter, I. and Murray, J. (2011). *Developing research in teacher education*. London and New York: Routledge.

Menter, I., Elliot, D., Hulme, M., Lewin, J. and Lowden, K. (2011). *A guide to practitioner research in education*. London and Los Angeles: Sage.

Mills, M. (2014). *Challenging the 'tyranny of no alternative': Teachers and students working towards socially just schooling*. Presentation to the Education and Social Research group, Manchester Metropolitan University, 22 January.

Milner, H. R. (2013a). Rethinking achievement gap talk in urban education. *Urban Education, 48*(1), 3–8.

Milner, H. R. (2013b). Analyzing poverty, learning and teaching through a critical race theory lens. *Review of Research in Education, 37*(1), 1–53.

Mockler, N. and Sachs, J. (2011) *Rethinking educational practice through reflexive inquiry: Essays in honour of Susan Groundwater-Smith*. New York: Springer. Retrieved from www.springer.com/gb/book/9789400708044

Moll, L., Amanti, C., Neff, D. and Gonzalez, N. (1992). Funds of knowledge for teaching: Using a qualitative approach to connect homes and classrooms. *Theory Into Practice, 31*(2), 132–141.

Mortimore, P. and Whitty, G. (1997/2000). *Can school improvement overcome the effects of disadvantage?* London: Institute of Education.

Mouffe, C. (2005). *On the political (thinking in action)*. London and New York: Routledge.

Munns, G., Sawyer, W. and Cole, B. (2013). *Exemplary teachers of students in poverty*. London and New York: Routledge.

Newmann, F. M. and Associates. (1996). *Authentic achievement: Restructuring schools for intellectual quality*. San Francisco, CA: Jossey-Bass.

Nuttall, A. (2014). *Raising the teachers' voice: The role of one research-active teacher in an urban English primary school*. Paper presented at the Annual Conference of the Australian Association for Education, Brisbane, 30 November–4 December.
Nuttall, A. and Doherty, J. (2014). Disaffected boys and the achievement gap: 'The wallpaper effect' and what is hidden by a focus on school results, *Urban Review, 46*(5). Retrieved from http://link.springer.com/article/10.1007/s11256-014-0303-8
Nuttall, A., Finn, B. and Beckett, L. (2015). *Teachers' constructions of poverty effects: Their research evidence*. Paper presented at the Annual Conference of the British Educational Research Association, Belfast, 15–17 September.
Offe, C. (1984). *Contradictions of the welfare state*. London: Hutchison.
Office for Standards in Education, Children's Services and Skills (Ofsted). (1993). *Access and achievement in urban education*. Retrieved from www.ofsted.gov.uk/accessandachievement
Office for Standards in Education, Children's Services and Skills (Ofsted). (2003). *Access and achievement in urban education: 10 years on*. Retrieved from www.ofsted.gov.uk/accessandachievement
Office for Standards in Education, Children's Services and Skills (Ofsted). (2012a). *New teacher standards*. Retrieved from www.education.gov.uk/schools/teachingandlearning/reviewofstandards/a00205581/teachers-standards1-sep-2012
Office for Standards in Education, Children's Services and Skills (Ofsted). (2012b). *The evaluation schedule for the inspection of maintained schools and academies: Guidance and grade descriptors for inspecting schools in England under Section 5 of the Education Action 2005, from January 2012*. Retrieved from http://dera.ioe.ac.uk/14076/1/The_evaluation_schedule_for_school_inspections_from_January_2012%5B1%5D.pdf
Office for Standards in Education, Children's Services and Skills (Ofsted). (2013). *Access and achievement in urban education: 20 years on*. Retrieved from www.ofsted.gov.uk/accessandachievement
Office for Standards in Education, Children's Services and Skills (Ofsted). (2014). *North East, Yorkshire and Humber Regional Report*. Retrieved from www.gov.uk/government/uploads/system/uploads/attachment_data/file/384717/Ofsted_Annual_Report_201314_North_East_Yorkshire_and_Humber.pdf
Ozga, J. (1990). Policy research and policy theory: A comment on Fitz and Halpin. *Journal of Education Policy, 5*(4), 359–362.
Park, J. (2013). *Detoxifying school accountability*. London: Demos.
Perry, E. and Francis, B. (2010). *Social class gap for educational achievement: A review of the literature*. London: RSA. Retrieved from www.thersa.org/__data/assets/pdf_file/0019/367003/RSA-Social-Justice-paper.pdf
Petersen, K. B., Reimer, D. and Qvortrup, A. (Eds). (2014). *Evidence and evidence-based education in Denmark*. Retrieved from http://edu.au.dk/fileadmin/edu/Cursiv/CURSIV_14_www.pdf
Philpott, C. (2014). *Theories of professional learning: A critical guide for teacher educators*. Plymouth, England: Critical.
Piketty, T. (2014a). *Capital in the twenty-first century*. London: Belknap Press.
Piketty, T. (2014b). Interview: Dynamics of inequality. *New Left Review, 85*, January-February. Retrieved from http://newleftreview.org/II/85/thomas-piketty-dynamics-of-inequality
Pink, W. (Ed.). (2012). *Schools for marginalized youth*. New York: Hampton Press.
Pink, W. and Noblit, G. W. (Eds) (2007). *International handbook of urban education*. New York and Philadelphia: Springer.
Pollard, A. and Oancea, A. (2010). *Unlocking learning? Towards evidence-informed policy and practice in education*. Final Report of the UK Strategic Forum for Research in Education 2008–2010. Retrieved from www.sfre.ac.uk

Power, S. (2006). Markets and misogyny: Educational research on educational choice. *British Journal of Educational Studies*, 54(2), 175–188.

Power, S. (2008). How should we respond to the continuing failure of compensatory education? *Orbis Scholae*, 2(2), 19–37.

Punch, K. F. (2009). *Introduction to research methods in education*. London: Sage.

Quartz, K. H. and the TEP Research Group. (2003). *Too angry to leave: Supporting new teachers' commitment to transform urban schools*. A Research Report prepared by UCLA's Institute for Democracy, Education, & Access. Retrieved from http://idea2.gseis.ucla.edu/publications/utec/reports/pdf/rrs-rr001–0902.pdf

Ray, A. (2006). *School value-added measures in England*. A paper for the OECD Project on the Development of Value-Added Models in Education Systems. Retrieved from http://webarchive.nationalarchives.gov.uk/20130401151715/http://www.education.gov.uk/publications/eOrderingDownload/RW85.pdf

Reay, D. (2009). Making sense of white working class educational underachievement, paper 3. In K. P. Sveinsson (Ed.), *Who cares about the white working class?* Retrieved from www.runnymedetrust.org/uploads/publications/pdfs/WhoCaresAboutTheWhiteWorkingClass-2009.pdf

Rizvi, F. and Lingard, B. (2010). *Globalizing education policy*. London and New York: Routledge.

Rudduck, J. (Ed.) (1995). *An education that empowers: A collection of lectures in memory of Lawrence Stenhouse*. BERA Dialogues 10. Clevedon, England: Multilingual Matters.

Rudduck, J. and Hopkins, D. (1985). *Research as a basis for teaching: Readings from the work of Lawrence Stenhouse*. London: Heinemann Educational Books.

Ryan, W. (1971). *Blaming the victim*. London: Random House.

Sahlberg, P. (2011). *Finnish lessons: What can the world learn from educational change in Finland?* New York and London: Teachers College Press.

Sahlberg, P. (2014). *Facts, true facts and research in improving education systems*. Inaugural BERA lecture. Retrieved from www.bera.ac.uk/news/inaugural-bera-annual-lecture

Sirotnik, K. A. and Goodlad, J. I. (1988). *School university partnerships in action: Concepts, cases and concerns*. New York: Teachers College Press.

Slee, R. and Weiner, G. with Tomlinson, S. (1998). *School effectiveness for whom? Challenges to the school effectiveness and school improvement movements*. London: The Falmer Press.

Smith, G. (1987). Plowden twenty years on: 'Whatever happened to educational priority areas?' *Oxford Review of Education*, 13(1), 23–38.

Smyth, J. and Wrigley, T. (2013). *Living on the edge: Re-thinking poverty, class and schooling*. New York: Peter Lang.

Smyth, J., Hattam, R. and Lawson, M. (1998). *Schooling for a fair go*. Sydney: The Federation Press.

Stenhouse, L. (1975). *An introduction to curriculum research and development*. London: Heinemann.

Sturman, A. (1997). *Social justice in education*. Camberwell, England: ACER Press.

Sveinsson, K. P. (2009). *Who cares about the white working class?* Retrieved from www.runnymedetrust.org/uploads/publications/pdfs/WhoCaresAboutTheWhiteWorkingClass-2009.pdf

Tan, J. (2013). RAISEonline, half-truths and other fictions about attainment gaps. In L. Beckett (Ed.), *Teacher education through active engagement: Raising the professional voice*. London and New York: Routledge.

Thompson, E. P. (2014). Commitment in politics. In C. Winslow (Ed.), *E.P. Thompson and the making of the new left*. New York: Monthly Review Press.

Thomson, P. (2007). Leading schools in high poverty neighbourhoods: The National College for School Leadership and beyond. In W. Pink and G. W. Noblit (Eds), *International handbook of urban education*. New York and Philadelphia: Springer.

Thomson, P., Lingard, B. and Wrigley, T. (2012). Reimagining school change: The necessity and reasons for hope. In T. Wrigley, P. Thomson and B. Lingard (Eds), *Changing schools: Alternative ways to make a world of difference*. London and New York: Routledge.

Thrupp, M. (1999). *Schools making a difference. Let's be realistic!* Maidenhead, England: Open University Press.

Thrupp, M. (2002). Making the difference: 20 years on. *Discourse: Studies in the Cultural Politics of Education*, 23(3), 340–345.

Thrupp, M. (2005). *School improvement: An unofficial approach*. London and New York: Continuum.

Thrupp, M. and Tomlinson, S. (2005). Introduction: Education policy, social justice and 'complex hope'. *British Educational Research Journal*, 31(5), 549–556.

Thrupp, M. and Lupton, R. (2006). Taking school contexts more seriously: The social justice challenge. *British Journal of Educational Studies*, 54(3), 269–271.

Thrupp, M. and Lupton, R. (2011). *The impact of school context: What headteachers say*. Paper published by Centre for Analysis of Social Exclusion, London School of Economics. Retrieved from http://sticerd.lse.ac.uk/dps/case/cp/CASEpaper158.pdf

Touraine, A. (1977). *The voice and the eye*. Cambridge: Cambridge University Press.

Toynbee, P. (2011). Chav: The vile word at the heart of fractured Britain. In Johnson (Ed.), *The Bedside Guardian*. London: Guardian Books.

Warren, C. A. B. and Hackney, J. K. (2000). *Gender issues in ethnography* (2nd ed.). Thousand Oaks, CA: Sage.

Whitty, G. (1974). Sociology and the problem of radical educational change. In M. Flude and J. Ahier (Eds), *Educability, schools and ideology* (pp. 112–137). London: Croom Helm.

Whitty, G. (1985). *Sociology and school knowledge: Curriculum theory, research and politics*. London: Methuen.

Whitty, G. (2008). Changing modes of teacher professionalism: Traditional, managerial, collaborative and democratic. In B. Cunningham (Ed.), *Exploring professionalism: Bedford Way papers*. London: Institute of Education.

Whitty, G. (2014). Recent developments in teacher training and their consequences for the 'university project' in education. *Oxford Review of Education*, 40(4), 466–481.

Wilson, R. (2014). Student absences and student abscesses: Impediments to quality teaching. *Urban Review*, 46(5), 831–845.

Wilkinson, R. and Pickett, K. (2010). *The spirit level: Why more equal societies almost always do better*. London: Allen Lane.

Winslow, C. (Ed.). (2014). *E.P. Thompson and the making of the new left*. New York: Monthly Review Press.

Wrigley T. (2000). *The power to learn: Stories of success in the education of Asian and other bilingual pupils*. Stoke-on-Trent, England: Trentham.

Wrigley T. (2003). *Schools of hope: A new agenda for school improvement*. Stoke-on-Trent, England: Trentham.

Wrigley, T. (2006). *Another school is possible*. Stoke-on-Trent, England: Trentham.

Wrigley, T. (2014). *The politics of curriculum (Policy paper)*. London: Centre for Labour and Social Studies. Retrieved from http://classonline.org.uk/docs/2014_Policy_Paper_-_The_politics_of_curriculum_in_schools.pdf

Wrigley, T. and Kalambouka, A. (n.d.). *Academies and achievement: Setting the record straight*. Retrieved from www.changingschools.org.uk/academiesfolder/complete%20report.pdf

Wrigley, T., Thomson, P. and Lingard, B. (Eds). (2012). *Changing schools: Alternative ways to make a world of difference*. London and New York: Routledge.

Wyse, D., Baumfield, V. M., Egan, D., Gallagher, C., Hayward, L., Hulme, M., Leitch, R., Livingston, K. and Menter, I. with Lingard, B. (Eds). (2013). *Creating the curriculum*. London and New York: Routledge.

Young, M. F. D. (1998). *The curriculum of the future: From the 'new sociology of education' to a critical theory of learning*. Lewes, England: The Falmer Press.

Young, M. F. D. (2008). *Bringing knowledge back in: From social constructivism to social realism in the sociology of education*. London and New York: Routledge.

"You're kidding! You count S.A.T.s?"

© Mike Twohy. Reproduced by permission of Cartoon Bank/Condé Naste.

INDEX

Aboriginal communities 9, 136
absenteeism 116, 130
academization 36–8
Access and Achievement in Education 26
accountability 2, 131
achievement 'hot spots' 71
'Achievement in City Schools' 63, 88, 104, 120
achieving success 26–7
ACORN 71, 97
advocacy of policy 147–51
AERA *see* American Educational Research Association
Aiming High 26
alienation 51, 116
American Educational Research Association 56, 82, 123
Anti-Academies Alliance 12, 49
anti-intellectualism 63
anti-technocracy 86, 104
Anyon, J. 8, 14, 123
Apple, M. 24, 43, 139
appropriate professional response 134–6, 142, 145–6, 149
Arthurs, N. 138
aspiration 6, 33, 51, 55, 57, 65
assimilation 51
attendance 64, 105, 116–17, 130
Austerity Britain x, 3, 14, 34, 46, 112, 128, 134, 139–40, 143

'Baker revolution' 139
Ball, S.J. 45, 55–6, 58, 62, 68, 86, 89–93, 140, 147
Balls, Ed 11–12
Beckett, L. 119, 138
behaviour management 106
Benn, Melissa 114, 137
BERA *see* British Educational Research Association
Best 8 *see* Progress 8 metric
Blair, Tony 11, 71
blame game 53
Blower, Christine 17–18, 145–8
Boomer, G. 151
Bradford Independent Labour Party 1–2
Brennan, Marie xi, 137
British Educational Research Association 46, 63, 115, 135, 138, 142, 147–9
Brown, Gordon 11, 22, 41
brute force 151
budding sociological practice 128–31

Cameron, David 16, 41, 45, 50, 142–4, 147, 150
capability procedures 57, 141
capacity-building program 31–2, 34
Carter, A. 8–9
channelling teachers' concerns 113–17
CHAVS 3, 108, 113, 120–21
Children's Services Directorate 115

Index

'choreography of policy conflict' 1–20
closing the gap 2, 15, 24–6, 45–6, 65, 69–76, 81, 88, 104, 113, 119, 125–37, 143–7
co-opting inquiry work 54–8
'coasting' schools 136, 150; *see also* failing schools
Cochran-Smith, M. 28, 38, 45, 51, 106, 123–4, 137
collective intelligence 22, 78, 88, 113–14
colonization of ethics 121–2
commitment 100–104
'Commitment in Politics' 144
common cause 85–111; conclusion 109; indicative commitment 100–104; introduction 85–7; populist hope 87–95; teacher partners' identified concerns 104–9; teachers' nascent criticality 95–100
complex hope xii, 25, 87, 117, 136
compliance 103
concerns 104–9, 113–17; channelling 113–17
confidence 29
conflict of policy 1–20
conformity 103
'Confronting Schools and Social Inequality' 98
Connell, R.W. xi, 100
consciousness raising 23
continuing professional development 5, 11, 14–17, 22–4, 28–33, 41–4
control over schooling 134–53; introduction 134–6; lessons learned 139–42; ongoing need for practical-politicized dialogue 142–5; professional-political arenas 145–7; standing on shoulders of giants 136–8; teachers political advocacy 147–51; teachers' research-informed voice 138–9
corporate sponsorship 72, 81–2, 141, 144
corruption 144
Courtney, Kevin 150
CPD *see* continuing professional development
crisis politics 5, 10–11, 13, 140–41
critical democratic work 41–60
critical engagement 97
critical friends 61–3

critical social explanations 123–5
criticality 95–100
Crossley, N. 138
culture of poverty 6, 34, 114
cumulative multiple deprivation 1, 15, 23–5, 29, 34–8, 55, 85–7, 114, 136

de-industrialization 128
delinquency 3
democratic collaboration 10, 42
democratic professionalism 5, 117
democratic work 41–60; conclusion 58–9; introduction 41–3; social/political realities 44–7; teacher inquiry work co-opted 54–8; teachers' nascent politicization 47–51; teachers' own accounts 51–4
demonization 3–4, 108, 113, 134
Department for Education 65–6, 71, 77
deprivation 3, 121
Deprivation and Education 26
deskilling 30
DfE *see* Department for Education
Dinkins, D. 123
disaffection 3, 116
disaggregated achievement data 120
discourse of derision 3
disengagement 116, 124, 129
disillusionment 124
divisiveness 100, 125
domain summary 26
dysfunction 50
dyslexia 94

economic disadvantage 1–2, 21–3, 26
Education Bill 15
Education Endowment Fund 7, 46
Education International 145–6
'Education Question Time' 149–50
Education Review 137
Educational Priority Areas xii, 23–4
emotional outbursts 94
enforced attendance 130
equity 123, 128–9
The Establishment 4
ethics 117–23
Evaluation Schedule for Inspection of Maintained Schools 89–90
exclusion 105
exhaustion 69, 116

failing schools 21–40; local solutions to 21–40; politics of 34–6
Fair and Equal Education manifesto 138, 142, 147–8
'feral underclass' 3
Finn, M.E. 10
fire-fighting 5
first trial 27–31
forced academies 61–3, 74, 81–2
forced academization 22, 36–8, 61
forewarnings 23–6
forging commitments 143
free school meals 1, 6–7, 13, 24, 33, 38, 51–2, 54, 63–4, 71, 105, 120–21, 128
free schools xii
From the Achievement Gap to the Education Debate 123
FSM *see* free school meals
'FSM Data & Poverty' 54
Funds of Knowledge for Teaching 123
Furlong, J. 109
futuristic teaching 138

G&T *see* gifted and talented children
Gale, T. 137
gap talk 123–5
GCSE *see* General Certificate of Secondary Education
General Certificate of Secondary Education 6, 43, 52, 55, 63, 71, 89, 141
GERM *see* global educational reform agenda
getting started 26–7
Ghale, B. 138
gifted and talented children 13
global educational reform agenda 2, 6, 16–18, 22, 30, 45, 58, 85–7, 115–16, 123, 135–6, 145–8
globalization 2
'going public' 114, 125–8, 144
Gove, Michael 2, 4–6, 10, 16, 41, 46–7, 62–6, 69, 76, 78, 97, 112–13, 115, 142, 150
Grace, Gerald xii, 24, 87
Gramsci, Antonio 87
Groundwater-Smith, Susan xi, 9, 23, 29–30, 33–4, 55, 78, 95, 119, 136–7, 147
Guardian 94
Gypsy Romany children 130

hard to reach students 75
Hargreaves, A. 125
Harvey, D. 3–4, 22, 49
Hayes, D. 28
high stakes accountability ix, 131
holding the professional line 87, 136
homelessness 122
Hopkins, D. 136
Human Rights Act 150

identified concerns 104–9
IMD *see* Index of Multiple Deprivation
Importance of Teaching 76
'Improving Underperforming Schools' 62–3, 65–6, 76, 78, 115
Index of Multiple Deprivation 1, 15, 23–5, 29, 34, 76, 121, 142–4
indicative commitment 100–104
industrial democracy 58
inequity 128–9
infant mortality 1–2
Inquiry into Research in Teacher Education 16, 63
Inquiry as Stance 124
inquiry work co-opted 54–8
insisting on school democracy 14–17
intake-related pressures 121
intellectual work 63–6
intelligent accountability 131
intentional investigation 106
interconnections 21–3, 113
intersectionality 13

jingoism 30
Johnson, L. 10
Johnson, R.S. 99, 108, 128
Jones, O. 3–4, 108

Kemmis, Stephen xi, 9, 23, 33–4, 95–6, 136, 147
knowledge building 9–11, 43, 69
knowledge of practice 43, 51, 54
knowledge-building partnerships 79–81

La Salle, R.A. 128
LAC *see* looked-after children
lack of motivation 51
Ladson-Billings, G. 123, 126
Laws, David 147

Leading Learning 17, 22, 24–5, 31–4, 43–7, 57–9, 81–2, 85–7
Leading Learning 31
league tables 71
lessons learned 139–42
Lewis, R. 10
Lieberman, Ann 28, 56, 68, 115–17, 137, 139, 143
life chances 121
Lingard, Bob xi, 7, 22, 28, 31, 43, 66, 68, 88–9, 97–8, 135, 137
literacy 57
local solutions to failing schools 21–40; conclusion 38; first trial 27–31; forced academization 36–8; forewarnings 23–6; getting started 26–7; introduction 21–3; politics of failing schools 34–6; scaling up 31–4
looked-after children 13
Loughran, J. 28
Lupton, Ruth xii, 10, 28, 46–7, 52, 55, 68, 82, 98, 106, 134, 136
Lytle, S. 28, 38, 45, 51, 78, 106, 123–4

MAACS 68, 82, 120
Maguire, M. 24, 137
making common cause 85–111
making a difference 7, 21, 28–9
marginalization 6, 125–6
marketization 113, 123
Menter, I. 24, 28, 88, 135, 138
mentoring 11, 61
method of intervention 33
Miller, L. 28, 117, 139, 143
Mills, M.D. 31, 137
Milner, H.R. 123–6
minority ethnic backgrounds 25–6, 29, 43, 46, 52, 63–4, 85
mitigating circumstances 3, 15, 55, 116, 144
mock inspections 69, 94, 100
Mockler, N. 119
Moll, L. 123
Morgan, Nicky 150
Mortimore, P. 23–4, 38
motivation 29, 49–51
multiple deprivation 1, 15, 23–5, 29, 34–8, 55, 85–7, 114, 136
Murdoch Press 4
Murray, J. 28

'naïve possibilitarianism' 23, 43, 50, 65, 76–8, 85, 117, 136
nascent criticality 95–100
nascent politicization 47–51
National Association of Head Teachers 4–5
National Challenge policy 11–12, 22, 36–8, 41–4
National Curriculum 5
National Teaching Service 142
National Union of Teachers 10–11, 17, 130, 137–8, 142, 145–50
need for interconnections 21–3
need for practical-political dialogue 142–5
Neighborhood Indices 26, 69, 76
neoliberalism 2, 4–7, 10, 17, 22, 29, 41–2, 51, 65, 79, 82, 85, 87, 112–14, 119, 136, 142
'New Approach to School Improvement' 65
New Labour 3, 11–12, 22, 41
No Child Left Behind ix
no-hopers 3–4
North East, Yorkshire and Humber Regional Report 2–3
Northern Education Challenge 66, 76–8
NTS *see* National Teaching Service
numbers game 14, 43
NUT *see* National Union of Teachers

Offe, C. 58
Office for Standards in Education 2–3, 5–8, 15, 25–6, 35–7, 41–3, 50–51, 67–9, 71, 82, 86, 89–100, 103, 112–15, 139–40
Ofsted *see* Office for Standards in Education
on the shoulders of giants 136–8
'one size fits all' approach 2, 69, 79, 124
ongoing practical-political dialogue 142–5
Operational Approval 67–9, 89
operational points of leverage 74–9
optimism of will 87
out-of-the-ordinary professional learning 109
Ozga, J. 56

Park, J. 137
PASP *see* Priority Action Schools Program
Patterns of Learning 11, 21–3, 31, 38, 79
pedagogies of poverty 14, 130–31

performativity ix, 58, 89–90, 139–40
pessimism of intellect 87
Piketty, T. 3, 10, 14, 38
Pink, W. 125
Plan B 108, 113
points of leverage 74–9
policy advocacy 16–17, 62, 147–51
policy conflict 1–20, 149–50; conclusion 17–18; insisting on school democracy 14–17; introduction 1–5; professional knowledge building 9–11; systemic difficulties 11–14; thinking strategically 5–9
Policy Exchange think tank 4
policy as numbers 6, 13, 43, 131
political realities 44–7
politicization 36, 47–51, 138
politics of blame 121–2, 138
politics of failing schools 34–6
Politics and Policy Making in Education 86
populist hope 87–95
possibilitarianism 21–3
poverty 1–8, 14, 23–4, 29, 38, 54–5, 116, 121, 130, 137
practical-political dialogue 142–5
Preire, Paulo xii
principles of procedure 95
Priority Action Schools Program 9–10, 22, 27, 29, 136, 139, 147
privatization 113, 123
probability of assimilation 51
problematizing achievement discourse 124; *see also* gap talk
productive pedagogies 30–31, 57
professed values 112–13
professional control over schooling 134–53
professional discretion 89
professional disquiet 26–7
professional knowledge building 9–11
professional-political arenas 145–7
professionalism 5
Progress 8 metric 6–8, 89, 121, 141
Pupil Premium 7, 13, 121, 130

QA process 67–9
QTS *see* Qualified Teacher Status
Qualified Teacher Status 8, 45–6
Quality Assurance 119
quality teaching 69–71, 129
quick fix solution 130

radical–conservative experiment 10, 112
Radio Times 108
RAISEonline report 5–7, 48, 71, 87, 105–6, 113, 121, 129
rationale for CPD participation 58–9
RaTs *see* research-active teachers
Reading Recovery 24
Reay, Diane xii, 52
regimes of truth 58
Renshaw, P. 28, 89, 97
Research and the Teaching Profession 8–9, 28
research-active teachers xv, 14–16, 54–64, 71–3, 81, 104, 113–15, 129–31, 134, 144–9
research-informed profession 89
research-informed teacher education 69–74
research-informed teachers' voice 138–9
resistance 38, 44–5, 140
reskilling 30
retail model of schooling 57, 74, 112
Rethinking Achievement Gap Talk in Education 123
Review of Initial Teacher Training 8–9
rich description 88, 108
Rizvi, F. 137
Robottom, I. 95–6
Rudduck, J. 136
Runnymede Trust 64

Sahlberg, P. 115–16
sameness agenda 124
sanctions 2, 5, 22
SATs 8
scaling up 31–4
school mix, 34, 64–5, 108, 121
school democracy 14–17
School Improvement Plan 2011–2015 115
Schools Direct 9
Schools for Marginalized Youth 125–6
Schools White Paper 15, 97
SCITT 9, 141
scrutiny 97
SEAL program 106
self-determination 38, 44
self-esteem 57, 64
self-evaluation 24, 38
self-identification 136
self-narratives 51–4
semi-privatized academies 112
SEN *see* special educational needs

Side-by-Side Learning 11, 22, 31–2, 36, 79
Sinnot, Steve 10
SMIS *see* Student Information Management System
Smyth, John xi
social class intake 34, 64–5
Social Class and School Knowledge 123
social determinants of learning 75
social disadvantage 1–2, 21–3, 26
social explanations 123–5
social justice 67, 123
social realities 44–7
socioeconomic disadvantage 46–7
sociological interventions 131
sociological practice 128–31
sociology of action 16
solutions to failing schools 21–40
special educational needs 13
sponsored academies 22
Stand Up for Education manifesto 138, 142, 145–8
standing on the shoulders of giants 136–8
'Standing up for education' 145
Stenhouse, Lawrence 10, 136
'Stepford wives' 63
Strategic Framework for Research in Education 16
strategic support 77
strategic thinking 5–9
Student Information Management System 71–3
support for intellectual work 63–6
surveillance 141
survival mind-set 116
sustainability 75, 141
systemic difficulties 11–14

'Taking Schools Seriously' 10
Teach First 9, 141
teacher education 69–74
teacher inquiry work 54–8
teacher partners' identified concerns 104–9
teachers' accounts 51–4
teachers' budding sociological practice 128–31
teachers' intellectual work 63–6
teachers' nascent criticality 95–100
teachers' nascent politicization 47–51
teachers' policy advocacy 147–51
teachers' research-informed voice 138–9
Teachers and Schooling Making a Difference 28
Teachers Talk about Race, Class and Achievement 123–4
teachers' voices 112–33; budding sociological practice 128–31; channelling teachers' concerns 113–17; conclusion 131; critical social explanations 123–5; 'going public' 125–8; introduction 112–13; turning point 117–23
teaching as craft 9, 69
teaching to the test 14, 130
Thatcher, Margaret 139
Thatcherism 9–10
thinking strategically 5–9
Thompson, Edward xiii, 1, 18, 42, 103–4, 144, 149
Thrupp, M. 127, 151
tick box mentality 82, 103
The Times 4
Touraine, Alain 16–18, 24, 36, 38, 44–5, 51, 58, 62, 81, 87, 104, 128, 138, 149–51
towards critical social explanations 123–5
Toynbee, P. 26, 108
trade unionism 145–6, 148–50
Trailblazers 15, 79–80, 87, 89, 95–6, 99–101, 104–9, 113–14, 117–31, 134, 143, 145
transformative pedagogies 7–8, 21–2, 29–30, 44, 57, 61
traveller children 130
triangulation 106
truancy 56–7
turning point 117–23

UCET *see* University Council for the Education of Teachers
Underachievement in Education in White Working Class Children 7
underperforming schools 1–4; *see also* failing schools
Understanding the Challenges for Disadvantaged Schools 46–7
University Council for the Education of Teachers 147, 149
'university project' 4, 9, 61–84; conclusion 81–2; introduction 61–3; knowledge-building partnerships 79–81; operational

points of leverage 74–9; QA process 67–9; research-informed teacher education 69–74; support for intellectual work 63–6
Urban Review 125–6, 145
urban school policy conflict 1–20

value added 105
vernacular neoliberalism 10
vigilance 43
Voice and the Eye 16–18, 149–51

wallpaper effect 128
Whitty, Geoff xii, 10, 17–18, 23–4, 38, 53, 117, 136

Who Cares about the White Working Class? 52, 64
widening participation 81
Williams, Raymond xiii
Williams, Zoe 94
Wilshaw, Michael 97
Winifred Mercier lectures 17–18, 98, 145, 148
worklessness 26
Wrigley, Terry 55, 68, 120, 137
writ of democracy 149–50

Young, M.F.D. 57

zero-sum game 55

Taylor & Francis eBooks

Helping you to choose the right eBooks for your Library

Add Routledge titles to your library's digital collection today. Taylor and Francis ebooks contains over 50,000 titles in the Humanities, Social Sciences, Behavioural Sciences, Built Environment and Law.

Choose from a range of subject packages or create your own!

Benefits for you
- Free MARC records
- COUNTER-compliant usage statistics
- Flexible purchase and pricing options
- All titles DRM-free.

Benefits for your user
- Off-site, anytime access via Athens or referring URL
- Print or copy pages or chapters
- Full content search
- Bookmark, highlight and annotate text
- Access to thousands of pages of quality research at the click of a button.

REQUEST YOUR FREE INSTITUTIONAL TRIAL TODAY

Free Trials Available
We offer free trials to qualifying academic, corporate and government customers.

eCollections – Choose from over 30 subject eCollections, including:

Archaeology	Language Learning
Architecture	Law
Asian Studies	Literature
Business & Management	Media & Communication
Classical Studies	Middle East Studies
Construction	Music
Creative & Media Arts	Philosophy
Criminology & Criminal Justice	Planning
Economics	Politics
Education	Psychology & Mental Health
Energy	Religion
Engineering	Security
English Language & Linguistics	Social Work
Environment & Sustainability	Sociology
Geography	Sport
Health Studies	Theatre & Performance
History	Tourism, Hospitality & Events

For more information, pricing enquiries or to order a free trial, please contact your local sales team:
www.tandfebooks.com/page/sales

The home of Routledge books

www.tandfebooks.com